# FAME

Fame is being paid a lot of money for what people think about you as well as for what you do . . . having strange women approach you and say they want to meet you, know you in every way, right now . . . misassessing the amount of interest other people have in you . . . trying to find yourself while under the scrutiny of thousands of eyes . . . reacting instead of acting, being passive instead of active . . . having people tell you what they want you to do with your life . . . learning to understand what others want from you . . . sensing people in a restaurant whispering and pointing toward your party . . . forgetting how hot the subways are in August . . . having someone write that if you visit this kid who is dying in a hospital he will get better . . . having strangers constantly test you and probe for the dimension of your "real" personality . . . coming into contact with ten times more people in a year than most people do in a lifetime . . . remaining unable to escape those few minutes or several years when what you did made you famous. . . .

# LIFE ON THE RUN

# Bill Bradley

BANTAM BOOKS
TORONTO • NEW YORK • LONDON • SYDNEY • AUCKLAND

LIFE ON THE RUN

*A Bantam Book / published by arrangement with
Quadrangle/The New York Times Book Co.*

PRINTING HISTORY

*Quadrangle edition published 1977
Three printings through August 1976*

*Bantam edition / October 1977*

| | |
|---|---|
| *2nd printing . . . October 1977* | *4th printing . . . February 1979* |
| *3rd printing . . . January 1978* | *5th printing . . . January 1987* |

ISBN 0-553-26152-5

*Published simultaneously in the United States and Canada*

# INTRODUCTION

## 1986

I wrote this book a decade ago. It is about my years on the road as a basketball player with the New York Knicks. It is about my teammates, the people we encountered, the cities we visited, and it is about the game, the influences around it, the rhythm of the life, and the thoughts provoked by experiencing each of those things in America during the first half of the 1970s.

The reader should know that what follows is not about politics or the United States Senate. Yet there is a continuity between my two careers.

I have always believed there was a larger purpose to basketball than individual achievements. Excellence has been defined for me in terms of the team's success.

In high school, it was whether our team from a very small school in a small town could defeat the bigger, city teams.

In college, it was whether a team of students who played basketball to their collective potential could compete with the best in the country.

In the pros, it was whether a team without a dominant star could be the best in the world.

And in the U.S. Senate, a moment of insight came when I realized that the passage of legislation, like teamwork, required getting people with different backgrounds, different interests, and different personal agendas to agree on a shared goal, and to work toward it.

Basketball seems very far away these days. The game is over, and life goes on.

What remains—beyond character influences, financial security, and enhanced human understanding—are the memories:

Standing in Tokyo in 1964 with the Olympic Gold Medal around my neck, the national anthem playing, and a lump in my throat;

Riding back to Princeton in 1965 with the Eastern Regional Championship and the knowledge that we had played a perfect game;

Seeing Willis Reed in the 1970 final series with Los Angeles hobble onto the court and hit his first and second shots;

Missing a last-second shot in the seventh game of the 1971 playoffs against Baltimore;

Knowing for 24 hours after a championship that you're the best in the world;

Going beyond the goose bumps of competition to a single play, executed perfectly, so that the moment has an inexorable rightness about it.

I'm proud of what we did together.

I'm proud if my days in basketball have reaffirmed an old truth: that only if you pull together can you succeed; only if you realize that who scores isn't important, but who wins is; and how you win is the most important of all.

*For Ernestine*

# Part I

"During those years, when most men of promise achieve an adult education, if only in the school of war, Ring moved in the company of a few dozen [men] . . . playing a boy's game. A boy's game, with no more possibility in it than a boy could master, a game bounded by walls which kept out novelty or danger, change or adventure. . . . It was never that he was completely sold on athletic virtuosity as the be-all and end-all of problems; the trouble was that he could find nothing finer. Imagine life conceived as a business of beautiful muscular organization— an arising, an effort, a good break, a sweat, a bath, a meal, a love, a sleep—imagine it achieved; then imagine trying to apply this standard to the horribly complicated mess of living, where nothing, even the greatest conceptions and workings and achievements, is else but messy, spotty, tortuous—and then one can imagine the confusion that Ring faced on coming out of the park."

(From "RING," an essay by *F. Scott Fitzgerald*)

THE APPLAUSE OF THE CROWD THUNDERS LOUDER AND longer with every shot my opponent sinks. The first quarter ends with him racing the full length of the court for a two-handed dunk, followed immediately by his clenched fist raised in triumph. Throughout the second and third quarters he talks to me as he plays:

"Hey, man, when you gonna guard me?"

"What's the matter, too old?"

"You just one no-playin' white motherfucker."

"I ain't even the doctor and I'm operatin' all over you."

The fourth quarter opens with me on the bench, fuming—at the coach for taking me out and at my opponent for his cocky derision. I look around and the faces of the crowd look familiar. My mother is on one side of the court yelling at the referees. My father sits across the floor from her, reading a newspaper. My high school coach is talking with a fourteen-year-old girl from my life-saving class. Most faces look blank, their features difficult to discern. A businessman who regularly sits behind our bench throws a hot dog bun at me. The woman next to him screams an obscenity, and then Mama Leone stands applauding my substitute.

With five minutes to go, I'm still waiting to get back into the game. Suddenly, the coach calls my name and I return to action. The first time I touch the ball, I hit a jump shot. During the next four minutes the running score sheet tells the story: "4:36—Bradley steals; 4:18—Bradley jump shot; 3:46—DeBusschere lay-up and Bradley assist; 3:28—Bradley rebound;

2:45—Bradley driving dunk; 1:20—Bradley two free throws; 1:05—Bradley jump shot." The crowd groans with each of my acts. With forty-five seconds to go in the game we have pulled to within one point. We score and go ahead by one. They score to recapture the lead. I'm fouled with eight seconds left. I have two free throws. The crowd is now in a frenzy. As I step to the line I notice an opposing player trying to divert my attention. I concentrate, blocking out all distractions so the pressure won't get through. Only two simple free throws.

Suddenly, something snaps. It is as if I do not remember the previous four minutes, but *only* the first three quarters—my failure and the fans' reaction. I pause to scan the audience and look at the taunting opponent. The grain of the leather ball feels natural in my hands. The crowd boos as I bounce it three times in preparation for the first free throw. I miss. The crowd explodes. I need to make the next shot to tie. I glance again at the fans and opponents. My fingers find their familiar spots on the ribs of the ball —three bounces, eyes on the rim, elbow under the ball. I take a deep breath, draw back my arm and in one quick motion I hurl the ball twenty feet over the backboard into the crowd. And I laugh and laugh and laugh. . . .

The phone rings. I roll over in bed and grab the receiver. The motel operator says, "Wake-up call. It's 9 A.M. Your bus leaves at 10." Dave DeBusschere, my roommate on the road, yawns and turns over. We are in Cleveland where last night we—the New York Knickerbockers—lost to the Cleveland Cavaliers. We lie still for 45 minutes, half awake, both wishing that we could sleep longer. Finally, DeBusschere opens the rubberized Holiday Inn curtains. Outside, a cold drizzle soaks the city and a thick fog encases its buildings. I draw a hot bath and sit in it for five minutes to loosen the stiffness from last night's game.

When I finish, DeBusschere has gone and the door to the motel hallway stands open. My socks, shoes, and Knick uniform hang drying over the chairs, the room heater, and the floor lamp. I dress, pack hastily, and leave. After paying my incidental charges at the front desk, I walk past the Hertz Rent-A-Car counter and out the front door. My mouth is dry and burning. My legs ache. I've slept poorly. I board an old bus with windows as small as portholes. It will take our group to the Cleveland airport. We are twelve players, a coach, a trainer, six reporters, and a public relations man.

Two sportswriters seated in front of me begin to talk, loudly and animatedly. "You know 0–2 Mc-Crory? Hell of a battler in the clutch."

"Yeah, but the best was Fighter Peru, used to play for the Albany Senators. He was a convict like Ali Amata."

"What you think of the Yankees this year?"

My attention drifts out through the bus window to Cleveland, one of America's northern industrial cities where furnaces of progress leave everything ashen, like the gray of a December morning. We pass buildings with their tops enveloped in mist. Car wheels hiss against the wet pavement.

Someday, I think, I want to write a book about what it is like to be a professional athlete in America.

The fog delays our flight to New York for thirty minutes. One by one the players file by the airline counter where small television screens show the schedule changes. They check the gate number and the new departure time. They exchange information on last night's women.

"How was she?" one player asks.

"Outa sight," says another. "I'll be sure and see her next time we're in town. And you?"

"Nothin', a real *chiwollephant.*"

"A what? You mean she was ugly?" (Pronounced you-g-ly.)

"Specially so—you know, part chimpanzee, wolf, and elephant. A real *chiwollephant.*"

The escalator is broken, so we walk up the steps to the main lobby. Jerry Lucas, the reserve center, magician, mnemonicist, and entrepreneur, overtakes me as I approach the newsstand. "Twelve and thirteen," he says. "Twelve and thirteen."

"What?" I ask.

"Twelve steps to the first landing and thirteen to the top. What's the matter, didn't you know that?"

"What do you mean?"

"Just what I said, twelve steps to the first landing and thirteen to the top. Counting is a good mental exercise."

Lucas counts steps everywhere. There are 93 steps from the Atlanta dressing room to the bus, and 62 steps from his locker to center court in Madison Square Garden. He says he walks the equivalent of 87 steps during the playing of the National Anthem at a normal tempo.

I buy the morning paper and head for the coffee shop. DeBusschere sits at the counter eating a sweet roll and drinking orange juice and a cup of coffee. Other players dot the restaurant, none sitting together —most of them reading the sports section of the morning paper. They missed breakfast at the hotel, too. I sit next to DeBusschere and order the same breakfast. A family sitting at the opposite counter whispers among themselves and then the mother walks over to DeBusschere and asks him for his autograph. Six other autograph requests interrupt breakfast. One man, who speaks with a Southern accent, says to Lucas, "Jer, ever since you was playin' high school ball down in Middletown, I been your number one fan."

I flip DeBusschere for the check. He wins.

We walk out of the coffee shop and start the long walk to Gate 48. A man stops me. He tells me that he went to Princeton (my alma mater) in 1958 and that he is a friend of a friend, who is in politics. He asks what I think of our friend's chances. When I catch up to Dave he grins and says in clipped military fashion, "Princeton—'58," as if the graduation year was the first name spoken after the surname Princeton.

At the departure gate a few Knicks are already sitting in the plastic chairs attached to the floor of the waiting area. DeBusschere makes his way to the seat next to Danny Whelan, the Knick trainer. He leans over and informs him that I had been stopped by "Princeton '58." Whelan, a man with foxlike features and carefully combed white hair, has been a trainer in either professional baseball or basketball for twenty-five years. "Hey, Red," he says to Red Holzman, the Knick coach, making sure I hear, "Bill just met 'Princeton '58.' Just think, Red, 'Princeton '58.' From the tables down at Mory's and all that rah rah. Makes you proud to know a Princeton man, doesn't it? Did he wear white bucks and a striped tie, Bill?"

A few waiting passengers seem puzzled. DeBusschere looks out the airport window, chuckling.

Dave DeBusschere is a man whose simple tastes are constantly at war with New York stardom. His great basketball ability has earned for him the loyalty of New York's basketball fans. His shock of dark hair, powerful legs, and wide smile make him a striking public figure. Drawn toward personal friends, his family, neighborhood bars, and other athletic men, he keeps himself apart from the New York celebrity atmosphere, which he regards as phony. Yet, he is a part of it and slowly he has come to live his role, though he is never comfortable as an idol. DeBusschere's personal strength lies in basics, such as loyalty, fairness, unselfishness, and consistency. His vulnerability lies in an occasional lack of grace, of self-esteem, of a sense of adventure. He never pretends to be anything but what he is.

━━━━━━━

Dave DeBusschere's grandfather emigrated to the United States from Trahoot, Belgium, with a bride his family had arranged for him. After living in

Canada for three years, they settled in Detroit where Renae DeBusschere worked as a bricklayer and later as a milkman on the city's East Side. He built his own home, using latches, nails, and tools which he had made himself. During the summer he tended an elaborate vegetable and flower garden. Self-reliance became the family trademark.

Renae DeBusschere's son, Marcel, grew up in Detroit and became a good athlete at De LaSalle High School. During the Depression, Marcel delivered beer to restaurants and bars located in the counties around Detroit. Later he purchased the local distributorship for O'Keefer, Baumeister, and Cincinnati Cream beers. He met and married the daughter of one of his customers, a restaurant owner in Irish Hills, Michigan.

Marcel's only son, David Albert DeBusschere, was born on October 16, 1940. Dave grew up on the East Side of Detroit in his father's old neighborhood. He attended an all-boy's Catholic high school and worked for his father after school. He spent many hours with the other employees—young blacks born in Detroit, white country people generally from the South. Together, they unloaded box cars of beer onto the trucks from which Dave made deliveries. "Our family was a real European family," he recalls. "The man was dominant. He provided. My mother was a housewife. She was totally dependent on my father."

Around 1958, his father sold the distributorship and bought the Lycast Bar. It stood across from one of the large Chrysler plants and only three miles from the family's frame house. The Lycast was dimly lit; a place that had last seen sunlight when the roof was nailed over it. A pool table stood in the center of the wooden floor and small tables lined three walls. In the back room, light food was served to supplement the drinking. A big bar extended the length of one wall and the Wurlitzer jukebox blared Country and Western tunes. "It was a factory bar," says Dave. "Guys coming off shifts at Chrysler would line up at seven in the morning to get in the joint. Each year brought another set of customers. They would migrate up from the South, work, and then they would get fired, or whatever the hell happens to them, but they'd be gone. There were a few regulars like Indian Pat and Tennessee Lee. When Tennessee walked in, singing, everyone would applaud and buy him a drink. So he'd sing again. He was the only live entertainment we had except for the old guys, sixty or seventy, who would get drunk and start fighting. Hell, they couldn't even see each other. It was a sad show, but it was a show. At that time, I wasn't looking at it as a sad show; it was sort of fascinating to me that that world existed."

Dave attended Detroit University, where he held to solid ecclesiastical tenets. He did "B" work in business administration, lived at home on the weekends, dated the same girl for four years, and developed into a great athlete. Baseball and basketball were his specialties. He excelled equally at both.

After college, DeBusschere signed a baseball bonus contract for $160,000 with the Chicago White Sox. They sent him and his blazing fast ball to the Sally League in North Carolina and then advanced him to the Triple A division in Indianapolis. At more or less the same time, he also signed a basketball contract with the Detroit Pistons and for four years he successfully played pro baseball in summer and pro basketball in winter. During his forty-eight straight months of sport travel, sitting alone in hotel lobbies or passing time with strangers in bars, Dave missed his close friends and family in Detroit. Although he was single and seeing most of the United States for the first time, the life got stale quickly, particularly the long, hot summers in minor league baseball. Once he made the White Sox, there were a few old-timers who befriended him, but Dave sensed that his curve wasn't good enough and his control too erratic for the major leagues. So, when the Pistons offered him the job of playing-coach at the age of twenty-four, he left the baseball world, casting his lot with basketball for better or worse. After two seasons as a coach

with disastrous records and one more year as a solid
but unheralded player, Dave was traded to the New
York Knicks in December 1968.

The Detroit team competed more against themselves than against their opponents. They were a
group of sensitive egotists who simply failed to fulfill
their potential. In New York, Dave could concentrate
on his specialties—defense and rebounding—and forget the pursuit of elusive personal statistics.

"My father never pushed me in sports," Dave says.
"He'd come to the games, but he never forced me to
play. From as early as I can remember, I just had
the drive to excel in sport—football, baseball, basketball, you name it. I had a fear of performing poorly.
I had to be good. I had to be competitive. I couldn't
stand to be embarrassed at what I was doing. I still
tell myself not to take it easy in a practice, a game,
or anytime. That's the only way I know how to play."

At 1:00 P.M., an hour and ten minutes late, the team
boards the plane, our steel cocoon where time stops
and familiarity brings comfort and security. I sit next
to the window, careful not to disturb the card game
that has already begun on the aisle. I fasten the
safety belt and slouch down so that my head rests
against the back of my seat. Moments later, I hear the
loud roar preparatory to take off. I feel the pressure
push me back into the cushioned backrest. The land-
scape outside passes, slowly at first, and then faster.
A creaking ascent follows a moment of fear. We're
aloft. The fog quickly denies us sight of the ground
as a gray mist whips around the edges of the wings.
Suddenly, moments after takeoff, we burst through
the white clouds to sunshine and blue sky. The experience is physical. My eyes open. I smile. The dull-
ness of Cleveland lies behind, and the brightness of
day stimulates my imagination. For the first time
since waking, I breathe faster and deeper and feel
alert.

After an hour and twenty minutes we swoop out of the clouds across New York harbor and up the East River. The skyscrapers of Manhattan rise from the island on our left like the monuments of a modern religion. On the right are Brooklyn and Queens, the square blocks of houses that provide contrast to the architectural feats across the river. "There it is," says a teammate looking out at the view, "the heart of urban America. That's where it's *all* happenin'." We veer away from the skyline, over a huge cemetery and Shea Stadium, landing at LaGuardia. Moments later we emerge into the unsure world of the city.

## 2

THE NEXT DAY, TUESDAY, I TAXI TO MADISON SQUARE
Garden around 6:15 for a 7:30 game. In the old Garden at 49th Street and Eighth Avenue, a game would
start at 8:30—or even 10:30, if it was the second game
of a doubleheader. Those were the days when for the
price of one ticket fans could see two games. The side
balconies hung directly over the court. Players heard
the fans' comments easily. Sometimes spectators
pelted stars of opposing teams with bottles, coins,
and programs and on a bad night, the home team
had to dodge the flying missiles. Occasionally, the
fans would shake the backboards which were suspended from long wires anchored in the balcony
concrete. Even so, players loved the baskets of the
old Garden. The rims hung loose on the backboards.
A shot landing on the rim was "softened" and usually
rolled in. The good shooters in the league called the
baskets "sewers" because almost everything went
down them. The portable floor, though, was a dribbler's hell. A few squares of the hardwood surface
were completely dead to the bounce. Often, a player
would be driving to the basket, only to find the ball
he had controlled seconds earlier unresponsive to his
dribble, as if it had turned to stone.

Backstage, behind the end seats were hockey goals,
ice-show scenery, an old circus cage, and a pulpit
from a Billy Graham crusade. In 1962 Marilyn Monroe sang Happy Birthday to JFK at the Eighth Avenue end of the arena. During the thirties the German-American *bund* held giant rallies there to support
Hitler's Germany. In 1924 the Democratic party

nominated John W. Davies there for President on the one hundred and third ballot. The old Garden was a social history of America. And, always, the smell of popcorn and burnt cooking oil filled the air.

The new Madison Square Garden opened in February 1968, three months after I joined the team. It occupies air space over the New York terminals of the Penn Central and Long Island railroads. It was privately financed and designed to be the ultimate indoor arena. Seats were cushioned and escalators assured quick exit. The design provided a powerful ventilating system and plenty of light. The promotional message encouraged the men of Wall Street and Madison Avenue to join the die-hard basketball fans from the garment center in the new Garden. The accommodating new atmosphere and the success of the Knicks increased attendance—particularly of women. Then, in an effort to attract more families and at the same time allow businessmen to see a game before catching the commuter train home to New Jersey or Long Island, the starting time was moved up to 7:30.

———

As I get out of the cab and head for the employees' entrance, Burt says hello. He is an avid fan who wishes me good luck before every game. He has a season ticket high up in the Garden's yellow section. Sometimes I give him better seats, and occasionally we have lunch. He knows the game well and likes to gossip about players and tactics. The Knicks make his life special, he says, and give him something to look forward to after a day at work in the post office. I am his favorite player. He is similar to other fans over the years who have identified with the team and me. They suffer with us when we lose and they are ecstatic when we win. They might criticize us when we play badly but they are never disloyal. They are the bedrock of our experience as professional players.

I get out of the elevator on the Garden's fifth floor, the arena level. Making my way through the back halls, I greet the carpenters, electricians, and guards of the building's staff.

"Go get 'em, Bill!"

"How you gonna do? Is Dave okay?"

I walk down a long hall past the twelve dressing rooms; I say hello to a man who stands with his son. Before almost every home game for four years, he has offered to get cut-rate diamonds for me. When he first made the offer his son was a small boy. Now he stands a head taller than his father. Another man nods hello—a wealthy bachelor who gives theater tickets to his favorite players. I shift my bag to my left hand and open the door.

The Knicks' locker room is small. The floor is covered with blue carpeting. At one end is a green blackboard and a bench where sportswriters or trainer's assistants usually sit. A roll-up movie screen is attached to the blackboard. At the opposite end of the room is a built-in storage cabinet and a closet. Inside the cabinet are towels, hundreds of towels. The Knicks will use sixty towels in one night, for showering, for applying liniment to muscles, for wiping perspiration, for drying hands and for providing a cushioning layer against the various therapies of hot sand packs, diathermy, and ultrasound. The closet holds all the equipment needed for the team: liniments, sprays, tape, pills, and wraps. There are uniforms, basketballs, socks (wool and cotton), jocks, and shoes. Each player maintains his year's supply of equipment in the closet. The only key belongs to Danny Whelan, who attends to the physical and mental whims of the team. Part of his job is to make sure every player is properly supplied, but not overly so. Some years ago, Whelan suspected a player of taking more than his share of equipment. He opened the player's private locker to discover a plentiful cache. Whelan returned the supply to the closet and left it to the player to wonder who had intervened. The player got the message and thereafter his equipment requests lessened considerably.

Whelan has to know who wears Puma shoes or

Adidas or Converse or Keds. He has to know which players want wool socks and which need special support in their shoes. He has to know which players use Vitamin C, which need nasal spray, which want B-12 shots and which will need and can have sleeping pills on the road. In his job, Whelan is assisted by eight ball boys who look after the players' immediate needs: band-aids, muscle wraps, gum, coffee, tickets, and messages. They are supervised by a special helper who runs the movie before each game while the players are dressing—always a film of the team we're playing that night—and fulfills any player's special request. When a player leaves his alotted tickets at home, it is the special helper who sees to it that the guests get to the proper seats. The special helper also arranges for the selling of any tickets on a player's behalf.

Locker stalls about three feet wide line opposite sides of the room. On the floor of each stall sits a big black trunk in which the player can store his personal items. At the top of the stall is a shelf, under which is a clothes hanger pole and a plastic name tag identifying the occupant. Dick Barnett has an advertisement pasted on the side of his stall—"WLIB, GROWN-UP BLACK RADIO." Under the ad is a picture of Barnett looking particularly dapper in a tweed suit, white turtleneck, and tilted hat. Walt Frazier and Willis Reed have boxes of unopened mail and extra copies of their books, *Rockin' Steady* and *The Comeback Year*, lying on their shelves. Dave DeBusschere has old, framed *Sports Illustrated* photos of himself stacked against the back of the locker, and a rosary dangles loosely from his shoes. On the outside of my locker, in clear view of everyone entering the room, is a poster about the horror of heroin addiction. I expropriated it from the locker of a player who was traded. On the edge of my shelf Whelan's special helper, who knows of my liking for the Canadian north, has attached a plastic strip with the lyric, "There's a town in North Ontario," from a Neil Young song. Taped to the side of Phil Jackson's stall are two letters from the same writer. They say: "You're one of the worst players ever. I challenge you one-on-one for any amount of dollars," and "Last year I hoped you'd get hurt and you sprained your ankle. This year I hope you die."

Between stalls on one side of the room, a door leads to the showers and to the trainer's room, which is shared by the New York Knicks and New York Rangers. Inside there are two rubbing tables, two refrigerators, scales, a whirlpool bath, therapy machines, a medicine cabinet, a cushioned platform for knee weight exercises, and a 5,000 pound iron safe. Players sit one at a time on the left rubbing table where Whelan tapes ankles and tells stories that keep everyone laughing. When the Ranger hockey trainer of 24 years comes in during the pregame preparations —he moonlights as a Garden usher at basketball games—Whelan usually reminds him of the hockey team's latest loss.

---

After taking off my coat and hanging it up, I look around and see a ten dollar bill on the floor. I ignore it. Dick Barnett walks in and sees the bill; in one quick swoop, as if reaching to brush his shoe, he picks it up and puts it in his pocket. The room erupts in shouts, for the bill is counterfeit and was planted on the floor for amusement. The old lost-bill trick works again. Phil Jackson says he knew Barnett would go for it. Everyone laughs, including Barnett, who now argues that he was "hip" to the trick from the beginning.

Barnett, one of the greatest jump shooters in basketball history and a starter on the Knicks' first championship team, has only recently become Red Holzman's Assistant Coach. The Knicks' acquisition of Earl "the Pearl" Monroe from Baltimore hastened Barnett's retirement. He remained a regular for the rest of that year but the next season he became a reserve guard seeing little action. After a brief comeback in the fall of 1973, he retired to the sidelines.

Red Holzman realized Barnett's value to a team and kept him on. He travels with us often and always comes to practices and home games. His voice should belong to the best drill sergeant in the world. It is as if the air from his lungs passes through uniquely built passages and comes out in sounds heard only from a tuba of the highest quality. People listen when he speaks in his deliberate manner, stretching words apart by the syllables. His sense of the locker-room situation is unsurpassed. He dominates it with a combination of candor, seriousness, and humor. What may seem a personal matter—beyond the probes of anyone but intimate friends—becomes fair game to Barnett's needling wit and frank observation: the differences between blacks and whites, the contrast between old players and young, the idiosyncracies of sex, the sophistications of the well-schooled man.

Dick Barnett was born in Gary, Indiana, in 1936, the youngest of three children. His father was a skilled laborer in the steel mills. When his supervisors ordered him to perform menial jobs as well, he quit rather than bow to their authority. He took a job with the Gary Parks Department. To make ends meet, he sold scrap iron and made deliveries for merchants. His greatest satisfaction according to Dick was that all his children finished high school and none went to jail— obedient to his fervent admonition, "Don't bring the police to my door." Mrs. Barnett was a loving, protective mother faced with economic hardship. "When I was hungry," Dick recalls, "she always came up with a piece of bread I didn't know was there, or she gave me twenty-five cents to go to a basketball game. When I was sick she was there to rub Vick's salve on my chest."

The neighborhood Barnett grew up in was a slum, ringed by more prosperous white areas. The air smelled from factories. Homes, including Dick's, were plagued by rats. Pollution was part of the living condition and the critical skill was survival. Dick's parents told him to stand up and be a man, not to rely on anyone but himself. And they said that he would have to be twice as good as any white man to make it.

"I lived a very secluded childhood," Barnett recalls. "I was self-conscious and shy. I probably had an inferiority complex about other kids' clothes and their new shoes. I just had one old pair of brogans. I wanted to be away from people. To play cowboys and Indians, you needed other kids, but I could play basketball by myself. I didn't need anybody else. All I needed was a ball and a basket, or at the beginning, when I was 10, only a ping-pong ball and a tin can."

By the time Dick was a sophomore in high school, basketball had become his consuming passion. He spent more time on the Roosevelt High School playground than anywhere else. A big concrete tennis court, long since abandoned, served as his gym. It had no lights but a basket stood at each end. That was all he needed. Dick played basketball every day during his sophomore, junior, and senior years, one thousand ninety-five straight days of basketball. Some days, he played from 9 A.M. until midnight, with an hour or two at home for meals of grits, lunchmeat, maple syrup, bread, and water. Other days, when the temperature shot up close to 100°, he played from six to ten in the morning and then came back at three and continued until midnight. One summer he got a job in the steel mills cleaning oil spills, coal bins, and lathes for seventy dollars a week. After working eight hours a day in the mills, he went to the playground for another four. When school was in session, he would get into the high school gym where he practiced from five until ten every evening. When the gym was closed and he couldn't break in, he would shovel the snow off the playground and return to his familiar concrete. At first, he stole a ball from the school. Later, the high school coach gave him one. He says that he did not imitate anyone, but just started playing. His imagination provided the opponent and the game situation. He dribbled, faked, and took his jumper. He hooked and practiced twisting lay-ups. Occasionally, there would be a one-on-one game, but that wouldn't last long. Dick was easily the best player in Gary. Still, he never relaxed his regimen. Even on the night of his senior prom, he was shooting. From the court, he watched his classmates in their tuxedos enter the prom. "I saw them, but they couldn't see me because it was dark," he says. "After a while, you'd adjust to the darkness and could play. You had a comfortable feeling about where you were. . . . Even when they couldn't see me, they could hear the ball and they knew that it was me, Barnett, alone, shooting on Roosevelt playground."

In his senior year, Dick's high school team lost in the Indiana State final to Indianapolis' Crispus Attucks, whose best player was Oscar Robertson. College scouts recognized Dick's ability and offered him scholarships. Dick chose Tennessee State, an all-black school in Nashville. High school had not prepared him for the academic side of college and when he got there he devoted little time to study.

His college years—1955–1959—were turbulent ones for race relations in the South. Barnett experienced outright segregation for the first time in his life when he sat in the first row of a bus during his freshman year. Everybody stared at him and then he saw the sign, "Whites Only," in the front of the bus. He experienced racial protest for the first time when he accompanied a group of students to a lunch counter sit-in. A white man spat in the face of one of his friends and the friend remained motionless. Such incidents had a lasting effect on Barnett's view of whites and fused with his parents' advice about self-reliance and the need to be better than a white man in order to succeed. Suspicion and distrust existed in him alongside great determination, pride, and good humor. Still, he was not a campus leader in the protest movement or the politics of race. He was first a basketball player; he didn't have the time or interest for much else. Besides, being a star gave him a special status with most people at the school.

After four years at Tennessee State, during which his team won three NAIA small college championships, Dick joined the Syracuse Nationals of the National Basketball Association. For two years, he suffered Syracuse winters and sparse soul cooking. After a few swings around the league he realized that he *really was* as good as most of the white stars he had read about. He also knew that he was not equally paid. During those years, a quota system for black players operated on each team in the NBA as an unwritten rule. It limited the number of black players on a team, and even the number that could be on the floor at the same time.

When the American Basketball League was formed in 1961, Barnett left the NBA for the ABL's Cleveland franchise, which was coached by his old Tennessee State coach John McClendon, the first black professional coach in any sport. The Cleveland franchise went bankrupt within a year, and Dick Barnett returned to the NBA, this time to play for the Los Angeles Lakers. During six years there, as third guard behind Jerry West and several (as Barnett put it) "white hopes," he remained underpaid, underpublicized, and unappreciated.

The day businessman Robert Short sold the Lakers to businessman Jack Kent Cooke for four million dollars, Short told the Laker players how much he appreciated their loyalty and hard work. To show his gratitude he said that everyone could have a steak at the hotel and charge it to him. Barnett went back to the hotel and ordered twenty steak dinners from room service. He stacked them up in the hallway and left them there. "Man just made four million dollars and he's going to buy me a steak dinner—shit," he says.

In 1966, Barnett was traded to the New York Knicks, where he became less a shooter and more a complete ball player. He promptly became a star—too late to be known as a superstar. He had already spent his best years as a substitute in Los Angeles. When the Knicks won the title by beating Los Angeles in 1970, Barnett's wife told me, "They never would understand. Jerry [West] and Elgin [Baylor] always had to be the stars. That's why they never won and that's why I'm glad we beat 'em tonight." Once during those same play-offs, a referee called a foul on Walt Frazier, giving Jerry West two free throws. Barnett, who was on the bench for a brief rest and who very, very rarely yelled at players or officials, shouted, "He doesn't deserve it. He doesn't deserve it. That sucker doesn't deserve it."

═══════════

Barnett, still making excuses for his lack of discretion with the ten dollar bill, walks to his locker carrying a plastic suit bag. He is wearing boots, blue jeans, a black turtleneck, a tan outer shirt with yellow and black suspenders, and a Dutch boat captain's hat. He asks Danny for a jock and changes to a practice outfit. He goes out for some exercise, one-on-one, with a chosen rookie, before the game.

DeBusschere reads his mail, much of which arrives in yellow and red envelopes with flowers around the edges. Walt Frazier tapes his ankle as if he were a master mason building a wall. Willis sits in street clothes talking to reporters. I undress, spray adherent on my leg, tape my ankle, put my uniform on, get a leg massage from Whelan, wash my hands, and sit waiting for Red Holzman's pregame talk, wiping my hands with a towel and biting my fingers. A few minutes before Holzman starts talking, Barnett walks in with the rookies who have been working out before the game. Perspiration rolls down his face and arms and legs. His face is wrinkled and he looks drawn, worn, old. "Chump, rookie," he says.

"Mothahfuckin' old man don't guard nobody," the rookie says after losing the one-on-one game. "He holds you—anywhere closer to the basket than 20 feet and he's got his arms pushing your hips, knocking you off balance."

"Hey, Barnett," says Frazier, "that belt's gettin' bigger and bigger. All that running isn't gonna do no good unless you stop eatin' all those chocolate bars and nuts."

Barnett looks dissatisfied with the comment. He walks over to his locker. One by one, pieces of his equipment come off: his shorts, jock, shoes. He sits, staring at his socks after he taken them off and lays them on top of his shoes. He gets up and walks into the shower, the roll of fat around his hips jiggling with each step. As Holzman finishes his pregame talk, Barnett opens the suit bag which hangs in his locker and takes out a tie, a clean shirt, new shoes, and a gray pin-stripe suit. With meticulous care he transforms himself into a model suitable for the pages of *Gentlemen's Quarterly*. As we leave the locker room Assistant Coach Barnett knots his tie and prepares to meet the public as a new part of the Madison Square Garden management. His blue jeans hang on a nail.

The game tonight is against Kansas City, coached by Bob Cousy. It is strange to see this former Boston Celtic great in street clothes and on the bench. For me he will forever be #14 in green and white. Everyone in my home town believed he was the most deceptive, smartest guard in basketball. I have never seen a better passer.

By 1969 he was coach of the Cincinnati Royals, and for a short time that year put himself on the roster as an active player. We played them one night, after we had won 17 in a row. If we beat Cincinnati we would set a new league record for consecutive victories. Oscar Robertson, then with Cincinnati, fouled out with one minute and forty-nine seconds to go in the game and Cincinnati leading by three. Cousy had not played for six years, but he put himself into the game. He would try to save it. This was supreme audacity or monumental foolishness. As he would have done ten years earlier in his prime he looked down the bench, took off his warm-ups, and motioned to the scorer. His long arms dangled and his head arched backward with a sort of haughty determination. I fouled him with 27 seconds left. He made both free throws, giving Cincinnati a five-point lead. Willis

Reed was fouled with 16 seconds remaining and hit two foul shots, cutting their lead to three. Then with eight seconds left, Cousy threw the ball away on an in-bounds pass, which led to a DeBusschere dunk. Then Cousy lost his man, Frazier, who got fouled on a rebound and hit two free throws, giving the Knicks a one-point victory, 106–105, and the record. At the point when Cousy put himself into the game, the official score sheet read, "Robertson out (P6, T4). Cousy goes in—yeah team."

I have heard rumors about Cousy's inability to communicate with his players. They don't seem to agree with his insistence on perfection. Only Nate Archibald, his best player (a 5'10" guard from the giant government housing projects in the South Bronx) who ironically plays with a style reminiscent of Cousy's, seems to understand such dedication. But tonight they start the game strong, hitting long jump shots and unmolested lay-ups. During the first half we seem unable to do anything right. We walk, double-dribble, and throw passes away frequently. The timing on our plays is awry. It is as if we are playing out of synchronization. Still we go into the locker room at halftime only five points behind.

Holzman is hot. "When we lose the ball," he begins, "don't hesitate. Get your ass back on defense. And stop flying around out there like crazy men. The first thing *all* of you did that first half when you got the ball was to put it down on the floor and dribble right into the pack. Play with some poise, look around, see what develops. Play like you're pros and not some fuckin' high school kids. This half get the ball to our good shooters at the right time. And that open man— take the shot. The way we played, I'm surprised we're not down more. Five points isn't much. Cut out the stupid mistakes and we'll win. Okay. Let's go."

Red proves the prophet again. We slow down our game and gradually roll over the young Kansas City team. They make mistakes not out of carelessness as we did the first half but because we force them into our traps. We run simple plays five or six times each, and they never catch on. They do not help one another on defense; our screens consistently pick off pursuing defensemen. DeBusschere takes every opportunity to shoot and hits most of his shots uncontested. We win by twenty points.

═══

Basketball players and politicians have at least one thing in common. They meet the press almost every working day. In basketball, the interaction leads to a charade. Reporters try to lead players to statements which will confirm the reporters' own preconceptions and players try to avoid saying anything that will make them look bad. So, every game must be followed with explanations of the self-evident. Each explanation must be short enough to fit into a five-hundred word story and perhaps interesting enough to sell papers.

On an October trip to Philadelphia, four sportswriters accompany us, but on a play-off trip to the West Coast, there might be fifty writers, TV announcers, magazine reporters, and public relations people. On a Tuesday night at the Garden, there will usually be twenty members of the press in the locker room after the game. A few players run to the showers to avoid reporters and others practically solicit attention. Often standing in the nude, players will explain their own play and describe the weakness and strength of the other team. Everyone knows the interviewing process is brief. It takes place in twenty to thirty minutes and varies little from game to game.

The newspaper press and the broadcasting media have a spirited rivalry and often come close to fighting for access to players. Four or five times I've seen pushing, and once I saw a blow thrown. Middle-aged writers have stood in the center of a locker room screaming, "I can't do my job with all those microphones in my way. I have to talk to the players. We were here first." The Knicks' public relations man usually resolves the dispute by giving the newspapers the first five minutes, then the microphones join the questioning.

Many journalists have a herd instinct. They cluster around two or three players, elbowing for position. At times they seem to work together, one reporter covering one player, another a second—later pooling their quotes. Sometimes those around one player will go to a second, where the same questions will be repeated. Often, after the pack leaves, a reporter will return to ask the questions which will distinguish his story from the others. If a player gives the persistent reporter the angle he is looking for, the reporter reciprocates by focusing attention on the player. Among the press, players get reputations as being "good copy" or "bad copy," depending on their quips and cooperation. I'm bad copy.

Wariness of the press comes from my years as a college player when much of what I said and did received exaggerated attention. For a while I lumped all reporters into one category and viewed them as people who imposed on my privacy, asking questions about many things unrelated to basketball. Later, I realized that in a pro locker room they are interested much more in the game than my life. I began to enjoy talking with a few, who were as aware of the charade as I. Still, immediately after playing, I am not capable of giving instant analysis. I am too involved with the game. Yet, when I do try to explain my version of what happened—and sometimes that is impossible in a few quick sentences—reporters frequently look at me with blank stares unwilling to take seriously the relation between my words and the game. Other times my explanation is incomplete because I leave out germane but occasionally derogatory references to teammates. The solution I have settled on is to help the reporter when I can but otherwise to utter a few standard comments so often that they lose interest in me.

Most reporters are hard-working family men making a living. Some are anxious young fans who stand somewhat in awe of their idols and write puff pieces which reinforce sports clichés. A few are fair, reflective commentators on the sociology of sport. A couple know the game themselves and are confident of their own analysis. Others are insecure, pseudo-journalists who will slant a story in any way that will promote their own careers. A newspaperman once told me, "When you come right down to it, the politician's very survival depends on me and journalists like me. That's why I have no mercy on them and never respect their privacy. But you, at root you don't need us and it's as simple as that. You have your performance."

But it is not so clear-cut, for no one outside the arena would know about our games without the press. If the only information in the newspapers after a game was a tiny box score, professional basketball would be a different kind of experience for the player. And any writer who says I don't need him is either misunderstanding his job or attempting to ingratiate himself to me. The players and the reporters are bound together inextricably, like partners in a dance.

━━━━━━

After the game, nine reporters rush to Frazier's locker. Five walk to the training room where De-Busschere sits on one of the rubbing tables sipping a beer. Another six spread out among the other players.

"What do you think?" asks one. "Why couldn't you score during that stretch in the second quarter?"

"Do you think Kansas City has improved?"

"How would you describe Dave's game tonight?"

"What did Red say at half time?"

*"Do you think Kansas City has improved?"*

Video Associates, in cooperation with WOR-TV and WNBC Radio, names Dave DeBusschere the star of the game. For this honor, he receives a gift certificate from a local haberdasher entitling him to three knitted shirts in the color of his choice. They probably will arrive some time next summer and there is a fifty-fifty chance they will be the wrong size.

After taking a long shower, I dry myself with my sixth towel of the evening. My home uniform already has been hung up by one of the ball boys. A blue road uniform is in my traveling bag. The home uniforms are cared for by the club. They are cleaned about five times a year. There are two sets, plus spares that Whelan keeps in his closet. Keeping road uniforms clean is the responsibility of the player, a responsibility individual players don't always fulfill. Fortunately the group can always express its dissatisfaction in such subtle ways as inviting a particularly ripe uniform to shower with the team.

After I dress, I stuff my wet socks, shoes, and jock into the leather traveling bag with my road uniform. I gulp two sodas, take a beer for the bus ride to the airport, and leave the locker room.

Outside the Garden, a black man waits, another diehard fan who in the old Garden sat under the basket. I see him less frequently since the new Garden opened because he can't afford the higher ticket prices. Tonight is the first time this season. "Hi ya, Bill," he says, "how you doin'? You guys will win it all again this year if you keep goin'. The Pearl is ready. You know, you can score more if you drive for the basket. You should shoot more, too. I remember you in college. . . ."

I finally get to the bus which will take us to Newark Airport for an 11:30 flight to Atlanta. I am cold and my eyes burn from the sweat and wind. Thirty teenagers stand outside the windows chanting "We're number one, we're number one."

"How can these kids be here," says DeBusschere, "don't they have school tomorrow?"

They jump up and down pointing at their favorite players and begging for an autograph. As we start moving they run along the street with us, for one block. Two slip and fall.

The bus enters the Lincoln Tunnel and the lights come through the bus window and strike my black leather bag. The brightness of one light quickly fades as we move through the tunnel. Just as the bag is about to become dark, we pass another light and brightness returns. The variations make the bag look like a neon light blinking outside a cheap hotel.

"Only 18 more," says DeBusschere.

"Not so soon," I say. "Too early to start counting."

On and off, shining and dull, light and dark; off to another city. Travelers in the dead of night.

At the entrance to Newark Airport stands a young Marine with his head shaved, his shoes spit-shined, and his hat tilted over his eyes. He rests at semi-attention, perhaps expecting the military bearing to conceal his human fragility. *His* team makes uniform dress a part of its overall discipline. My team emphasizes individuality in dress. Yet we both work to achieve disciplined cooperation. It occurs to me that he might be going home tonight; unprepared for a life without the platoon-certainties both he and I have come to depend on.

On board there is the usual struggle of a late night flight. We are tired but can't sleep. Card games start. One is going on in the seats in front of me. I sit next to Jerry Lucas, who sometimes keeps the card game results in his head; when each player wants to know if he is ahead or behind he can ask Lucas, who reports for instance that Barnett is $268 behind for the year and $18 ahead for the evening. The team calls Lucas "The Computer." Tonight he does not keep score but concentrates on a piece of paper (the card players will have to settle up when the plane lands). About halfway through the flight, he looks over at me and says, "I just made a million."

"How?" I ask.

"This puzzle I just figured up. I'll sell it to Mattel or Cross and it's bound to market like wildfire."

Jerry Lucas is an eternal optimist. If twenty people before him had placed their hands into a basket and had been bitten by a snake, Lucas, the twenty-first, would be sure he could hypnotize the snake with his fingers. His positive approach to life meshes well with his quest to make millions overnight. When I met him, I was a junior in college and he was a successful pro. He spent two hours telling me about some children's games he had designed which were going to be big national sellers. He reasoned that because Kroger Inc. was located in Cincinnati and he was then a hero for the Cincinnati Royals, Kroger would love to market his games in their stores.

After playing at Middletown High School and Ohio State, and starring for the 1960 U.S. Olympic team, Jerry Lucas was the most famous basketball player in Ohio history, even more famous than Oscar Robertson. He was Phi Beta Kappa—a straight A student in marketing. Handsome, with thick black hair and perfectly formed teeth, he was every mother's hope and every coed's dream. The national press pictured him as an All-American boy who drank postgame milk shakes, married a barber's daughter at age 20, and knew where he was going in life. Important things always took priority with Jerry. When he and a few other Ohio State seniors (including John Havlicek and Larry Siegfried) barnstormed the state, Lucas apparently was careful to announce to his teammates that since he was the star attraction his share of the gate would be 50 percent. The other four players divided the rest.

For Lucas basketball could never satisfy his thirst for activity or wealth. During his fifth year with the Cincinnati Royals, he started a restaurant business. Bringing in some of his teammates as investors, "Jerry Lucas' Beef 'n' Shakes" prospered. According to Lucas, in 1968 a prospective buyer offered him $1.5 million, which he turned down because he wanted to maintain control and was convinced that an even bigger payoff would come in the future. Besides, the buyer demanded that Lucas quit basketball to manage the business. Jerry refused because he knew he had some good money years left.

Lucas took a set of expansion plans for his company to various banks. One gave him a verbal commitment for financing, and he began extensive construction. During the recession of 1969 the bank canceled his credit line. In 1970, Jerry Lucas declared bankruptcy.

He was traded to San Francisco, moved to California, and began anew. After two successful and happy years on the coast, he was dealt to New York. He brought with him his penchant for deals and mental games. He has an odd talent for pulling words apart and rearranging their letters alphabetically. The first day he was in the Knick training camp I drove him to practice. We stopped behind a car and he said in rapid-fire order, "E-E-E-J-N-R-S-W-Y. That's New Jersey spelled alphabetically." Another time after one of his early games as a Knick I saw him confound the chess champion, Bobby Fischer, with his memory of the Manhattan phone book. "What is number 34 in the first column on page 146?" Fischer asked. "The number," Lucas replied, "is 758-4010." Fischer became so perplexed by the feat that he sat on a stool alone in the kitchen of our host's apartment for fifty-five minutes trying unsuccessfully to figure it out.

Armed with a Knick contract, new business opportunities, and no debts, Lucas prospered. He looked for ways to avoid paying taxes. He constantly hunted for bonanza tax shelters. Once, trying to encourage me to join him in an apartment deal guaranteed to yield triple deductions and a 15 percent annual tax-free income, he said, "Those fuckers have stopped auditing me. They used to audit me every year until finally I told 'em it was ridiculous. They didn't find anything wrong in seven years. To continue was harassment. I don't pay taxes, period, but I do it legally. I'm not stupid." With no taxes to pay, he dreams of other jackpots in puzzles and magic seminars. He has even begun to write a book about memory which he thinks will be a bestseller. If it was 1849 and Jerry Lucas was living in New England he would be on a clipper ship bound for California, along with many of the other fortune hunters who helped build America, convinced that he'd find the biggest gold strike in the West on his first day of prospecting.

We land in Atlanta at 1 A.M. It is 21 degrees outside and the frost makes the runway sparkle as if it were sprinkled with bits of glass. Inside the gate three other groups wait to board planes to Miami, San Antonio, and New York. Two hundred people in such a small space so late at night confirms the strangeness of the travel world. Some of them sleep while others, unable to rest, read with bloodshot eyes. Wiry men with leathery skin stare at our entourage as it passes.

"Is this the circus?" asks a tiny woman with a bouffant hairdo that adds a foot to her height.

"No, must be ballplayers."

We wait forty minutes for our bags, which delays our arrival at the Atlanta Marriott Hotel until 3 A.M. Even at that hour, a fan with a New York accent approaches me in the lobby. He says he came all the way from Miami and could I spare some time tomorrow to talk basketball. He tells me he knows everything about me. I nod, yes, force a smile and keep walking. This is Atlanta, after all, and tomorrow is another day.

I put my leather bag in the room and go to the coffee shop, where I eat two eggs over easy with sausage, toast and jam, milk, and grits. The first time we played in Atlanta we also arrived early in the morning and everyone was hungry. Most of us didn't go to our rooms first but went directly to eat. Barnett, who usually was the first one to the coffee shop late at night, said he was going to his room. All the way in from the airport the black players had been making allusions to "bossman," "boy," "sit in the back of the bus," revealing the abiding wariness many blacks have about parts of the South. Several of us were eating our eggs, ordered from a black headwaitress, when Barnett walked in wearing a Dashiki. He had changed just for the Marriott coffee shop in Atlanta. He claimed he did it only for comfort.

## 3

THE NEXT DAY, WEDNESDAY, AFTER BREAKFAST AT noon with the late-night fan, I discover that the week's convention at the Marriott is for Georgia beauticians. Carefully coiffed ladies fill the halls, lobbies, and restaurants of the hotel. They try to resemble the women in *Cosmopolitan* magazine ads, but only succeed in looking like the women in department stores who spend all day, every day, demonstrating the proper application of various cosmetics. The beauticians giggle, pat their permanents, and look at themselves in their compact mirrors. Six of them crowd into a restaurant booth made for four, and order cherry cokes.

At 2 P.M., Dave and I sit across from each other, both ordering the same lunch: green salad with Thousand Island dressing, steak medium with french fries, coke, chocolate sundae, and a cup of coffee. I remain seated after he leaves and overhear two college students in the next booth talking about their future. At other tables I catch bits of conversation dealing with life insurance, pregnancy, and local construction projects.

For all the camaraderie of DeBusschere and the rest of the team, there is an overpowering feeling of loneliness on the road. I telephone friends and conduct business over long distance, hoping to connect with someone who will share my life's experience and understand. The day passes. Local acquaintances may show up. There is chit-chat with them of times past and superficial discussions of contemporary events—his job, and my activities outside of basketball. After that exchange, it's over. There is nothing more to say, little common interest. Sometimes I take in an art exhibit, call on a local politician, or visit an unusual section of town. There is too little time, though, and there are too many towns, each one different and exclusive, yet all part of a whole too large to know well in the time available. So I sit in a hotel room reading books, listening to the radio, and arguing with DeBusschere about whether the TV should be on—dropped into a city of which I'm not a part, unable to explore it or to know its people as much as I would like. I remain a performer traveling from city to city with only my work to sustain me.

Some day, I say to myself, I won't be spending 100 days a year on the road. Travel disrupts the continuities of life. Seasons of the year become merely months of basketball games. Some day I'll wake up in the same place every morning and that will lend wholeness to my life. Flying away to play and returning one week later destroys that possibility, not because of what happened to the place, but by what has happened to me while away. When I travel constantly the experience I have seems to consist largely of observations and moments of enjoyment—the 80 degree weather in San Diego, the desert nights in Phoenix, the days in the mountain ranges of the Northwest—but never are they lived through and absorbed. I miss that sense of sharing that comes from people living together in one place, over time. I miss permanence.

In my hotel room the day passes slowly. In the late afternoon, Country-Western singer Bill Anderson comes on the radio and sings his super-patriotic hit, "Where Have All the Heroes Gone?" He speaks for the common man. He touches the hearts of descendants from the strong Scots-Irish stock that settled the Revolutionary South and lived with the economic pressure that a slave economy generated. They rarely held slaves but they still managed to eke out a substance in the backwoods of the Piedmont. Their descendants proudly sent sons to Vietnam and, as Anderson sings, they can't understand why others did not want to.

Plantation art covers three walls of my hotel room. One scene shows four ladies dressed in highcut flowing dresses carrying bonnets and parasols; they are having tea on a columned porch with a gazebo in the background. Another picture is of a man in a waistcoat, white pants, and black boots. He is walking with a woman who picks flowers under a moss-filled oak. A third picture is of the grand hall: A Confederate officer chats with a woman who wears a long red gown, while a second Confederate officer awaits his lady as she descends a sweeping staircase. These scenes, with all their assumptions about power and position in the Old South, are the past of Atlanta's new look, progressivism.

Inside the chambers of Marriott modernity Bill Anderson's words clash with these scenes from the aristocratic past. Atlanta styles itself as leader of the "New South." Hank Aaron's marriage to a civil rights activist makes the society columns of the newspapers. The Marriott, opening its doors to anyone who has money, the great American leveler, fills its ballrooms with black cotillions and its banquet rooms with black businessmen's luncheons. Never mind that white lawyers and real estate tycoons still control much of Atlanta's future. The opinion leaders of the city see Atlanta as cosmopolitan, prosperous, black and beautiful, aristocratic, powerful, and most of all, in the vanguard of progressivism. Atlanta, the capital of the Confederacy, is the home of Martin Luther King, Julian Bond, Lester Maddox, and Scarlett O'Hara. Atlanta sells its municipal bonds easily while mayoral candidates make crime the number one issue of a campaign. Atlanta is a deceptive study in contrasts.

Around 5 P.M., I take a 45-minute nap and then board the game bus two minutes late.

"That'll be a five dollar fine," Holzman says.

An elaborate structure of fines punishes tardiness: a five dollar fine for arriving from ten seconds to five minutes late, a ten dollar fine for being up to ten minutes late, and five dollars for each additional minute over ten. Holzman established the fine system with approval from the team. The money collected goes into a pot that is used for a team party at the end of the year. Therefore, it is to everyone's advantage for Holzman to fine.

"Boo-ay-ay," shout the fellows in the back of the bus.

"On behalf of the team I want to thank you for the contribution, Bill," says Phil Jackson.

We wind through the residential streets of Atlanta to the Omni (as in *omni*potent or *omni*scient), the new home of the Atlanta Hawks. The Hawks, formerly in St. Louis, were the team of my childhood fantasies. Bob Pettit, Cliff Hagen, Clyde Lovellette—they made my interest in the game burn. They provided examples of individual moves to develop. During high school summers in my home town of Crystal City, Missouri, I would drive sixty miles a day to play in pick-up games against the best players in the St. Louis area. One night I hit a hook shot against Cliff Hagen, and another night a Hawk rookie, Zelmo Beaty, split my face with an elbow under the eye, which the Hawk doctor had to stitch up. Every other Saturday night during my grade school years my friends and I would go to a pro game in St. Louis, and the Boston Celtics became our bitterest rival. Those were my days as a fan. Sunday afternoons we watched the Hawks on TV and later tried to imitate them in backyard games. The high point of those years came when Pettit scored 52 points and the Hawks won the world championship. The low point came a year later when the Celtics regained the title.

In many ways I will never be as much from anywhere as from Crystal City—that small cluster of houses tucked between two limestone bluffs on the banks of the Mississippi River. When I was growing up, it was a town dominated by the Pittsburgh Plate Glass Co. and populated by workers of many ethnic backgrounds, melding together in the heartland of America.

The mythic hero of my youth was Ozark Ike, the funny-paper athlete with one enormous blond curl and the Daisy Mae girlfriend, and a tantalizing penchant for making last-second shots, scoring touchdowns, and hitting home runs. Then there were the real-life heroes with less fantasy and more flesh—like Basil, Perry, Cook, Hicks, LaRose, Carter, King, and the Jennings brothers, all of them high school basketball players in a factory town.

I was an only child born to an energetic mother who spent a lot of time at church, and a banker father who suffered from severe arthritis. We lived in comfortable circumstances. As early as I can remember I was programmed to become a successful gentleman. My father insisted on manners and my mother on success. I took lessons in practically everything: dancing, trumpet, french horn, piano, boxing, tennis, golf, swimming, canoeing, typing, French, and horseback riding. Our home served as a meeting place for my friends, and my mother arranged excursions to museums, baseball games, swimming holes. By the time I was fourteen I had become self-motivated. Whatever raced inside me was more demanding than any pressure applied by parents or teachers.

At about that time I began in earnest to play basketball, spending four hours a day, alone, in the high school gymnasium, choreographing the smallest detail of particular moves I had learned at Easy Ed Macauley's basketball camp. Gone were the leisurely hikes with my grandfather along the banks of the Mississippi listening to stories of his youth in Germany. The river road became only a track along which I ran for miles, training for my sophomore season. Basketball was my preoccupation about which I never talked with my parents and about which they manifested little interest. At fifteen, when a girl called me up one night in a playful mood, I told her I was already dating someone—a basketball.

The high school coach, the only man who would ever be "the coach" to me, was like a monk, withdrawn personally and unsociable in town circles; unreachable by the power of the company, the church, the bank, or the mayor; rigid with discipline and sparse with compliments; inspiring to boys like me, cruel to those unprepared or unwilling. Never did he confuse his roles. He was not the college counselor, family advisor, tutor, athletic businessman, or budding politician. He aspired only to be the coach. It was a calling. If in the years as a New York Knick there would be thousands of words written about passing and teamwork and hitting the open man, it would all be true but it would not be new. It would be "the coach's" game, which by age seventeen was second-nature to me.

An education at Princeton placed a layer between adolescence and manhood and pressed me toward a traditionally acceptable career. But it was my two years of study at Oxford that proved the more rewarding experience. I was determined when I left the United States in 1965 that I was finished with basketball, or more appropriately I was finished with the public acclaim that surrounded the game. My last year in college I had received fifty letters a day and had become something of a symbol as the Christian scholar-athlete. Although it was true that I studied, practiced, and went to church, the media exaggerated each facet of my life until expectations were generated in the public that I could never fulfill. When I told reporters I was interested in politics they wrote that I wanted to be President or Secretary of State. When I told ministers that I could not speak at their church they accused me of being unChristian. When I told coaches that I could not play in post-season all-star games they said I was ungrateful to the sport which had given me so much. The greater the acclaim became, the more certain it was that the public appetite could never be satisfied. The only way out, I thought, was to reject basketball and become a lawyer or a businessman.

At Oxford I had time to experiment with every aspect of my life. For the first time since I was fourteen I took chances with my body—hiking, racing cars, and playing contact sports—without fear of injury. Eating five meals a day I even gained 30 pounds. I questioned my religious faith and sought workable moral values instead of simply rules. I became more playful and rebellious, responding to events in a way that discipline and obligation had outlawed before. I began to enjoy people more, at first only if they were interesting foreigners and then even a few of the less serious-minded Americans. I traveled widely in Russia, the Middle East, and western Europe. Specific studies were neglected without guilt. I stopped taking myself so seriously, recognizing that life is as much a good laugh as a stirring sermon. I began to see how far I had to grow and change if I was to become a person that even I would like to know.

Toward the end of my second year, after not touching a basketball for nine months, I went to the Oxford gym simply for some long overdue exercise. There I shot alone—just the ball, the basket, and my imagination. As I heard the swish and felt my body loosen into familiar movements—the jumper, the hook, the reverse pivot—I could hear the crowd though I was alone on the floor. A feeling came over me that stirred something deep inside. I realized that I missed the game and that the law could not replace it. I knew that never to play again, never to play against the best, the pros, would be to deny an aspect of my personality perhaps more fundamental than any other. Uneasiness about the public would not, I vowed, prevent me from doing what I loved. Three weeks later I signed a contract with the New York Knicks.

The Atlanta locker room is quiet. Walt Frazier has not arrived. Atlanta is his home, and because he visits relatives when we're here he usually arrives at the Omni late. Some of the players go out early to practice. That leaves Whelan, Barnett, DeBusschere, and me in the taping room. The talk as always is of crime, death, money, sex—visions of the real world through the locker-room lens.

"When I was a trainer for Rochester in the International League," says Danny, "we used to play in Cuba. A guy in a white suit used to visit in the locker room after the game. See, he was a Batista man. He would offer a ring to players for $800 and he'd say it was worth $2,000. Of course, the players didn't believe him, so the guy in the white suit would say, 'Take it to New York, have it appraised at Tiffany's. That'll cost you $25 and if it's not worth what I say, keep it and don't pay me nothing.' Well, a couple of guys started doing this, and the rings were worth what he said, ya see, 'cause he got 'em real cheap from Switzerland.

"One day I asked Jesus, one of the Cubans on our team, if he was for Castro or Batista. He stared at me, pulled me over into the corner, whispered, 'I for Castro, but don't tell any of the other Cubans or I die.'

"When Castro finally did take over, the guy in the white suit," Danny says, pausing and aiming an imaginary gun at an imaginary line of traitors, "shit, he fell into the ditch with a lot of other people I used to know around baseball when we traveled there in the International League."

Barnett picks up the general thread of discussion. "Yeah, but in the United States rich people never go to jail. When did you ever hear of a rich man going to jail? They pay off the judges and everyone else. Shit, where there's millions to be made, no court is going to stop the big men with the money."

"Yeah," Danny says, "you can always find a crooked lawyer. I've seen enough of them to know."

"Motherfucker steals a loaf of bread and gets ten years, and there are big fuckin' corporation presidents rippin' us all off and gettin' suspended sentences," says Barnett. "That's justice?"

The other players return and listen to Red go over the Atlanta team, its strengths, it weaknesses, what might work and what we have to do to win. We leave the locker room and begin taking warm-up lay-ins. In the ceiling a latticework of lights and speakers comes alive with sound and brightness. The steep pastel seats become darker as they lead at one end to a big American flag. At the opposite end are signs which say, "Kristel Kritters" and "Junior Hawk Corner." Only a few people are in the Omni. A band assembles at one end of the court and begins playing. It is the Reedsville, Georgia, State Penitentiary Band. In the middle of lay-ins, the public relations director for Atlanta pulls Walt Frazier aside. A member of the band who is doing time for armed robbery stands with both of them. He is an old high school classmate of Frazier's.

The scene is about a common heritage which is never completely a thing of the past. Four years earlier in Atlanta, before the Omni was built, the Hawks played in the Georgia Tech fieldhouse, a place Frazier remembers from his childhood as a "real white groove." That night there was an all-white band playing during warm-ups. They played several popular songs and then played "Dixie." Every black player on both teams reacted. Their heads turned, they looked at each other and at their opposite number on the other team; one or two glared at me. After a few uncomfortable minutes Bill Bridges, the black Hawk captain, told the band to stop playing "Dixie." They did.

Walt Frazier controls the game from the opening buzzer, putting on a show for the eight members of his family in attendance. He scores 34 points against Pete

Maravich, the white darling of Atlanta, and the Knicks win by 8. Frazier's family is dressed in their Sunday best. Clyde (a name Frazier acquired because of his preference for the wide brimmed hats and 1930s styles seen in the movie *Bonnie and Clyde*) arrived at the game in clothes a little more conservative than usual. He, too, respects his past. The first time he came to Atlanta, for example, he shortened his Afro because his grandmother didn't like hippie long-haired kids, regardless of how "cool" they were.

Walt Frazier is the oldest of ten children. His grandparents on his father's side come from farm country near Augusta. Since slavery ended, people in his mother's family have continuously done subsistence farming on a plot of land near Sandersville. During most summers of his first ten years, Walt, along with his sisters, mother, and grandmother, visited their country relatives. From those days, he remembers the taste of freshly picked corn and newly plucked chicken, fried Southern style. He recalls the near impossibility of catching a baby pig on the run, however quick your hands. Then, at night, conversations about snakes filtered into the kids' bedroom from the living room where relatives spoke in cautious tones. Finally, the midnight train with its shrill whistle passed so close to the house that Clyde and his sisters feared it might come crashing through the bedroom door one night.

In Atlanta, Walt lived with his mother, father, brother, and sisters. His father's parents lived next door. His grandfather worked from dawn to sundown. "You're not a man unless you have credit," he said. He worked on an assembly line at the Atlanta Paper Company for thirty years, until he was forced to retire at age sixty-five. He got a good pension, but he still insisted on doing work such as lawn and building maintenance at homes where his wife was employed as a domestic.

From his grandfather, Walt heard the familiar Puritan litany about hard work and frugality. From his father, he saw the rewards of the fast life. Walter, Sr., was a hustler in the Summerhill section of Atlanta and provided his family with a comfortable lifestyle. "As a kid," Clyde remembers, "whatever I wanted my father got me, from spending money to tickets for the Globetrotters. We went shopping every Saturday." Whenever someone in his family wanted to go somewhere, Walter, Sr., sent one of his employees in a Cadillac to drive him. A maid came once a week to cook and to clean and there was always plenty of food and clothing. "I can remember trying on my father's clothes alone in front of the mirror," Clyde says, "wishing I was big enough to wear the bright two-button sport shirts that opened in front, or the brown and white Stacey Adams shoes. I liked the way they looked on him and I wanted to look the same."

When Walt was twelve years old, his father lost his territory. Clyde's grandfather had always urged his son to save his money, but Walter, Sr., was an incurable spendthrift. Abruptly, the pockets that used to be full of twenties, fifties, and hundred dollar bills had only fives in them. "The house was always crowded with people," Frazier says, "and then suddenly, nothing. Nobody came when he no longer had cash, except some whites who came around looking for money he owed them. He started coming home only three nights a week. It was bad but I never asked him what happened. In my own mind, it was like some guy in power who let things go to pot. Everybody played the numbers. He was just the man lucky enough to control it—for awhile. I don't think my father had worked a day in his life until then. I don't think he ever had a job."

When Walt was eleven years old, he stopped going to the farm and devoted all his summers to sports and work. At the playground three blocks from his house, he spent long hours playing baseball, basketball, and football. When it rained, the instructor introduced Clyde to ping-pong, Scrabble, and Monopoly. Clyde gained a reputation as a ballplayer, and this, strangely, exempted him from the gambling that the older teen-agers went in for after playground hours. "Go home," they would say as they rolled the dice. "You're going to be an athlete."

One summer, Clyde got a job cleaning up the old Atlanta Cracker baseball park during the day. Then he and his buddies returned at night, sneaked under the stands and gave hotfoots to the paying fans. Other jobs were cutting grass in the white sections of Atlanta, cleaning carpets in private homes, and working as a bus boy in a restaurant or as a curb attendant at a Zesto ice cream stand.

The Atlanta of his childhood was a world of separate and unequal societies for white and black people. The wrestling matches, the buses, and the ballparks had special black sections; even the drinking fountains were segregated. Clyde and his friends called whites "crackers." They often played with them in pick-up games or swam with them in creeks, but, as Clyde recalls, "Once you left that field, you went your separate ways. I never had a run-in with adult white people when I was young. I was never too many places where they could call me 'Nigger' for long. There were places or neighborhoods you knew you shouldn't go, but the other guys would. I would always mind my own business."

His all-black high school did not compete against white athletic teams. When the time came for him to go to college, he wanted to choose Tennessee State or Grambling, each a black school. His grandmother and mother, however, wanted him to go to an integrated school, and he dutifully chose Southern Illinois University. He led Southern Illinois to the NIT championship of 1967. After seeing the all-around play he demonstrated in that tournament, the New York Knicks drafted him number one, and two months later he signed a contract to play professional basketball in New York.

━━━━━━

Now, after the game in the Omni, eight members of the press crowd around the players in the steaming locker room.

"How would you describe Clyde's game tonight?"

"Why were you hitting so well in the third quarter?"

"Do you think the Hawks will make the play-offs?"

"How would you compare Maravich and Frazier?"

Star of the game: Walt Frazier. He is promised two knitted shirts. We shower, stuff our wet clothes into our bags, and head for the bus.

Back at the hotel, the beauticians are partying. I notice that the door across from mine is open. There are people inside laughing. I drape my uniform across chairs to dry and wander across the hall. Three men and three women sit on the beds drinking and talking of sex, clothes, make-up and what they used to do in high school "up at Van Buren." One of the men, a Georgia Congressman who spoke at the beautician's dinner, makes a hasty exit after no one listens to his discussion of taxation and political integrity. With the departure of the Congressman, I am the third male. A man pours more bourbon. The talk decreases. I hesitate briefly, but what the hell I'm only young and single once.

After so many nights on the road in so many different hotels encountering so many different situations, everything takes on an ephemeral quality; everything ends with the payment at the cashier's desk the next morning. What normally would be out of the question for me becomes acceptable in the self-contained world of Mt. Marriott or Holiday Valley. Normal shyness would prevent me from entering a stranger's hotel room, but on the road there seems to be nothing to lose. Everyone in the hotel sleeps under the same roof for one night and moves on. Loneliness can be overcome only by reaching out for

contact: a conversation in the bar, a sharing of dinner,
a question in an elevator, a direct invitation, a telephone call to a room, or a helping hand with doors,
windows, TVs, locks, or ice machines. The percentages are that if a man spends enough nights in hotels
he will meet a woman with whom for that night he
will share a bed, giving each a brief escape from
boredom and loneliness. Make no mistake: Life in
hotels is no continuous orgy. There are months of
nights in one's room, alone. And it is rare that an en-
counter develops beyond the verbal level. It is very
unusual when everything feels right and the loneliness
of the road oppresses two strangers equally at the
same time.

## 4

"THIS IS THE LAST CALL FOR FLIGHT 623 TO CHI-
cago, departing from Gate 54 on the East Concourse."
I hurriedly swallow my orange juice, roll and coffee
and head for the gate. The plane ride is full of familiar sounds, sights, superstitions, and annoyances.

Generally, I prefer to sit next to a team member.
After a few years of trying to meet and talk with
strangers on planes, I began to put more value on
being alone while in the air. There are no telephones
or interruptions up there. A trip to the West Coast
guarantees five uninterrupted hours of splendid soli-
tude. It is different from the loneliness of hotels and
terminals, or the yearning for permanence that
glimpses of cities and mountains generate. Seated
next to a window with a book in hand and the hum
of jet engines as backdrop, I enjoy flying. The movement of the plane and the knowledge of changing
environments imply that things are being accomplished, while I rest in total comfort. Some of my best
moments come on airplane flights. In the off-season, I
sometimes fly off somewhere just so I can concentrate
during the flight. The fuselage of a jet airplane
serves as a mechanical sanctuary for me.

As I get on the plane, all the seats are taken except
one—next to a man wearing a dark suit, white shirt,
and striped tie. I sit down and immediately start to
read. The man looks at me between glances out the
window and at his *Sports Illustrated*. "Pardon me,"
he finally says, "but aren't you Bill Bradley?"

"Yes."

"I'm Jack . . . I went to basketball camp with you fifteen years ago."

"Yeah, what do you do now?"

"I work for Kimberly Clark, the paper company."

"How do you like your job?"

"You know, I've learned a lot. Once you sell Kotex as a man you can sell anything."

We talk about the basketball season, players salaries, his family, and his athletic past for ten minutes.

"You still play ball?" I ask.

"Not much, but I help organize teams for our athletic club in Detroit."

"That must be enjoyable."

"Yeah, usually things go all right," he says, "but one of the basketball nights a member invited a friend who invited another friend who was black. Now, you know, I don't think I have much prejudice. I don't care if blacks are members, but I know how the guys felt. Thirty percent of our club is Detroit policemen and they hate them. Anyway, I went up to the black guy and told him to leave, that this was an all white club. He took it the wrong way and next thing I knew the NAACP was suing the club. It's terrible the way things are. I think some day we'll all be one race. As long as people know what they're getting into and what it means for the kids, it's okay with me. Take our company, for example. There is only one black at our regional meetings. He's really sharp but that's one of the things wrong with the company. They say they won't hire a guy if he's not a graduate of college. I say you don't need no degree to be a good salesman."

Our conversation dries up after lunch and then I ease into reading my book. The rest of the trip to Chicago is uneventful and silent. When we land, the salesman says to be sure and look him up in Detroit —maybe I might want to visit the athletic club.

After getting off the plane, I go directly to the soda fountain at O'Hare Airport, where I buy the only genuine vanilla ice cream cone available in an American airport. As we pick up our suitcases from the baggage conveyor, one black porter says to another, "They're the Knicks. Did you see the one in the long black maxi with the fur collar and hat? He was somethin'." We board a city bus, the kind whose sides are all windows, whose seats face each other, and whose bright fluorescent lights are either all on or all off. Lucas's bag is lost. We sit in the bus waiting twenty minutes until the airline authorities assure him it will be at the hotel by evening. People on the sidewalk stare at us in the bus. Lucas finally boards with the team's public relations man and we pull away. Like an illuminated fishbowl in the rush hour traffic, we move toward Chicago.

I find a message at the hotel which says to call a Chicago friend. When I reach him, he says that he has arranged a little party in my honor at his apartment. He lives off Rush Street in a brownstone. People start arriving around 9:30 and the evening quickly turns into an interrogation.

"What is Frazier really like?"

"Is Holzman the best coach?"

"Will Willis ever be 100 percent again?"

"Is DeBusschere a good guy?" a girl asks.

"Yes."

"Who is the toughest guy for you to guard?" asks her boyfriend.

"Havlicek."

"Tougher than McMillian?"

"Yeah."

"No, how can you say that? McMillian is so much bigger and better at one-on-one. McMillian's the best. He's better than Havlicek. He's harder for you to guard."

"No, he isn't."

"I think he is."

"Okay, whatever you say."

Finally, one of the members of the group says, "Do you really like to play basketball?"

"Yeah, more than anything else I could be doing now," I reply.

"That's great. You know, I once played the trumpet. I think I know what you feel. I played in a little band. We were good. We'd play on weekends at colleges. In my last year we had an offer to tour and make records. Everyone wanted to, except me."

"Why didn't you?"

"My father thought it wasn't secure enough."

"What about you?"

"Well, I didn't know, I guess I agreed," he says. "The life is so transient. You're always on the road. No sureness that you'll get your next job. It just doesn't fit into a life plan. So, I went to law school and quit playing the trumpet, except every once in a while. Now, I don't have time."

"Do you like law?"

"It's okay, but nothing like playing the trumpet."

# 5

THE NEXT MORNING, DEBUSSCHERE GETS UP BEFORE 10 and walks to the nearby office of Merrill Lynch, Pierce, Fenner & Smith to check the progress of the market. He is going to have lunch with a vice president of a Chicago bank to obtain information on the McDonalds Co. He has been toying with the idea of getting one of the New York franchises and believes that since his banker is a personal friend of the president of McDonalds, he has a chance.

I eat breakfast with a friend who is thinking about running for Congress in Chicago if he can get the Daley machine's endorsement. The talk is of fundraising, political intrigues, and political organization.

After breakfast, I go to a luncheon put on by the Chicago Bulls Boosters, where I am scheduled to be the principal speaker. It is held in a downtown Chicago hotel and about 200 men attend. Part of being a professional basketball player is speaking at many kinds of affairs: shopping center openings, charity fund raisers, sports banquets, high school and college assemblies, bar mitzvahs, annual company dinners, and church services. You learn to sense the mood of an audience. The element of performance in a speech often outweighs substance. The hard thing for me is to strike the balance between preaching on the one hand and slapstick on the other. Somewhere between those two extremes lies the craft of a professional speaker, be he lawyer or teacher, politician or basketball player.

The expectations of an audience to which one speaks are much different from those of 20,000 basketball fans. They aren't nearly as demanding. During my senior year at college, I spoke in the area of New Jersey around Princeton. When my college coach would accompany me, he'd say the audience laughed at my jokes, not because they were funny, but because I told them. In a way he was right. I have often heard Walt Frazier or Willis Reed or Red Holzman tell stories that are not side-splitting but that made audiences roll in the aisles. The temptation as a speaker is to adopt a standard pose and to work from it to any audience. Willis acts as if he were a politician at a county fund-raising dinner, giving recognition to all the other politicians in the audience. He unfailingly directs compliments to the Knick organization—owners, general manager, coach, publicity man, and secretary—and to the fans, and to his hosts of the evening. Frazier, on the other hand, always conveys a cocky aloofness with an occasional good-natured jibe at Holzman, other players, or the toastmaster. For example, he will say, "Red Holzman is a smart coach. Smart enough to draft me." Holzman's approach is self-deprecating. He becomes the put-upon little guy who just tries to get by against all the odds. He will say, "I heard what the toastmaster said about baldness. I don't think that's so nice. [Pause.] I feel lucky to be here tonight. Out of place with all these stars, but lucky. [Pause.] And that's why you people shouldn't make fun of me. Besides, Willis Reed said it was okay if I came tonight. [Pause.] He knows I need a free meal."

For me, the challenge of improvisation is the most important element of public speaking. I will arrive at the dinner or luncheon without specific preparation and, as the meal progresses, I'll write my speech, particularly the humor. Sometimes I surprise myself. Occasionally I fall flat, like the time I got up at a formal dinner and introduced Mr. Vanderbilt as Mr. Rockefeller.

The luncheon lasts two hours. The businessmen seem to be entertained with my locker-room humor and informed about the inequities of the reserve

clause. I return to the hotel room, where I find De-
Busschere asleep with the television on. The room is
strewn with the residue of our stay: soda cans, books,
odorous drying uniforms and gym shoes, an emptied
suitcase, and a promotional packet from McDonalds.
I undress and sleep for an hour. The TV awakens
me. A talk show, one of America's consciousness
raisers, blasts away into the late afternoon. The guest
is Woody Hayes, the football coach at Ohio State
University. He says, "Anyone who will tear down
sports will tear down America. Sports and religion
have made America what it is today."

"Why doesn't he tell that to the official he kicked,"
DeBusschere says as he changes the channel.

Most arenas in the league are modern structures
built in the path of urban growth. Chicago Stadium is
a relic from the past. Built in 1929, it stands like a
mountain of Depression concrete, in the center of
urban decay. When I first started playing professionally in 1967, there was an operating McDonalds restaurant across the street. Now, all that remains is the
sign with the golden arches. The rest was leveled.
Outside the arena black kids ask for tickets. Stores in
the area are boarded up. Those that remain won't last
long. The crime rate in the nearby housing projects is
high. One of the reasons that Chicago never draws
well is the physical danger involved in parking. There
are three lots near the stadium with spotlights shining
on them. For those who come late, there are more
distant lots which are safe only if you leave with the
crowd. A year ago, two friends waited for me after a
game for half an hour and as we approached their
car, a young kid robbed us at gunpoint.

Inside the stadium, things look as if they hadn't
changed for twenty years. Vintage popcorn smells
permeate the arena. Vendors in blue uniforms load
their boxes with an evening's supply of hotdogs, beer,
and soda. The court and hallways are so dirty I
change shoes after we play here. The arena itself is
cold and the locker rooms are cramped. It is difficult
for twelve players to dress or shower at the same time.

Chicago is a city in which many of our players bump into their pasts. Barnett's father shows up from Gary occasionally, or some long-lost Tennessee State friend, living in Chicago, says hello. Frazier's wife lives in Chicago. He always arrives at the stadium separately from the team after spending the day with his son. The mother of Cazzie Russell (a former Knick) sometimes stops by to say hello to Cazzie's old teammates.

As we change into our uniforms, Danny opens the evening's banter. "I knew a boy who came to the clubhouse one day in San Francisco in the old Pacific Coast League. He complained of a stomach ache. The doctor said it was overeating. He continued to complain. His father took him to another doctor who diagnosed it as a sore throat. The kid died that night of a ruptured appendix."

"Doctors are just like anybody else," I offer. "There are good ones and bad ones."

"Yeah, and some of them are terrible," says Danny. "You ever hear what happened to Jeff Chandler? He had a simple operation but the doctor left some tool inside him. He bled to death. Sinatra sued the hospital for I don't know how many millions, which went to Chandler's wife, but that didn't do fuckin' Jeff any good. He'd already gone West."

"Some doctors are as counterfeit as wrestlers," says Clyde, who has just arrived. "You know my grandmother used to believe that wrestlers were for real on TV."

"Yeah," says Barnett, "all those wrestlers rehearse. Man, some of them cats make the big bankroll, $100,000 or $200,000 a year. Ernie Ladd, my man, is making more now wrestling than he ever did in football."

The door of the locker room opens and in walks Ernie Banks, the Chicago Cubs baseball player who does sports broadcasting in the winter. His Afro is clipped close and the slightness of his build is surprising. He has a wide smile and a button on his lapel that says "Get Excited." He opens with "Hey, how you doin'? You're real professionals now; right, how you doin'?"

As Banks walks over to Frazier for an interview, Barnett turns away and says, "No motherfucker's suppose to be *that* happy, man."

━━━━━━

Effective defense in basketball requires good body position (keeping yourself between the offensive man and the basket) and knowledge of where the ball is —all the time. Each player must remain alert to help if a teammate's man breaks free. No player, though, can stop another player every time down the court; that's just the nature of a game played by talented individuals. Two offensive maneuvers, the screen and roll and the jump shot, one old and one new, decrease every team's defensive capabilities.

When the jump shot was first introduced, it was particularly devastating because conventional defensive wisdom urged that the defender never leave his feet. Bill Russell, the Boston Celtic great, changed the game by demonstrating that a player could not only jump to block shots successfully but could also control the game by selecting when and where to block shots. Now players regularly attempt to "reject" (block) opponents' shots, an act that has added more grace and excitement to the game. But, the shooter still has the advantage of knowing when he will release the ball.

A screen and roll is a basic basketball play. One player "screens" or "picks" (impedes with his stationary body) the defensive man of his teammate, who is then free to shoot unmolested in the open space behind the screener. If the screener's defensive man "switches" (jumps from guarding the screener to guarding the newly freed man), the screener rolls (moves in a straight line) to the basket before the other defensive man can get into his path. While in motion, he receives a pass for what should be an extremely easy shot. Thus the screen and roll is complete.

Sometimes a screen is set for the purpose of freeing a player to receive a pass. Team patterns can be designed so as to spring open men at any point on the court. Proper timing and placement (when and where to set screens, when and how to use the screens, when and how to pass the ball to the newly freed man) can make defense very difficult.

If team defense is to be even partly effective, it requires determination, considerable effort, and group coordination. The Chicago Bulls display all three. Under the leadership of their coach, Dick Motta, an iron-disciplined Mormon who frequently reminds me of Holzman in his pugnacity and competitiveness, the Bulls harass players all over the court. While it is usually easy to dribble the ball three quarters of the court deep into your own offensive zone, the Bulls make it difficult to dribble anywhere. The players guard their men chest to chest for the full length of the court. They dive to the floor for loose balls and into the stands for lost balls. They fall down in front of offensive players at the slightest brush and if a charging foul is not called they bounce up and continue hounding. They communicate effectively among themselves. They know when and how to switch. If a screen is set, the man who switches tries to smother the ball handler so that he cannot pass the ball to the man rolling. If the screen is away from the ball, they frequently see it far enough in advance to alert each other and prevent receipt of an uncontested pass.

Ironically, the Chicago offense revolves around the assumption that defenses make mistakes. They run rigid offensive patterns. They remain patient until the defense's concentration or determination lapses and then they exploit it. For example, they run a simple screen away from the ball and wait until the defense either doesn't switch, which gives the shot or switches too soon, which gives the roll. Only on rare occasions can a defense prevent both options, particularly when the offense sets good screens and has the patience to take only good shots. Many of their baskets come from "offensive turnovers" (mistakes, such as bad passes, and violations, such as steps, double dribbles, and offensive fouls). One of the anomalies of their offense is the presence on the team of Chet Walker, who is one of basketball's great one-on-one forwards. Not a flashy player, he makes his moves with such perfect timing that his one-on-one action does not disrupt Chicago's patient offense.

One-on-one is a game within a game. Every pro has played it. Sometime before his involvement with the complexity of team ball, the need to develop pride and confidence made individual confrontation necessary. A few players continue to feel such soaring confidence in their abilities that they *prefer* to duel with a single opponent rather than coordinate their movements within the team. When two one-on-one stars play against each other, there is a lot of "get-backing" (when one scores, the other must reciprocate). Screens bother them, for screens crowd at least two more people (the screener and his defensive man) in upon them. One-on-one stars want the ball, an open court, and a single defensive man. Then they operate with imagination and uncanny skill. There are nights when one-on-one players can so easily beat any defense that they seem to be reaching heights of invincibility unknown to other mortals.

"When I was younger coming up, everything was a constant one-on-one battle," says Dick Barnett. "Even if you were in a game you were still playing against your man in a one-on-one situation. As you mature in the pros, you no longer feel like you have to go out and build a reputation. The game isn't as personal. You have so many games that your approach is more workmanlike." A more controlled one-on-one is practiced by Walker and by most veterans. They don't shoot every time.

Walker is an excellent basketball player standing 6'6" and weighing 230 pounds. He is a handsome man with a close-cropped Afro. I first saw him play in college, and even then his body and mind seemed in balance. He does pretty much what he wants on a basketball court, getting a good shot at his whim. He will dribble to the middle of the court or to the baseline, and will go into his shooting motion as if he is going to jump and shoot. If the defender does not jump, Walker will "fake his shot" another time and perhaps even a third time. By the last fake, the defender will at least be off balance and will probably have jumped into the air to block the anticipated shot. Walker will then take his jump shot unmolested, or will be fouled as he shoots.

If he chooses to fake his shot before he dribbles, he retains the option of driving to the basket when his defender jumps for the faked shot. In addition to Walker's mastery of these basic moves, he is a very smart player. He senses when to make the explosive drive to the basket and when to play nonchalantly within the pattern of the team. He senses when he has the advantage and he knows that he has to be patient to use it most effectively. Above all, Walker is confident in the clutch—shooting during the last quarter— and, eight times out of ten, if there is a last-second shot, he is the one to take it.

Holzman finishes his pregame talk. Everyone claps and we walk down a linoleumed hallway, up a set of steps, and into a still empty Chicago Stadium. The three tiers of seats are newly painted in red, white, and black. The steel beams cross the ceiling and disappear into the sides of the building's old brick walls. Radio booths hang at the Bulls' end with the station's call letters, WGN and WMAQ, embroidered on the giant banners which cover the bottom half of the booths. Concession stands sit at the same spot on each tier, looking as if they were carefully stacked toy blocks. The old pipe organ with its red and white ornate wood decoration high above the visitors' end soon will be raised into position and the organist will play the national anthem. We go through our warm-ups. People start to fill the midcourt area seats.

DeBusschere looks distracted and tired. He takes a warm-up hook that misses the rim. Chicago for Dave is the best and worst of cities. He played baseball here with the White Sox. There isn't too much left from those years but the friends. There's one in particular, a Greek-American with whom he usually spends most of the night before the game, drinking in "just a few joints Nick and I found." DeBusschere sometimes surprises me the next night by playing a great game, but often he is fatigued. He is 33 years old. Still, he prepares for the game and expects himself to perform as if he had rested for two weeks.

DeBusschere is the best defensive forward in basketball. There is always physical contact between him and the man he is guarding. Resting his forearm on his opponent's chest or waist, he rarely gets screened; sometimes pushing his man in order to get past the screen and not to switch. He places his body chest to chest with his opponent's, somehow avoiding a foul and still preventing his man from beating him on a drive. DeBusschere plays the percentages. He knows he can't block the shot of a good jump shooter, so he tries to force his man to shoot while off balance. There are areas of the court in which he allows his man to maneuver uncontested and other areas in which he fights his man for every inch. He channels a player toward areas of the floor that are out of that man's optimum shooting range. Given the choice of battling Dave for 48 minutes to get good shots or of taking more difficult shots farther from the basket, many players resign themselves to the bad shots. When DeBusschere guards a taller player or a great one-on-one player, he tries to deny him the ball by "overplaying" (placing his arms or body between the offensive man and the passer rather than between his man and the basket). If the ball moves quickly to the opposite side of the court, DeBusschere beats his man to the spot on that side of the court at which the player is most likely to receive a pass. Like all great defensive players, he enjoys playing defense. "You are always in a game when you play good defense," he says. "I like to hound my man constantly—make him feel like I'm never going to let him breathe. I don't want him to feel I am ever an inch away from him. Wherever he goes, whatever he does, I anticipate first. I start in the afternoon before the game, thinking about how I can upset the man I guard. It is hard work, but you can make it fun."

Tonight, as usual, DeBusschere will guard Chet Walker. Theirs is a rivalry which dates back to high school. DeBusschere was from a Catholic, all-boys high school in Detroit. Walker grew up in Benton Harbor in southwestern Michigan and went to the public high school there. DeBusschere shot well from the outside and played with good fundamentals. Walker was the first player in his high school's history to dunk the ball. They met in the Michigan State High School Finals at East Lansing before a crowd of 15,000. Both played well. DeBusschere, who had a stronger supporting cast than Walker, fouled out with five minutes left in the game, but his team pulled it out for the 1958 state title.

In professional basketball two athletes' careers often become intertwined. They may be friends and may even have come from the same city or neighborhood, but only when they are on the court do they feel the intense rivalry that exists between them. The more times one player meets another, the better he gets to know not only the other's abilities, but also his personality. Subtle weaknesses become glaring shortcomings to one who knows how to exploit them: a tendency to lose your temper, a hesitation to take a pressure shot, a preference for the flashy low-percentage move, a fear of losing, an inability to cope with changing tactics. Mutual respect develops between many pairs of players. Mutual enmity festers between others.

The buzzer sounds to start the game, and DeBusschere, unstrung by the warm-up, is already on the bench drinking water. I ask him how he feels. He says he's ready. I'm not convinced. Holzman and Barnett suggest an opening play. The game begins.

The Bulls are at their best, and soon they lead us by ten points. Walker takes DeBusschere to the baseline twice, fakes, and scores easily. Dave does not discourage him with aggressiveness. He is a step behind as Walker flashes across the lane and takes a pass for an easy lay-up. He can't seem to keep him away from the ball. The Knick guards do not move the ball to the open man, or go into quick one-on-one moves. Instead, they dribble without penetrating to the basket until the twenty-four second clock is about to run out. Then they force shots. I am smaller than the Chicago forward I play against so I try to overplay him. He takes me low, near the basket, and simply shoots over me. I draw three quick fouls. I also miss four open jump shots. Holzman replaces me with Phil Jackson, the Knicks' third forward, who at 6'7" and with extremely long arms, is a better defender.

Phil envelops opponents. His specialty is the "double team" in which, flailing his arms, he drives the man with the ball toward one of the corners, preferably where the half-court line meets the out-of-bounds line. Once there, a second defender leaves his man and plugs the only outlet, thus trapping the man with the ball. A bad pass or a steal often results. When Phil makes his move, you can see panic on the face of an inexperienced player. Generating pressure and threatening contact are at the core of Phil's defensive game.

━━━━━━

John Jackson, a shipbuilder from Bristol, England, came to America in the 1660s with his brother, Jay. They settled in what is now Portsmouth, New Hampshire, where the family practiced its trade until the American Revolution. At that point John's grandson sided with the English and, as a loyal Tory, chose to leave the newly formed United States of America. King George III of England deeded 50,000 acres to him on the Ottawa River in Pembroke, Ontario. There, the offspring of John Jackson farmed the fertile river valley soil, and intermarried with neighboring O'Briens and Clemonses. To this day, Joe Jackson, Jr., Phil's older brother, retains the deed to the Jackson home in Portsmouth which they held throughout their years in Canada. It has been preserved as the oldest frame house in the state.

Joe Jackson, Phil's father, is part of the John Jackson branch of the family. He quit school in Ontario at fourteen and worked on the farm, which, after generations of split inheritances, had dwindled to 200 acres. Winters, he traveled north to the lumber camps at Hudson Bay, where he labored first as a cook's assistant and later as a lumberjack. He devoted more and more time to his work as a lay preacher in the Lutheran Church. He married and had one girl. During a second pregnancy, both mother and child died. Simultaneously, the Great Depression hit the farm, bankrupting him. Mr. Jackson took these events as signs from God. He headed west to become a lay preacher in Montana. There he met an evangelist named Elizabeth Funk.

She was the daughter of Peter Funk, who came to Montana from Weyruth, Saskatchewan, when strong anti-German sentiment during World War I had forced him and his family to leave. Mr. Funk set up a stable and boarding house business for Indians at Wolfpoint, Montana. He worked as a wrangler of wild horses. After breaking them he would sell them to individuals for riding or to the U.S. Army for meat. "My gramps was out to make his fortune," says Phil, "which he never did. It was a tough land to make money in."

Elizabeth Funk was valedictorian of her high school class and captain of the girls' basketball team. She received a teacher's certificate and worked in a one-room schoolhouse for two years. At 22 she went to a Penetecostal seminary in Winnipeg, Manitoba.

After leaving there, she joined her brother Peter and sister Nell, and formed a team of traveling evangelists. Nell would later become a missionary in China, be placed in a concentration camp by the Japanese, and, after World War II, teach on rooftop schools in Hong Kong, but now she was busy telling the people of Montana about Pentecostalism. The procedure for the Funk family was the same in every prairie town. They stood on street corners playing the accordion, proclaiming the imminent arrival of Christ, and asking people to come to a service that night. In the upper room they had rented for the occasion, they sang. They played the piano, the guitar, the accordion; they encouraged the "spirit of the Lord" to move among the congregation. Sometimes they spoke in tongues. The Funks became well known throughout Montana during their seven years of constant travel. Once, it is said, Betty Funk, the blond, blue-eyed proselytizer, even performed a miracle on a boy born without eyes.

When Joe Jackson met Betty Funk, they fell in love and married. Phil Jackson was their third child. The Jacksons were a ministerial couple "living for the Lord." Their first parish was in Haver, Montana, followed by churches in towns of the Northwest such as Hamilton, Anaconda, Miles City, Great Falls, Williston, and Fairfield. Betty preached Sunday night. Joe preached Sunday morning and took care of the church finances. "My father was compassionate and thorough," Phil says. "My mother was competitive and brilliant—a prophetic evangelist who dealt with the books of the Bible like Revelations and Isaiah and the concept of the world's end. Every Sunday since I was born the apocalypse has been coming next year. My parents saw it as their job to get everyone ready."

Phil didn't see a doctor until he was six, and he did not receive a penicillin shot until age fourteen. When he was injured, the first act, in accordance with Biblical tradition, was the laying on of hands and the rubbing on of olive oil. Other than eyewash, Mercurochrome, and band-aids, the only treatments for illness were the herbal remedies of the old West. For example, a staph infection was treated by a poultice of old bread crusts, onion, oatmeal, and milk wrapped in a hot towel. Every fall for one week each Jackson child had to take a cold preventative made of sulphur, honey, and deer lard.

At age sixteen, when Phil stood six feet five inches, he abandoned his first love, baseball, and chose basketball as his favorite sport. He acquired keys to the Williston, North Dakota, town armory. Alone, he sneaked past the stage that stood at one end of the hall to the tile basketball court, where for hours he worked on his hook shot.

Phil's high school team became known statewide. Their nearest opponent was a hundred and twenty miles away and some games involved round-trip journeys of six hundred miles. The team traveled in the cars of the coach and assistant coach, driving along Highway 2 through the butte country and the Badlands of North Dakota. Slowly, they crossed into the north central part of the state, where the land became flat, and grazing land gave way to farms and trees. The high school gyms held 1,500, with bleachers on the stage. At many games, fans stood three deep along the sidelines and under the basket. Outside, the temperature was ten degrees below, and the wind made it feel like forty below. If the windows had to be opened to cool the crowd, condensation formed on the playing surface and occasionally it froze, leaving a thin layer of ice on the court. Win or lose, the memory of a game passed quickly, for the team spent most nights of away games in the motels of North Dakota. One might feel down about losing, but sleeping four players to a room, two to a bed, made any prolonged depression difficult.

Jackson's style as a player developed in accordance with his build, which reminds me of a clothes hanger turned upside down. Tall and thin, with long arms (42-inch sleeve), he seemed to be off balance constantly. When he ran or jumped or shot he seemed to be caroming off unseen opponents, able to right himself with just enough time to make the necessary move. It was as if his arms served as separate sides of a scale which never achieved equilibrium but constantly fluctuated from side to side. He surprised big men by his defensive skills and made them feel they were being guarded by a man with three sets of arms. He shot his hook with great accuracy while coming across the middle. In high school he led his team to a second-place finish one year and a first the next in the North Dakota State Schoolboy Tournament. A center from a rival school surpassed Phil in individual statistics, but together they were easily the two best players ever to compete in North Dakota. The other high school star failed to improve in college and faded like so many before him; but Phil continued to improve each year at the University of North Dakota, and New York drafted him in 1967.

With Jackson's substitution, the Knicks seem revitalized. He blocks two shots, steals three passes, and over a span of four minutes gets six rebounds. Frazier hits four jumpers and we tie the score. Chicago seems befuddled. Jackson hits a hook across the middle and then takes a lead pass from DeBusschere and dribbles the length of the floor for a reverse lay-up. Barnett smiles and shakes his head, unable to comprehend how, despite his apparent awkwardness, Phil can get the job done. On the last series of plays in the first half, Jackson blocks his man from a rebound, only to see the ball bounce to a Chicago guard, who attempts a drive for a lay-up. Phil leaves his man, lunges across the lane as if out of control, and swats away the ball just as it is about to hit the backboard. Goal tending is not called. The buzzer sounds. The Knicks are up by three at the half.

I believe that basketball, when a certain level of unselfish team play is realized can serve as a kind of metaphor for ultimate cooperation. It is a sport where success, as symbolized by the championship, requires that the dictates of community prevail over selfish personal impulses. An exceptional player is simply one point on a five-pointed star. Statistics—such as points, rebounds, or assists per game—can never explain the remarkable range of human interaction that takes place on a successful pro team. Personal conflicts between team members will never surface if there is a strong enough agreement on the community's values and goals. Members of the Budapest String Quartet disliked each other personally, but collectively still made exquisite music. They did so in part because they had a rigid score that limited the range of personal interpretation. The cooperation in basketball is remarkable because the flow of action always includes a role for creative spontaneity; the potential for variation is unlimited. Players improvise constantly. The unity they form is not achieved at the expense of individual imagination. That creative freedom highlights the game's beauty and its complexity, making the moment when the ideal is realized inspiring for the players, thrilling for the fans.

As the New York Knicks meshed in 1969, Red Holzman's role in the development of unselfish team play was crucial. With rules, personal manner and organization he clearly established himself as boss. But, he also encouraged contributions from players, sometimes deferring to their judgment. A player rarely made a suggestion that Red had not thought of before. Still, he allowed each player to believe that his help was essential. He told us we were as good as any team and that potentially we were the best. He had no technical secrets or remarkable innovations. As he said, "Everything done today was done twenty years ago, you guys just do it better."

The real genius of Holzman lies in his handling of players. A comment on a plane or in an airport might relate tangentially to a previous game, but it is always delivered low key. He never tells players exactly what he wants them to do beyond the general rules of "seeing the ball" on defense and "hitting the open man" on offense. He prefers to shape a player as he performs. Toward some players he is stern; others he cajoles and flatters. A few he abuses verbally. Each of his moves is calculated to manipulate the player toward action which Red thinks will bring victory.

Most men would have failed as coach of the New York Knickerbockers. Great college coaches often can not make the adjustment from coaching boys to controlling men. Holzman does not beg players to do good deeds, nor does he set up elaborate codes of conduct. He expects everyone to act as a responsible adult and he treats players accordingly. To rookies and substitutes he says, "If we miss a practice, it's up to you to find a place to work out on your own. Just make sure when and if you're ever called upon to play you're in shape." To veterans he says, "No one drinks in the main bar of the hotel where the team stays. That one belongs to me." And, "If you manage to get lucky, don't fall asleep on top of the covers. I don't want any colds." To all players he says, "If we win you will have a lot of free time; if we lose you belong to me." In his first year as coach we lost often, and during one twenty-five day stretch we played eight games and had twenty-one two-hour practices. Everyone learned quickly that life was more pleasant if we won.

Other men Holzman's age who become coaches in the NBA have difficulty communicating with black players. They overdo their understanding of blackness so that it comes off artificial. Or, they can't understand black pride or individuality, and sometimes even slip into a careless use of a code word like "boy." Holzman never makes racial mistakes. Everyone is subject to the same treatment. It seems natural that he senses the right course, for he grew up a Jew in a non-Jewish world, where discrimination was a very real part of his own life. He understands the dividing line between paranoia and reality. He also had coached black and Latin players in Puerto Rico for four summers prior to becoming the Knicks' head coach. It was there that he learned the flexibility in approach that allows for different life-styles and different values on his teams. It was there that he learned to discard his own non-basketball perceptions when they clashed with a player's in an area unrelated to the game. It was there that he learned to enjoy a way of life different from his own in New York.

Holzman knows that whatever happens on the team, the next day brings another game. Whenever crowds become vicious he says that it is nothing compared to Ponce, Puerto Rico, where frequently after games the visiting teams had to wait at center court for an hour, surrounded by police, until the fans calmed down. I have the feeling that the Ponce experience has given him confidence in handling any player in any situation.

Some coaches who try the professional ranks can't take the road schedule physically or emotionally; being away from home for 100 nights a year is too disorienting. But for almost ten years Holzman was the New York Knicks' chief scout, traveling constantly throughout the United States from November to April. He set his own schedule, booked his own plane and motel reservations, made his own appointments, and picked his own game to watch. He became accustomed to the vagaries of road life. The strain of the away-from-home schedule as a professional coach is for him merely a continuation of well-formed travel habits.

Many coaches in the NBA do not understand the press and public relations job that a coach has to master. Holzman had seen six Knick coaches fired while he was the chief scout. At a certain point, the press had always contributed to each coach's downfall and each victim had assisted his own demise with careless remarks in unguarded moments. Holzman never says anything bad about anybody to the press; if possible, he says nothing. That way, players do not read the paper to find out what the coach thinks of their game, and no sportswriter can extract from him the name of a player on whom to pin defeat. Left with little material from the source, the writer develops his own interpretations. Holzman's "cooperation" exasperates some reporters, but it works beautifully. He has mastered probably the most tricky aspect of being a New York coach. He will probably never be a celebrity. But then, he only wants to be the Knick coach.

In technical terms, Holzman avoids the average professional coach's mistaken emphasis on offense. Many coaches assume that a professional team can run more plays than in fact is possible. They insist on rigid adherence to a pattern, and then after their approach brings losses, they are not flexible. Instead, they develop major personality clashes with players, which brings more losses, or they give up trying to coach and watch one-on-one chaos, which also brings more losses. "If you play good, hard defense, the offense will take care of itself," Holzman says. All the things Chicago does well on defense, the Knicks do equally well when we play Red's way. He believes that at least a third of offense should come from defense. A quick steal or a double team or an interception can lead to a basket with very little offensive effort. Wearing a button-down Oxford shirt, a striped tie, and dress slacks at a practice during the season, Holzman crouches and pivots, explaining what he means by "seeing the ball." He urges us never to turn our backs to the ball, always keeping our men and the ball in sight. Even when there is too much one-on-one, he emphasizes defense before he admits that there is an offensive problem. In all these ways, Holzman is the right man, in the right place, at the right time, and as a team the Knicks prosper—most of the time.

═══════

The second half play in Chicago takes a turn for the worse. I quickly get my fourth foul. Phil returns but he gets three quick fouls, too. Meanwhile, Walker is having a great night against DeBusschere. Chicago wins by sixteen. Even in defeat, there is a star of the game. Frazier, who in the fourth quarter led a desperate charge for recovery, is awarded two knitted shirts.

The tiny locker room is now jammed. I am in the shower. Reporters are asking me questions and spray is soaking their notebooks. They want to know about Walker's night, about the Chicago defense, and about our inability to sustain our second and fourth quarter spurts. I retreat into the hot water which offers a more peaceful state of mind. My neck muscles loosen. I hear only the hiss of hot pellets striking my head. I think back over the nights on the road. I chuckle about the time in Cincinnati two years earlier when DeBusschere bet me $50 I couldn't monopolize the post-game TV interview conducted by an opinionated announcer who frequently criticized players. I talked for four straight minutes in answer to one question, much to the consternation of the interviewer, who glanced hurriedly at the camera several times from under his toupee. He never realized what was happening. I won the bet and the following week received four letters from viewers who said the interview was either a great practical joke or I was crazy.

Phil asks me what I am grinning about. I say it's just a joke I remembered. Then I turn to the soap which has softened into a yellow mush stuck to its tray. As I stand in the cramped shower stall I think about the insulated world we professional basketball players live in. We travel from city to city, sometimes as if we were unaware of a larger world beyond our own. Every city we enter is full of crises and problems that never reach us in a hotel room. The daily worries and pressures of workers concerned about how to pay for food, housing, or medical care never penetrate the glass of our bus window. To do our job, we have to remain healthy and follow orders. In any airline terminal even the sad scene of a soldier's farewell or the joy of a family reunion often by-pass us making no impression. In the airports that have become our commuter stations we see so many dramatic personal moments that we are calloused. To some, we live romantic lives. To me, every day is a struggle to stay in touch with life's subtleties.

Yet events of the larger world do buffet us sometimes. I remember a phone call that interrupted a press conference I was having with the local sports reporters on my first visit to Chicago as a Knick. It was 1967 and a former college classmate had been killed two months earlier in Vietnam. His wife, whom I had met twice, had read in the newspaper that I was in town. She wanted to talk with somebody since things were tough for her just then. There was not much to say.

A night in early 1973 at the Chicago Stadium stands out in my memory too. I was kneeling at the scorer's table, preparing to reenter the game in the second quarter, when I heard the public address announcer say, "Ladies and gentlemen, attention please. President Nixon announced tonight that a cease-fire in Vietnam will be signed on Saturday, all POWs will be returned and all American troops will be home in sixty days." Scattered pockets of twelve and fourteen among the 17,000 in attendance stood and applauded. There was none of the catharsis of a V-J Day. It was as if people had forgotten the war. The turmoil of those years flashed across my mind and I thought about my friend's wife.

I towel dry and dress in silence. The reporters have gone. Danny Whelan zips his equipment bag. I grab a beer and head for the bus.

I wonder sometimes what effect our group has on other people as we travel around the country. Here we are at Chicago's O'Hare Airport. We saunter, limp, swear, and tug at our tight-fitting clothes. The Filipino bartender draws us five glasses of draft beer. We guzzle them. Three soldiers at the end of the plastic bar look up from their glasses full of Scotch. They can't be more than nineteen years old. Our conversation trails off after the first beer. Two players leave to make late night calls to Chicago girl friends. Silence, then the heads of soldiers and players alike rotate, turning left to right as a lady with peroxide hair walks past the bar window. "What an ass!" the bartender says. No one responds. We are too tired. We down one last beer, pick up our bags, and head for the Knick charter. The automatic ramp is broken so we walk down concrete stairs to the outside. The night is clear and cold. Looking under the tail of the plane I see others lined up at angles. The pavement is wet and gritty from the salt spread to melt the ice. Then, the freshness of a winter night becomes the staleness of a grounded airplane reeking of gasoline fumes. We taxi down the runway. Planes are being repaired in big hangars; searchlights pierce the black night like white arrows. A quick jolt, speed, momentum, lift, ascent, flight, the deep hum of engines. It is 1:15 in the morning. I eat Macadamia nuts, shrimp cocktail, salad, steak, baked potato, five pats of butter, brussels sprouts, and cherry pie. I drink a beer, three Seven-Ups, three Cokes, and milk. There are card games, crossword puzzles, scotch, the *Chicago Sun Times* and *Chicago Tribune*, news of yesterday, today; the unmemorable reflex of another flight.

One of the stewardesses sits across the aisle from me and we talk. Her name is June and she has flown for seven years. She has soft brown hair, an attractive face with blue eyes, and a careful manner. She ranks high in stewardess seniority. That's why she chooses the Knick charter—four girls to handle twenty-five people. A veteran of the Cincinnati-Detroit-Columbus route and the New York-Los Angeles transcontinental flights, she can now choose among any routes or charters available. She says that she has just visited the two stewardesses with whom she shared an apartment in her first year of flying. One of them was recently given a bonus for heroic work during a crash landing. The other just had a difficult abortion. For June the thrill of working at a decent salary in the so-called romantic world of travel has passed. She left her parents in a small Minnesota town where her picture appeared in a local paper when she won her wings. The life no longer holds excitement, or escape, or independence for her. She shopped the Loop in Chicago, visited Disneyland in Los Angeles, toured the Empire State Building and the Statue of Liberty in New York, learned how to move around San Francisco—until her destinations held little interest for her. She turned then to people because, "After all, they're more important than buildings." She had affairs in some cities where friends began an evening with a quiet dinner or invited her to a loud party. The affairs came from the plane, from the men who understood the road and its disorienting quality. She had thought at separate times of marriage with two of them, one of whom seriously thought of marrying her. But it didn't work out.

Flying keeps many stewardesses in a limbo between Hollywood and Duluth. Many have expectations they can never meet, and all run the risk of becoming impersonal after so many passes, so many invitations, so many unrealized dreams. There are those who see the deception of the exaggerated glamour; after several years they quit or get married or take an office job. The rest, as long as the schedule is hectic enough, don't have to think about the past or the future, just about making the airport bus on time.

The plane touches down at 3:45 A.M. Frazier, Jackson, and I share a cab as usual. The driver takes the Van Wyck Expressway to Grand Central Parkway to the Long Island Expressway to Van Dam Street to the 59th Street Bridge. As we cross the bridge the smell of freshly baked bread filters into the car, one of the few pleasures of early morning travel.

Manhattan is between day and night. Only a few floors are lit in the skyscrapers as janitors wrap up their night's work. Newspaper trucks and garbage trucks move on empty streets below the skyscrapers, preparing the city for another day. Cabs pass us taking night people home. A couple on Second Avenue, leaning against each other for balance, hail a cab. She wears his suit coat. Men leave the massage parlors of

53rd Street. A lone hooker stands at the corner by the New York Hilton. A few people talk outside the doughnut shop on Eighth Avenue, waiting for it to open. The doorman of my apartment building tells me he is sorry about the loss in Chicago but he can't feel too badly because he made $100 betting against us. I get into bed around 5:30 A.M.

My legs ache. Just one more game this week, then we have two days off. We will have played five games in seven days in four different cities.

I toss restlessly in bed, unable to relax. I remember that I forgot to take the telephone off the hook; I don't want anyone to wake me early Saturday morning. I pick up the receiver and stuff it in a drawer under my undershirts. After twenty more sleepless minutes, I draw a hot bath and ease into its relaxing warmth. Foam from the liquid soap covers the water's surface. After ten minutes of soaking and a slow towel-dry, I fall into bed and sleep. It is dawn.

## 6

SATURDAY DOES NOT BEGIN FOR ME UNTIL 1 P.M. Whenever we return from a road trip late, the next day is always a jumble. Breakfast and dinner seem to fuse. At 1:15 I have a cup of coffee and a doughnut and at 3 P.M. I have my usual pregame meal. I will not eat again until a midnight supper after the game. A friend and I walk for fifteen minutes through the streets of midtown Manhattan. Back at the apartment I read for half an hour. At 5 P.M. I sleep for an hour. The alarm goes off at six. In preparation for the game, I stack several Rolling Stones records, dipping into my imagination to gather some aggressive enthusiasm. "You can't always get what you want," sings Mick the Jag, "but if you try sometime, you might find you get what you need." Predestination with a rock beat, courtesy of satanic public relations. "I met a gin-soaked ballroom queen in Memphis . . ." That's more like it—the throbbing beat, the intensity. "I can't get no satisfaction, uh huh huh and I tried, tried, tried . . . can't get no satisfaction."

The cab ride to the Garden takes six minutes. The driver says that he went to junior high school with Holzman at P. S. 89 in Brooklyn. As I enter the Garden employees' entrance, Frankie La Greca, the security man, waits at the desk. I joke with him about his weight, my weight, his Italian, my Italian, his job, my job, concluding in a jumbled yelling exchange consisting of a string of more-or-less connected monosyllables. I arrive in the locker room just before Red's deadline, one hour before the game. Everyone is there.

Willis announces my arrival, "The Senator from New York, the President of the United Socialist Republic."

"What you gonna be, Dollar, a Democrat or what?" says Frazier. I was given the nickname "Dollar Bill" because of the glint of my big initial contract, and because I'm celebrated among my teammates for my frugality. I've always said Frazier gave me the nickname as an incentive for me to buy some new clothes.

"He's a liberal," Whelan says.

"I bet his old man, the banker, ain't liberal," adds Barnett. "How about it, can I get a loan in Crystal City? Do they give loans to black people?"

"The liberal candidate from what?" asks Willis. "Where you gonna live, Dollar? When you gonna run? Give me a job as the bodyguard."

"No, Willis," says Frazier. "You gotta be the chauffeur."

The locker room has become a kind of home for me, not simply a resting place. I often enter tense and uneasy, disturbed by some event of the day. Slowly my worries fade as I see their unimportance to my male peers. I relax; my concerns lost among relationships which are close and real but never intimate; lost among the constants of an athlete's life. Athletes may be crude and immature, but they are genuine when it comes to loyalty, responsibility, and honesty. The lines of communication are clear and simple. The humor is repetitious, generally, but occasionally a brilliant spontaneity flashes—only because we are at ease in the setting of satin uniforms and shower nozzles.

On the road, the team is together constantly weeks at a time. As DeBusschere's roommate for six years, I probably know him better than anyone except his wife. I sleep eight feet away from him for one hundred nights a year. At home, we see each other for games and practices. The members of my team have seen me, and I them, in more moods and predicaments than I care to remember. Our lives intertwine far beyond the court. It is a good life with congenial people. If victory and unity fuse on one team, life becomes a joy. It is a life that truly makes sense only while you're living it. A few old friends can't understand why I do it. I wrote in my journal during the 1970 exhibition season:

We left the University of Hartford yesterday. The Connecticut countryside in late September is a rich green, covered with thick trees just beginning to turn. Homes of stone, wood beams, and glass fill only small parts of spacious estates. The bus passes a Jewish community center. The road winds through the upper middle-class suburbs of Hartford, where everything looks in perfect order: finely trimmed hedges, manicured lawns, circle drives, thick walls, and station wagons.

The noises on the bus tell our story. Aretha Franklin, the original soul sister, sings from Willis' tape recorder. "You and me, together, for eternity." Dick McGuire, the assistant coach, mumbles about basketball, saying something inaudible. Cazzie sits talking with a reporter, "This year I feel stronger. . . ." Danny Whelan sits in the front seat with Red Holzman and says, "You know this guy's angle was never told. Fred Saigh, the owner of the Cardinals who went to jail for income tax evasion. Why he . . ." DeBusschere reads *The New York Times* and Barnett looks out the window at a college campus and says, "I bet they got fifty million dollars' worth of buildings on this place. . . ." The hum of the bus and "You and me, we shall be, together, for eternity."

Bound together we ride, unmindful of the distinctive nature of our trip. We look through glass. People walk in the yards and on the drives. House after house passes. I wonder who they are and how they live. Are they like us? Could they know what our life is like? Everything seems to pass so quickly, never to appear again. The houses, the people, the cities will disappear. The life on the bus, our self-contained community, is the thing which shall remain for this year.

Willis says, "Connecticut is a nice state; there are good towns here. Yeah, this part of Connecticut is one of the nicest places in the country to live in."

I hear him talk and think, "You couldn't live here, Willis. You must believe that you are another man. Your life flows toward the big city, the wilderness, and the South. You wouldn't like a community of wealthy landowners, corporate managers, and insurance executives. You can only guess what might be good if you had lived another profession and had another past. Maybe your opinion is not a misplaced dream but rather a disguise that your fame has allowed you to assume so that even you don't recognize that you, as I, would be unhappy in this prim and proper Connecticut town."

The airport tower looms on the horizon. We are flying to Atlanta on an Eastern 727 Silver Bird and then on to Memphis. We are grown men, driving to an airport together, living together, giving each other identity through our association, never realizing that that identity on a team in a bus or locker room is what we will lose upon retirement. We will miss this life of prolonged adolescence, caged from even the passing countryside and its people by the hum of the bus, the dreams of impossible relocation, and the strains of "You and me, together, for eternity."

I hang my street clothes in my locker and put on my uniform. A rookie walks in and says, "Who can help me out? I need two tickets in different locations."

"Don't want your bitches to meet each other?" asks Barnett.

"I'll give you a ticket if you let me have the lady sittin' in it," says a veteran.

"Forget it," says the rookie.

As I walk out of the locker room a reporter is asking Frazier about his youth in Atlanta. "The white high school had all the best equipment and books," says Frazier. "We got second-hand books and our school had no science labs. I thought I was okay because I did well in what we had. But then I got to college and found I wasn't prepared. There was no way to know that in Georgia."

I enter the training room to get two band-aids, the skin adherent, and tape for my ankles. Barnett and Jackson are talking about politics and they seem to agree for once.

"No, I didn't vote last time," says Barnett. "What's the difference? The rich get richer and the poor get poorer, whoever wins."

"Yeah," says Jackson, "both candidates are controlled by the same interests."

"You better vote if you want *any* say," says Danny, who is busy taping Jackson's ankle.

Danny's new assistant is Barry, a boy about 24. He stood outside the employees' entrance every game for two years asking for autographs before Danny invited him to the locker room. Now he works as a trainer's assistant and Danny treats him like a son. Barry has limited powers of concentration. Yet he imitates perfectly the radio broadcasts of the Knick games including the advertisements. He also imitates the court mannerisms of Red and all the players. His life is literally Danny and the Knicks. "Hey, Barry," a player shouts, "give us Red." Barry puts his hands on his hips, glances at an imaginary scoreboard, stamps his foot, glares, shakes his head, mimes the words "bull shit" at an imaginary referee, and brings his hands together in a "T" to signal for a time-out. Everyone laughs, but Barry can't stop for three more minutes.

Willis, who just walked into the training room, smiles. "Hey, boy," he says to the rookie with the two women, "here's your ticket." He delivers the ticket and then takes two hot sand packs from the hydroculator and places them on his knee.

Willis Reed is making a comeback from an injury for the third time in as many years. During the 1970–71 season, an area about the size of a quarter above his left knee became inflamed. Doctors said he had tendonitis. "When they don't know what's wrong, they call it tendonitis," teammates said jokingly. For Willis, it was no joke. An operation to remove the shredded portion of his kneecap tendon was declared a success in May 1971. By the beginning of the next basketball season, six months later, the pain had returned and spread to both sides of the knee. Another doctor brought in on the case said that only rest would heal tendonitis. Willis rested for the remainder of the season. The tendonitis had obliterated two seasons, 1970–71 and 1971–72, during which he played in thirty and thirteen games, respectively. Throughout the early summer of 1972, Willis worked on weights. Then, gradually, he started to run and began to shoot. He came to training camp in reasonable shape and said he felt no pain in his left leg. It took him most of the year to get back a modicum of timing. His quickness was gone forever. With his knowledge of the game and his sheer physical bulk, Willis helped us sporadically during the 1972–73 regular season. Slowly, he began to try the old moves and rebound without fear of reinjury. A touch of the old Willis returned in the final play-off series against Los Angeles, when he out-hustled and out-shot Wilt Chamberlain and we won our second world championship. The comeback year had a glorious ending. After the second championship, Willis signed a four-year contract in expectation of a complete return to form. Then in November, on the same Los Angeles court that six months earlier we had left as World Champions, Willis tore a cartilage in his right knee. After a two-week observation period, Dr. Donald O'Donoghue, of Oklahoma City, removed the cartilage.

The long months of rehabilitation with a weighted boot ended two weeks ago. He has begun again to run and shoot and he probably will play a little tonight. There is a long road ahead even if he wants only to regain his 1973 quickness. Forget 1970. But who could forget Willis then?

In 1970, Willis was the dominant member of the

Knick team that won the World Championship, and he was the Most Valuable Player in the NBA. He combined power and mobility, playing the pivot with surprising inventiveness. Other centers were stronger and a few were quicker, but at some point in the game Willis would find and exploit the weak spot in his opponent's style. Against seven-footers, he went outside where he shot with a feather touch. A series of quick "fakes" followed by a soft jump shot were his most effective tools against men of his own size. If, after a switch, he found himself with a smaller forward or guard, he simply turned and overpowered him. The move I liked best came after he had hit several jumpers moving to his left. He would turn with the same motion in the same place, as if to shoot again, but this time he would only show the ball. Then he would cross his left leg in front of his right, take a big step to put himself on the opposite side of the basket, stretch his left arm out, and flip a reverse lay-up against the glass.

He was the perfect center for our team that year. He set the best screen in the league. On defense, he sacrificed himself constantly, leaving his man open for the brief seconds necessary to stop opponents driving to the basket. After an opposing guard had his shot blocked, or collided with Willis, he usually gave up trying to reach the basket, choosing instead the safety of 20-foot jump shots. When called upon, Willis could score, though he rarely forced shots. Above all, Willis was an extraordinary rebounder. He had good timing and a sense of where the ball would bounce. If someone tried to block him from a rebound, Willis usually delivered an elbow to the sternum with audible impact. When he got his hands on the ball, no one took it away.

Willis was also the captain and leader of the Knicks during two championships. The role seemed natural for him and he was accepted by everyone. He was always the one to speak up when Holzman asked if anyone had something to add, and when Red was absent, Willis would sometimes speak to the team alone.

If Holzman was "the boss," Willis was "the player boss," yet he kept enough distance from management to maintain his integrity in the team's eyes. He also acted as counselor, talking individually with a depressed or angry player. His dominance came in part with his position: A team is only as strong as its big man. A center has to fight for his teammates or, more specifically, has to make the opponents believe he will fight. Willis never had trouble convincing anyone.

Willis Reed is six feet nine inches tall and weighs two hundred forty pounds. A close-cropped Afro frames his face and adds stateliness to his scarred eyebrows and wrinkled forehead. His lips are thin and they often part to reveal an engaging smile. When he grimaces, these same lips pinch together and his usually gentle brown eyes narrow until they are fiery slits.

On a hot night in the Garden when his muscles and skin glisten in the spotlight, there is something startlingly elemental about him. It is as if every pore opens and Willis cleanses himself nightly with his effort. I feel better for being a part of *his* effort. For spectators and teammates alike, the special awesomeness Willis conveys makes one wonder about his past, his background.

━━━━━━━

Born an only child on his grandfather's 200-acre farm ten miles east of Bernice, Louisiana, Willis knew hard work early. He grew up a country person in the strongest positive sense. Grandparents on both sides of his family were rural Baptists who never touched liquor and preached hard work and self-reliance. After living with the eleven relatives who worked the farm, his parents moved to Bernice, where his father worked for the Linsay Sawmill Company. As a kid of nine, Willis would get up at 4 A.M. to go fishing on the stream that crossed his grandfather's property. Sometimes he would sneak out his grandfather's shotgun and hunt birds. When he was twelve, Willis was picking 210 pounds of cotton a day at $3.25 per hundredweight. He picked watermelons. He hauled hay. At thirteen, he was "cutting those people's grass" in the white section of Bernice. He saw that all the merchants and gasoline dealers were white, but he did not allow himself to hate. A strong home and good teachers gave him his preparation for life. "My parents taught me to be a good Christian," Willis says, "to work hard and give my boss an honest day on the job and to attend church. When I was in high school, my father still demanded that I be home by 9:30, unless we had a football or basketball game. My mother and father didn't care what I chose for a career, but they wanted me to be a good human being. If that meant haulin' hay ... well, it was no disgrace."

As a thirteen-year-old, Willis came under the influence of a high school basketball coach who stayed after practice with him, teaching him the things about shooting, rebounding, and finesse that Willis's teammates didn't want to know or couldn't do. The coach talked of proper conduct and sportsmanship, and when Willis once lost his temper in the middle of a game, he sent him to the locker room. When Willis had completed the tenth grade the coach at Grambling College promised him a basketball scholarship upon graduation. Although many other schools made the same offer when he was a senior in high school, Willis selected Grambling because he thought its representatives were "honest" and their team played with style like Boston. Willis's hero was Bill Russell. It wasn't until Grambling went to the national small college tournament that Willis played against a white player. Grambling won the title that year and Willis kept Grambling in the winning column for the next three years. The Knicks, though, made him only their number two draft pick and the Olympic selectors chose Lucius Jackson instead of Willis for the center position on the 1964 Olympic team. Willis was hurt. He thought he deserved to be number one and vowed he would prove that the experts had guessed wrong about his talent. People underestimated his skill and determination; and throughout the period that followed, and during his later comebacks from injury, Willis lived by the aphorisms of his high school and college coaches who said, "There's no harm in failing. Just pick yourself up and get back into the race. You run a little harder than the next guy and nobody will ever know you fell." "A man's reach should exceed his grasp." "Go for the moon. If you don't get it, you'll still be heading for a star."

---

Willis leaves the training room and slumps on his locker-room stool. The team doctor talks to him. Willis nods his head but doesn't look up. Tonight's opponent is Milwaukee, with Kareem Abdul-Jabbar at center. Willis knows he's not prepared for the best offensive center in basketball. He knows that his body will never be the same after two operations and almost three years of little active competition. Still, he sends his complimentary tickets down to the will-call window, as usual, and tells the Knick publicity man that he feels good. He sprays his knees with skin adherent and pulls on the braces which give his weakened joints support. Then he tapes his fingers to avoid jamming them. A hot pack lies over a shoulder as he rubs liniment on the tendon area above the knee. Self-respect is still as much a part of him as ever, but the pride is less apparent. He plays against his real opponent, pain, with the knowledge that someday he will lose to it. But, his will forces him on and he is ready to work, believing that his team needs him—and we do—if only for a few minutes. Basketball is his living. He holds on, and who can fault him? Still, it's not the same, and that's sad.

I return to my locker stall, tape my ankles and put on my uniform. I watch the first quarter of the Milwaukee film, and then turn to the stack of mail that the ball boy has just delivered from the administrative office downstairs. I usually get forty letters a week, less than in my college years, but still a sizable amount, almost none of it from people I know. Total strangers write to "Bill Bradley of the New York Knicks." I quickly break the mail into four categories: autograph request, business proposal, personal invitation, other. For four years, I tried to answer every letter. Eventually, I realized that although each letter meant something very important to the person who sent it, I could not form forty personal relationships each week, no matter how important it was to the sender. The ones with the letterheads I recognize, or ones that are marked "Personal," I open and read. The rest I try to forget by placing them in the black trunk, which I empty at the end of each year into big cardboard boxes. I save them all. I have nearly every fan letter written to me since 1965.

Willis answers some of his mail with the help of the Knick administrative secretaries. Barnett does the same. DeBusschere's sister-in-law, overseen by his wife, answers most of his mail. Monroe, Jackson, and Lucas rarely answer any mail. Frazier has one of his secretaries at Walt Frazier Enterprises (a company that represents players in contract negotiations) cope with the problem. He receives more than a hundred letters each week.

The first letter I open is from a Rotary Club president in New Jersey who wants me to speak at his club's next luncheon. Then there are a few autograph requests. A woman in Jersey City writes to ask if I could send her anything for a celebrity auction her church is having. A man from Sparta, New Jersey, asks me to assure him better season tickets. A letterhead from the Dean of Students Office from a local New York college catches my eye. It is from the Assistant Dean of Students and it begins, "I find myself increasingly interested in the effects of greatness on athletes. It is of course practically impossible to get any kind of accurate clues from such sources as television commercials, sportscasters, and popular literature; nevertheless, some consistencies do emerge sometimes. Take Dave DeBusschere. I first saw Dave doing a hair commercial in which I recall he flashed a smile that was dazzling. His radio voice, which I heard next, was moderate and pleasing. His image, coupled with his brilliance as a ballplayer, added up to an affable, easy, relaxed kind of guy. But now I think this is not so. Dave, apparently, wrote *The Open Man*, in which he inadvertently reveals quite a bit about himself. . . ." The assistant dean, a woman, then launches into a brief psychiatric profile of De-Busschere, as revealed in his book. Predictably, it is a negative portrait because the assistant dean is angry. What is she mad at? DeBusschere did not respond to a letter she sent him, so he is now on her enemy list.

The assistant dean continues, "To me, this portrait is a great disappointment, almost a tragedy, not because it reveals a great man to be a fallible human, but because it exposes the enormous pressure under which the man lives. Were I to write to Dave instead of you, I would surely wound him, even though I am a total stranger.

"I believe athletes lead the sort of life that is highly destructive to them in many ways. Constantly on the run, subject to incredible hardships on the road, it would take a highly insensitive person, or one with fantastic insight, to maintain equilibrium. Given one who starts off less than confident, the results must be progressively difficult, not only for the star himself, but for those who live with him."

She asks me to comment if I desire. Two days later I write to her, saying that I find Dave to be a warm, confident, and genuine friend and that I'm sure she would, too, if she got to know him better. I write that the questions she raises about athletes in general are good ones, except that I would put quotes around "greatness" in her question about the effects of greatness on the athletes. I never show DeBusschere the letter or tell him about it.

Another letter is from a man who is angry because I did not comport myself properly during the playing of the National Anthem before a recent game in Maryland. "You looked very uninterested in your country's anthem," he says. "Then, before the music had even stopped, you broke away from the other players and headed toward the bench. I realize that standing even at half attention is not the 'in' thing to do among basketball players, but for someone who it is rumored has political aspirations, it may not be a bad idea. Also for thousands of kids watching these games you would be giving a good example. . . ."

There is a note from the "Famous Peoples Eye Glasses Museum" in Henderson, Nevada: "We would like to add a pair of your eye glasses to the growing FPEGM." There is an invitation to a sculpture exhibit on Sutton Place in New York. Inside the invitation is a note scribbled, "I sit in my seat 16 feet from yours and watch you perform 1782 minutes each season (54 home games $\times$ 33 average minutes). Therefore I demand 60 minutes of your time knowing of your appreciation for art."

The last letter I open is from Kentucky. It is marked "Important." Inside is a letter from the doctor-father of a boy whom I had met four years earlier. The son was then a sophomore at the University of Kentucky. He came all the way from Kentucky to ask me to show him how to shoot a basketball. He just appeared at my apartment one day. We went up to Riverside Drive Park where there are some empty baskets. After three minutes, I knew what I had suspected. He couldn't shoot well but he kept asking how to get off his jump shot under heavy guarding. He said that Adolph Rupp, the coach, had told him he might have a slim chance to make the team. He insisted that he intended to work day and night, for his lifelong goal was to play basketball for Kentucky. We talked and shot about an hour. He thanked me for the help and boarded a bus back home. I saw him later that year in Cincinnati. He had been cut from the Kentucky team. He was down, and convinced that his sprained ankle had something to do with it. I wrote him a letter two years later, after his sister had written that he had cancer. My letter arrived too late. The boy's father thanks me for the letter but says that his son had died six months earlier. He goes on to relate the grief and pain of losing his only son. I put the letter down. Holzman begins his pregame conversation. I can't concentrate. I should have written sooner. I feel numbed with anger and sorrow.

———

We leave the locker room with a clap of hands, pass between the tan burlap curtains under the loge seats and onto the hardwood surface of Madison Square Garden. The spotlights shining down from the spoked-wheel ceiling make the court warm, even hot. As we form two lines for warm-up lay-ins, the Garden audio department blasts a record whose high-speed percussion ratchets through the enormous loud speakers hanging suspended over center court. During the first game that was played in the new Garden, in 1968, a large metal plate fell from the ceiling to the floor, and since then I have thought about what might happen if the gigantic speaker fell. The players who never get back on defense or never go for rebounds would be the most likely victims.

I approach the basket slowly, take the pass from Frazier and lay the ball against the backboard. The pace is slow and jerky. As you get older, the warm-up becomes more important. Muscles are tight and restrict movement. They need to be slowly stretched and loosened for the running and jumping to follow. A rhythm develops which puts me in tune with the game rhythm.

Before play-off games, nervousness and determination mark the faces of players. There are shouts of encouragement to teammates and glares at opponents. Each player tries to convince his body to perform beyond its capability. But during the regular season the warm-ups are a time of hellos to opponents, smiling inquiries about families, and occasionally the making of post-game plans.

The record fades into the more familiar accompaniment of organ music. Stiff muscles yield, the tempo picks up. I see the ball drop through the hoop. I start, fake left, and then cut right; going toward the basket at an angle. The ball thuds into my hands. I feel the grain, bring the ball up to my chest, and drop it softly against the backboard. Coming down on my toes, I take five steps to slow down, then jog to the end of the rebounding line. The music plays, people watch, and a mood begins to form.

As the lay-ins draw to a close, the younger players start the playful movement of basketball, the dunk shot, literally stuffing the ball into the basket. There are many varieties. The straight one-hand and two-hand dunks are elementary. The reverse dunk, however, requires a player to approach the basket frontally and then at the last moment turn at a right angle in the air and slam the ball over the left backside of the rim with the right hand. For the hesitation dunk, a player "skies" (jumps very high). As he approaches the level of the basket, he ducks his head aside to miss the rim or net and at the last moment, after his body is past the basket but before it descends, he reaches back with one hand and stuffs the ball through. The self-assist dunk is the most violent: a player tosses the ball against the backboard and as it caroms off, he jumps, catches it above the rim and slams it through, all in one motion. With my limited jumping ability I'm not much on the dunk. The standing locker-room joke is that a daily *New York Times* can't be slipped under my feet even on my highest jump. So, in between the "oohing" and "aahing" the crowd gives for the practice dunks, I shoot driving hooks and reverse lay-ups against the glass. After my last lay-in made running flatout down the center, I go to the right corner of the court to tighten my shoelaces. A little boy and girl shout, "Dollar, look up, look up. Please. We want your picture. You're our favorite Knick." I look up, but they don't take the picture so I return to my sneakers. The two young voices call again, "Look up, look up, you jerk!" No player can blot out the comments from the crowd. He can only pretend he doesn't hear.

After the lay-ins, the team starts individual warm-up shots, using six balls. A jumper, a free throw, a hook, a running one-hander—each player will run through his repertoire until he has reaffirmed it against the imaginary opponents of the warm-up.

DeBusschere practices his long jumper from the corners and his full-speed drives across the middle to the basket. He jump-shoots three from the low post and tips in a few rebounds off the glass. Lucas stands twenty-five feet from the basket. He shoots with a piston-like motion—one bounce, fix the ball into shooting position, jump, fade, kick one leg forward, release the ball near the right ear. Monroe works on his rhythm, faking his shot, driving to the basket, pulling up for the jumper from the hip. Frazier dribbles from baseline to halfcourt five times. I shoot fouls and take jumpers at points on the court where our plays are designed to spring me for the open shot.

Muscles loosen even more and confidence grows. Sometimes you can sink every shot in the warm-ups, but the shots in the game fail to drop. Other times just the reverse. Each player has his own superstitions: taking the last shot, swishing the last shot, walking to the bench last or first, shooting with one ball only, saying hello to a friend in the stands.

Frazier and DeBusschere rarely use the full ten minutes for shooting; they prefer to sit on the bench for two or three minutes, thinking about their opponent.

Several years ago, I took to surveying the crowd for lovely women, and now in Madison Square Garden three women are part of my pregame fantasy ritual. They sit in different places and they attend games often. At some point during the warm-ups, I will stare at each of the three. I don't want to meet them and I'm sure they aren't aware of their strange role in my preparation. After two years, one of them made it known through friends that she was available, but somehow it didn't seem right. From what I saw, she was extremely attractive and alluring; meeting her might dispel that image. I knew she was bound to be different. Anyway, I did not want to find out, because the very act of meeting her would destroy the role she played in my warm-ups. So, I continued just to look. She caught my glances with recognition for several more months, but finally ignored me altogether. I still notice her dress, her hair, and the remarkably impassive manner with which she regards the scene. Three times I have seen her from a cab walking down a New York street. She looked the same, but her allure was less, insufficient without the Garden and the game.

The buzzer sounds, indicating that players should return to their benches for the start of the game. Players take last-second shots not unlike students cramming, minutes before an exam.

"Welcome to the magical world of Madison Square Garden," says John Condon, the Garden's public address announcer, "where tonight it's the New York Knicks against the Milwaukee Bucks. And now for the Milwaukee starting lineup . . ."

"Boooooo." The Garden vibrates like a bass violin string. Few opposing teams escape the New York boo.

"Now the World Champion New York Knicks . . ."

Sound of waterfalls, a continuous roar.

"Playing forward, No. 22, Dave DeBusschere."

Waterfalls.

"Playing forward, No. 24, Bill Bradley."

Waterfalls.

"Playing center, No. 32, Jerry Lucas."

More waterfalls.

DeBusschere and I stand stonefaced as the remaining introductions are made. DeBusschere says, "I found her. I'm playing for her tonight."

"Where, which one?" I ask.

"The blonde in the blue sweater up to the right of Gate 13."

I glance up the wall of faces, past Wall Street types in their three-piece suits, past blue-jeaned bearded kids, until I focus on an unknown woman in a gray skirt and a blue turtleneck sweater. She gazes down at us as the National Anthem is announced. "Okay, we'll do it for her tonight," I say.

During the National Anthem, while a fan in the front row does toe raises, I stare at the balcony where the signs of Knick sponsors hang—Coca Cola, Manufacturers Hanover Trust, Schaefer Beer, Eastern Airlines. I fix on the red and black Coke sign. The colors jump and then fuse. "O'er the land of the free and the . . ." I can't wait. I spring to the sidelines, ready to play, excited. I catch a towel from the ballboy as the singer finishes, ". . . home of the brave." I take off my warm-ups and towel my legs dry. Holzman gives last-minute instructions. Barnett calls our first play and we head out for the center jump. Game number 66 begins.

Milwaukee gets the tip. Oscar Robertson passes to Kareem Abdul-Jabbar, who hits a drifting hook shot from the middle of the lane. Oscar hits a jumper and passes for three more. Milwaukee takes a 10-to-2 lead. They are running well.

Oscar and Kareem, the old and the young, make Milwaukee a devastating team. Kareem's calmness engulfs opponents. With a beard covering his face and his alert eyes darting back and forth across the court, he looks like a member of some royal family. He does things on a basketball court that are truly astounding. At 7'3", he is as graceful as any player in basketball. In one game, I saw him grab a rebound two feet over the basket, dribble the full length of the floor ending with one dribble behind the back, leap from about the foul line, and dunk it. He does not have the massive bulk of Wilt Chamberlain or the coiled reflexes of Bill Russell; but he seems to be flying effortlessly, giving and taking at his whim.

Oscar's play has been my model since I was in high school, when I saw him play against St. Louis University. He never wastes a movement; the form is always perfect. His arm fits under the ball as if its sole function is shooting baskets. The same motion releases the ball in the same manner every time. The Robertson body fake frees him time after time for the short jump shot. He dribbles at you slowly, then fakes right with his head, shoulders, and arms. His man jumps right, and he brings his body back left for a clear shot or drive to the basket. His passes are crisp and pinpointed. He is unselfish with the ball but demands that the game be played properly—his way.

Who is the best, Jerry West or Oscar Robertson?

"Jerry's a great shooter," Barnett says, "but Oscar is the best all-around basketball player ever. He makes it look so easy. He's not fancy, just fundamental. He is going to take the shot he wants, not the one you want him to take, and the motherfucker isn't going to shoot further out than fifteen feet. When he was younger he could have scored 100 points in a game if he went for the shot every time instead of averaging ten assists a game. No mistaking it either, Oscar is boss. One night we were playing Cincinnati and Wayne Embry [a 6'8", 250-pound center] sets a pick for Oscar. As he attempts to roll I try to hold him. Embry looks at me and says, 'Don't hold me, man, Oscar will yell at me if I don't roll.' "

Oscar dissects situations on the court. Basketball for him has never been a matter of emotion. The only obstacle between him and a perfect game has been the ability of his teammates, which, until he joined Kareem, could not compare with his own. Perhaps he doesn't give lesser players a large enough margin for error, but when they listen to him he makes All-Stars of meager talents. He controls events on the court with the aplomb and authoritarian hand of a symphony conductor. The NBA finals in 1971 showed Oscar's mood as he sensed the possibility of his first championship. He drove his young teammates, placing blame on those who made mistakes, urging them never to let up, telling them when and where to move, and insisting on perfect execution.

Oscar perceives the game from the pinnacle of his own self-confidence. When pretenders to his throne of preeminence arose (Jo Jo White, Dave Bing, Pete Maravich), they were challenges only of a moment, coming up from a lower class. Once in a crucial All-

Star game between the NBA and ABA, his team trailed by eight points with three minutes to go. Dribbling the ball downcourt, he caught sight of a few glum faces on his NBA bench. "Don't worry," he said impatiently as he passed the bench, "we're not gonna lose." He knew that three minutes was enough time for a lead of eight points to vanish twice over. He knew that steals, bad calls, panic, experience, and luck still could brew quite a different result. He felt in control—and was. The NBA won by five.

Except for Oscar's berating of officials (he believes that their incompetence has hurt the game) and instructing of teammates, he plays impersonally, and sometimes even seems to react mechanically. Other players also school themselves in detachment. Walt Frazier, the Knick's exponent of cool, wrote a book about it, in which he said, "Cool is my style. I almost never show any emotion on the court. A guy might harass me, and it might be working, but if you look at my face, I always look cool. So they never know what I'm thinking." Oscar never talks about his cool— he plays in Milwaukee.

When I was in college, I, too, played with detachment. I was careful to control my emotions and to let out only those feelings that made me more productive. I even described my play as if I were a machine. But as a pro I was no longer leading crusades for Princeton to show the world that a team of student athletes could prevail in the best competition. After surviving my NBA initiation and winning a starting position on the team, I had stopped struggling. I was in a safe, if competitive, status as a regular professional, and my play became more personalized. No longer did the severe discipline of the court prevent me from accepting the gentler half of my personality.

Now, I allow myself expression on the court. If I am angry or nervous, I show it. If I am in a great mood, I show it. As I give expression to my feelings during play, I have a greater satisfaction and calmness afterwards. Playing creates a release for my emotional energy. I have become dependent on the action, the physical contact, and the verbal bantering of the game. I know that when I finish with basketball for good and can no longer experience the catharsis of game and locker room, I will have to find something to take its place. Basketball has fulfilled more emotional functions for me than I can imagine.

Phil Jackson says you can tell more about a person when he loses. Some players don't care about winning and make excuses because they're interested only in themselves, not team victory. Other players, like me, learn only reluctantly to accept defeat as part of the life. My second game in the NBA, I scored 25 points but threw the ball away with nine seconds left. The other team then scored and won in overtime. I took the defeat hard and afterwards didn't speak to anyone, I was so depressed. Later that night in the hotel, Dick Barnett ended up as my roommate. We had exchanged about ten words since I joined the team. I had replayed the game about fifteen times when he walked into the room, looked at me, soaked in a hot tub for ten minutes, then got into bed. Before he turned over to sleep he picked up a statistics sheet of the game and read my line of points, assists, rebounds, free throws, field goals, and minutes played. Looking first at the sheet and then at me, he finally uttered his only comment of the night, putting the game in perspective. "Forty-six minutes—that's a whole lotta' minutes."

When the game is over, the most important thing is the next game. A player must be able to recuperate from a loss within twenty-four hours. Such resiliency is not a bad character trait to take away from the sport. But like so many of "sport's lessons" it becomes oversimplified and even leads to insensitivity when applied to life. Once, for example, I heard an old basketball man say that a coach had a bad year, as if to say a bad season. The coach's wife had died and he had lost a large lawsuit. There are some things for which there will not be another season.

Yet winning and losing is all around us. From the high school level on, athletes are prepared to win and they in turn convey to a larger public what it is to be a winner. Locker-room champagne, humility in victory, and irrefutable knowledge of a favorable, clear-cut resolution are what championships resemble from the outside. The winning team like the conquering army claims everything in its path and seems to say that only winning is important. Yet like getting into a college of your choice or winning an election or marrying a beautiful mate victory is fraught with as much danger as glory. Victory has very narrow meanings and, if exaggerated or misused, can become a destructive force. The taste of defeat has a richness of experience all its own.

===

Toward the end of the third quarter we begin to make our move against Milwaukee. DeBusschere hits from the corner. I hit on a jumper from the key and Earl Monroe scores on a drive. The next three times down the floor Earl makes a move for a basket. Once, he jumps, changes the position of the ball three times, and floats the ball just over the outstretched hand of Kareem Abdul-Jabbar. The next two times he drives directly at his man, then spins to the left, takes two more dribbles and shoots from the baseline. Earl Monroe plays like a man whose body was assembled through a mail order catalog. Each part seems to move independently yet is controlled from a single command center. He has an uncanny skill for gauging the distance between himself and anyone who can block his shot. When his timing is off, as it is when he is returning from an injury, his shots are often blocked. When he is healthy, he can loft the ball over anyone's outstretched hand. Sometimes the defensive man misses a block by a foot, sometimes by an inch, but when Earl is right no one can stop him. He is one of the few players who openly challenges Kareem with a drive. Seventy percent of the time, Earl finds a way to get a shot off: He shoots it hard against the backboard; he goes straight for the rim; he steps back, jumps, tucks the ball in and then shoots it between Kareem's arm and his head.

=====

More than any other Knick, Earl Monroe grew up in an atmosphere shaped by the rhythms of urban change during the post-World War II decades. He was born November 21, 1944, at the University of Pennsylvania Hospital in central Philadelphia. His mother, Rose, came north from New Bern, North Carolina, with her family when she was fourteen. Of her twelve brothers and sisters only two survived until Earl's birth. One brother died in prison. Another died swallowing a baked potato. Disease and violence took the other eight, with the last death occurring on November 23, 1944.

Earl's maternal grandmother lived next door to Earl in a Philadelphia row house. She ran a little business in her home, selling candy and flavored ice cones. She served liquor to the adults from a home bar that came to be known in the neighborhood as "The Speakeasy." Earl's mother and father divorced when he was five. He did not see his father again until he was twenty-one years old. His early childhood memories center on his grandmother's business, the non-stop weekend card games that his mother ran in her home, and the vacation Bible school that he attended every summer from age four to fourteen.

At home there was little talk of the family's past in North Carolina. "Very seldom people like to look back on that," Earl says. "They just said some very bad things happened. They won't be out of mind but they try to keep it off the mind."

Rose remarried, and Earl developed friendships with kids on the block, one of whom, a ten-year-old, fell to his death from a Schuylkill River bridge. He also grew to fear his three older cousins, who frequently jumped from shadows to frighten him and beat him up. When Rose found out, she beat up the cousins, but she couldn't be around all the time. Earl started playing basketball with a rubber handball and a trash can when he was nine. He was not good immediately. His shyness affected his play.

In 1961 the family bought a three-story building with a grocery store on the first floor. Earl's mother, stepfather, and two sisters ran the store. The family lived on the third floor. "I don't remember growing up when I wanted something that I couldn't or didn't get," Earl says. "That may be because what you don't see you don't want. Bicycle, ping-pong table—I got all that stuff. I never felt pain, so to speak, but I did have a quick temper. I'd get mad, turn chairs over in the house and punch glass out of windows. Afterward I'd say, 'I'm sorry, Ma.' She was the only person I could, or would, say I'm sorry to. She wouldn't let anyone hurt me. She'd do anything for me."

When Earl grew older his cousins became less antagonistic and more protective. They were the gang leaders in their section of Philadelphia. Violence was commonplace. Every summer during Earl's adolescence, racial battles erupted on the streets, and gang wars continued the year around. When Earl was eight years old he saw a stabbing in which the assailant literally cut the heart out of his victim and threw it on the street in front of twelve petrified onlookers. It was the first of three killings he was to witness.

A few years later one of Earl's friends led him to the roof of a nearby steakhouse where he took a Tommy-gun and began spraying the street with bullets just to frighten the passersby. Earl did not participate in the rumbles of his friends. Whenever the action started, he faded toward the rear. As a 6'3" fourteen-year-old ballplayer, he had a different status. Still, he kept his leather coat which certified him as a member of a gang that was called "The Road."

Earl learned basketball on the playgrounds—first watching, then imitating. He played earnestly wherever there was a good game. On the court, the competition sometimes became heated, and anger turned to violence. "When we played in another section of town," he remembers, "we would tie our clothes in a bundle and put them next to the court with an extra guy watching in case we had to leave quickly. If we played indoors and the lights went out, it was best to stay on the court because the home team fans would be waiting for you at the exits. If you were outside, you'd try to climb the wire fence to escape. At one place, Lanier playground, if you won you got an automatic fight. But you had to play. That was the only way to improve. I always tried to get the best competition. Whatever happened happened."

After high school, Earl went to college in Winston-Salem, North Carolina, where he majored in English and personally encountered segregation for the first time. Playing basketball in the southeastern United States in an all-black conference, Earl developed into a local folk hero. His feats inspired nicknames that soon became the trappings of his reputation. Among his manifold skills his spin move became unstoppable. He drove toward the defensive man only to turn his back to him at the last possible second before collision, pivot with his left foot and head away from his first path at a forty-five-degree angle. The aspect of the move that was different from any other player's spin was Earl's control of the ball with one hand, as if he had attached a short string from his fingers to the ball. When he was in a playful mood he spun, let the ball hang suspended in air, crossed his hands as if he were calling a baseball player safe, grabbed the ball, looked one way and passed it in the opposite direction. At such moments a murmur would ripple through the crowd and burst into an explosion of shouting, clapping, laughing, and stamping of feet. It was then that Earl became "The Pearl," named after a sportswriter's characterization of five high-scoring games as pearls, and, more appropriately, "Magic," because he made things happen with the ball that defied normal explanation. Earl's fans were not surprised when the Baltimore Bullets made him their number one draft choice in 1967. They were shocked, however, when the Bullets traded him to their biggest rival, the New York Knicks, in December 1971.

———

Jerry Lucas, hits several long jumpers, Kareem remains close to the basket, conceding Lucas the open shot. The Knick lead is now four points. DeBusschere and I shut off the Milwaukee forwards, while Monroe and Frazier score steadily, with an unusual array of one-on-one moves. Oscar cannot match them. He begins to fade. Fatigue saps the spirit of competition that once grew ferocious in the waning moments of a game. The Bucks begin to crumble. Sixteen times the Knicks have met them in Madison Square Garden during the last six years, and fifteen times we have won. Often, victory has required seemingly impossible efforts. Once, for example, Milwaukee led us by nineteen points with five minutes left in the game. Fans were already leaving the Garden to get an early start home. Suddenly, we "caught fire." Everything we shot went in and our defense held Milwaukee scoreless for five minutes. We won by three points, accomplishing what came to be known as "a believer feat." Those who saw it believed in our invincibility. I even think we did.

The Knick lead increases to nine points as time runs out. Kareem, though he misses two shots in the last minute and a half, remains impassive. Oscar swears, with a look of disgust on his face. Larry Costello, the Milwaukee coach, places his red face between his knees as if they were the walls of a vise. He holds a clipboard stacked with the diagrams and plays which failed again to provide a blueprint for a Garden victory.

"See you Monday for practice," Red says in the locker room after the victory. "Take Sunday off. Okay, let the press in."

The star of the game is Earl Monroe. He wins two knitted shirts. The writers crowd around his locker.

"How do you account for your streak tonight?"

"Is Milwaukee psyched out in the Garden?"

"Will a game like this have any influence on the play-offs?"

"Where are Milwaukee's weaknesses?"

Monroe is still talking with the press when I leave the locker room.

My guest for the evening has seen her first professional basketball game. I like her detached perspective. She waits for me with the wives, girl friends, and acquaintances of the other players. Twenty people sit in empty seats at halfcourt while the Garden maintenance crew dismantles the hardwood floor. As we leave the building, she comments, "What's so strange is how quickly everyone leaves. There are these frantic emotional moments with everyone sky high. Then it's over, just like that." She is right. Although it will take me four hours to come down from the game's high, it *is* over "just like that." Massive amounts of energy are expended, and then there is a silent void. There is a feeling of desolation about the Garden after a game. Paper cups, hot dog wrappers, programs, and popcorn boxes litter the arena floor— the residue of the same appetite that consumed the players' performance. The cleaning women, shrieking at each other in three languages and sounding like jungle birds in the vacant arena, soon sweep it all away, and tomorrow the excitement of another game will recharge the air.

The abruptness of a game's end, however, never strikes me as much as the change that comes with the season's end. For eight months you play basketball and think about basketball; your happiness depends on basketball. Then it is over. Nothing fills the void. Fans and reporters seem to accept it, unaware that for some of us it can never be just the conclusion of a natural cycle. At the end of the season I find myself struggling awkwardly for a proper rhythm, like a novice drummer. For a few days I wander aimlessly, unaccustomed to the slowed pace, to the absence of flights and new cities, to the prospect of no work for four months. Gradually other interests impose routines on daily living and purpose replaces restlessness. Then, as September approaches, preparation for another season speeds up activity and basketball again dominates. But when there are no more Septembers with basketball, what happens then? Will it be over "just like that?"

## 7

$S$UNDAY PASSES QUICKLY. I SLEEP UNTIL 11, EAT
breakfast, and read *The New York Times*. Around
4 P.M. I go to a movie with a friend, then to a Chinese
restaurant. Later I read and then more sleep.

New York Knick practices rarely take place at Madison Square Garden, because it is filled almost every
day of the year with other events. The first two years
I played for the Knicks, we practiced at a city recreation hall in Queens. It had a buckled floor, no hot
water, and a low steel-beamed ceiling. Kids sometimes crowded the court so that it was difficult to work
on plays. The building was called the Lost Battalion.
The next site was the Columbia School for the Deaf,
also in Queens. Now we practice at Pace College,
across from City Hall in lower Manhattan. The
gymnasium is on "C" floor, the third floor underground. The court is not regulation length, and the
rims are always bent. You can easily hear the rumble
of passing subways. Holzman likes the location because it gives him the privacy he needs to work
with the team.

Danny Whelan arrives at 9:30 Monday morning for
the 11 A.M. practice. He checks the basketballs for
air pressure and makes sure there is the proper number of dry, clean towels for post-practice showers.
He takes tape and elastic wraps from his equipment
bag, lights a cigar, and reads *The New York Times*,
waiting for the team. The rookies and substitutes
begin arriving around 10:15. Danny tapes their ankles and they begin working on their shots or playing

one-on-one. The pre-practice session is necessary for the non-regulars. In order to improve and stay in condition, they need extra practice. The whole team will work out only eighty minutes. The regulars arrive just in time to be on the court by 11.

DeBusschere calls attention to the fact that I am taking my first shot with my left shoe untied. Holzman says that will cost me five dollars.

"At least," says Earl.

"Way to go, Dollar," says Frazier.

"Who else we gonna get today?" says Barnett, who then notices that only eleven players are present.

"Willis called in sick," says Danny.

"Sick," says Lucas. "I bet he got sick after he knew he was going to be late."

"Okay, let's have the shooting game," says Holzman. He divides the squad into four teams, two at each end of the floor, competing against each other. Players shoot, fetch their shot and give the ball to the man on their team that is next in line. The object is to hit five shots from the corner, ten from the edge of the circle, and fifteen from the middle of the circle. The winners at each end play to see who will be the champion for the day. Each player on a winning team gets a point. At the end of the year the player with the most points (last year a rookie) gets one hundred dollars from the fine money before the party. Success depends upon having good shooters as teammates, since the shots are alternated. Holzman tries to balance teams, but usually there are half-serious complaints about "loading up" one team with all the better shooters.

"Look at the two blind mice," Lucas says to a team of two rookies.

"Who is blind, chump?"

"You only chump here, plumber."

"José, hey José," shouts Barnett. "We got José Feliciano and Ray Charles shooting against Anvil Akins and the Computer. Hey, Computer, don't lose count of the score."

After the shooting game we run a full-court drill to loosen up the muscles. Players run at their own pace, passing the ball among themselves.

"Gimme two," shouts Frazier as half of the team runs to the other end of the court and back, twice.

"Gimme three," says Barnett. The other half goes for three round trips.

"Gimme four," says Barnett.

"Okay," Holzman says, "everybody loose. Let's go to work."

For the next half hour we work on the timing of our offensive plays. A full-court scrimmage follows. Holzman does not believe in keeping score during a practice scrimmage. He stops play occasionally to point out mistakes, but most of the scrimmage is left to the players. The veteran starters poke fun at the substitutes while executing plays and utilizing their experience to great advantage. The red shirts, or second team, often outplay the blue shirts, or first team. Today the reds start out fast, filling the baskets with shots and the air with epithets for the regulars: "He's just an old man"; "Get a pension"; "I shot one in your eye."

"We just warming up for you chumps," shouts Frazier. "Now the pressure's on. Let's see what happens now that we're ready."

Frazier steals three passes. "Oh, oh," he starts, "you 'boys' need help. Bring out the oxygen tent."

"Nice try," says Earl to his man, as he spins and drives to the basket, untouched. "You still young, you not ready yet."

Holzman blows the whistle calling an end to practice, which concludes with everyone shooting free throws.

For a player who, like me, works thirty to forty minutes a game, the practices serve primarily to keep my body toned and my timing sharp, to "break a sweat," and to shoot. By now, I can sense when the purpose has been served. Rest is often more important than practice. As one gets older, practice is less for improvement and more for combating the erosion of age. For me, practices are work and fun. The personalities of the players and the sense of team contribute more to that feeling than anything else does. I used to hate practice, though, when I first came into the league.

Now, when I think about my first four years with the Knicks I'm surprised how little joy there was in comparison with these later years. The tangible changes between the two periods were in Holzman's manner and in the composition of the team. During Red's early years, he was by design a super-authoritarian and I was often one of his targets for abuse. At the Garden all he had to do was walk into the locker room and say one word, or just use a certain tone of voice, and there was total silence. At practices he would yell at me until I was as tight as a guitar string. On the road I would be afraid to run into him in the hotel elevator because I was sure he would remind me that he was "the boss." I would go for days without speaking to him and once, for a week, I didn't even look at him. I felt he talked to me as if I was a punk kid and whatever he said often angered me. Once during the play-offs when I asked to miss a team flight so I could take examinations for graduate school he said, "You know, don't you, that your contract gives me complete control over your body for nine months a year. Didn't you know when the playoffs were?" I had never felt about anyone in my life the way I did about Red. As I wrote in my journal then, "Recently Red kills much potential joy for me. I don't want to leave New York but if he trades me what choice do I have? If he wanted to keep me on the bench forever he could. It's always the tyranny of the unspoken. I feel helpless before his power over my life."

But, after the first championship in 1970, Red began to mellow. He had become general manager as well as coach and though he had more power he acted more gently. He retired his dictatorial manner and adopted a friendlier attitude toward the team, in part because it must be draining on a coach always to play the villain and in part because Red knew everyone well enough to get exactly what he needed from each at the proper time without much shouting. Still, the major breakthrough in my relations with Holzman came only when he traded Cazzie Russell to San Francisco for Jerry Lucas. Red had picked *me*. The effect was exhilarating. Before, when he had consulted me about strategy as he had with other players, I resented it, fearing it was some plot to cut my playing time. Formerly, when he came into the locker room and made some comment about me having gone to Princeton and him "only" to CCNY. I burned with anger. But, once Russell was gone, things changed. I began to laugh when he kidded me about Princeton or talked about going to CCNY with his greasy paper bag full of lunchmeat; he seemed to be laughing himself. Never was there a word spoken between us about such things, but the atmosphere became noticeably more congenial.

The addition of Monroe and Lucas brought to the team two players of exceptional abilities and unusual personalities. But, the departure of Cazzie was more important for my greater enjoyment of the game because we had spent three years as constant competitors for the same starting forward position.

Despite the rivalry between Cazzie and me, I liked him very much (and continue to). I've seen few athletes more dedicated to their sport. In that sense he was like Barnett and, to a lesser degree, me. But we shared other, more striking, similarities. We both came from strong religious backgrounds. We both had strong mothers, a stable family, and an acceptance of conscientious hard work as a virtue. In our college years, he at Ann Arbor, I at Princeton, we both gained respect from people for things we did beyond playing basketball. Both of us had big contracts to turn pro— Cazzie in 1966, I one year later—and experienced the concomitant jealousies of other players who had not yet benefited from a higher salary structure. Each of us spent his rookie year on the bench, coming to terms with failure for the first time in his life. Cazzie's exuberance for the game, above all, made me fond of him. Critics called him a showboat, but I sensed that the raised fists, the shoulder shakes, and the prolonged follow-throughs that marked his style were signs of the same love I felt for basketball.

To the fans our competition highlighted our differences. He was flamboyant; I was not. He was black; I was white. He verbalized constantly; I was careful with words, preferring to listen. He was an explosive player who generated much excitement through his one-on-one skills; I was a methodical player who often needed a screen to get my shot and concentrated on floor play (play without the ball). Finally, we had a history of competition that dated back to 1964 when my Princeton team played Cazzie's Michigan team twice. The game in Madison Square Garden on December 28, 1964, permanently etched our adversary roles in the minds of the basketball public. Princeton had a fourteen-point lead when I fouled out with four minutes remaining. Cazzie and Michigan caught and beat Princeton in the stretch, avoiding a loss which would have jolted them from their number one national ranking. Although I had outscored Cazzie, his team won.

The Knicks drafted both of us. I went to Oxford for two years, then broke in as a guard. Cazzie made his way as a starting forward. When Cazzie broke his ankle, in January 1969, I took his spot. The switch from guard to forward placed me in a position I had played in college and, more important, the team began to win consistently. After Cazzie's ankle healed our competition began in earnest.

We divided the basketball fans in New York into warring camps. The press and public emphasized our dissimilarities. Cab drivers would tell me Cazzie should start. Cab drivers would tell me I should start. People at courtside would do the same. If Cazzie or I missed several shots during warm-ups, someone would invariably yell that the other one of us should be starting. Both of us had a hard time accepting anything less.

I came to view our competition as a sad but necessary aspect of professional basketball. Playing time is like food for a player; without it, he cannot survive. However much Cazzie and I respected each other, since neither of us was prepared to accept twenty minutes of playing time as sufficient, every game and every practice became a battle to show Holzman that one of us was better than the other. Our head-to-head competition drained me of much emotional energy, for I was never sure that I would win. I thought about how best to defense him before every practice. Since he was such a great clutch shooter I could never give him room to maneuver. Above all, I could never relax. I felt the tension the moment I stepped onto the court. When Cazzie was on an opposite team in the practice shooting game, we were really shooting against each other. During scrimmages, every rebound and shot was contested fiercely. Each of us looked for any kind of edge, so much so that often we remained shooting after practice until the court closed, both determined not to be the first to leave. The constant rivalry might have made us better players, but it did not make life enjoyable. Even off the court, the anger and aggressive drive spilled over and prevented closeness.

The tension between us never became bitter or hostile, though, for two reasons. First, I think we understood each other and possessed a mutual respect more basic than words could convey. It was as if a fragile, arbitrary frame of competition with its own set of distinctive rules and requirements had been placed on a foundation of solid and natural understanding. Second, each of us directed much of our hostility toward Holzman, for it was he who controlled our supply of playing time, our food. I finally realized that Cazzie and I were pawns in a larger game, like corporate executives apparently competing for promotion but most directly benefiting the corporation that established the arena for competition. So we were competing between ourselves and against the team's opponent. There was vertical and horizontal competition, just as in any good capitalist organization. Many fans saw the familiar signs of their own work situations in our competition; their interest in part derived from the anxieties generated in their own lives and projected onto us.

Holzman stood at the top of the hierarchy. He controlled our destiny. The players under him might try to please him, impress him, or help him, but they could never be sure that they had security as long as even his smiles, his glares, and his unexplained actions perpetuated the competition. I developed elaborate explanations (however erroneous they were in fact) of how Holzman was intentionally sabotaging my game. In retrospect I realize that Red, as coach, had to view the dictates of the game as a whole, which brought him into a necessary clash with the players who often viewed only their own needs for self-fulfillment as important. The predicament that Cazzie and I found ourselves in was as much a product of our own paranoias and egos as it was of Holzman's design.

But with Cazzie's departure everything changed. I was no longer pouting about playing time and the bitter competition for the starting position had ended. Holzman's already mellowed manner became downright paternal and kind. Playing basketball became more fun than I had ever envisioned.

———

After practice, I cut the tape from my ankles. I put my foot on an ice bag for fifteen minutes to decrease the pain in an inflamed arch. Finally, I shower—long after the other players have finished, dressed, and left. Danny Whelan and I are the last to leave Pace College. I give him a ride to the Garden. We are free until the game against Boston the next night.

From the middle of September until May there is usually no longer than one day at a time without basketball. There are no long weekends or national holidays for players. It is impossible to take a trip to the mountains or fly to Florida even for two days. We are a part of show business, providing public entertainment. We work on Christmas night and New Year's Eve. A player remains on call by his team. Occasionally decisions about practice, films, and trips are made day to day so it is difficult to make any firm plans during the season. If a coach wants to demand a player's presence every day of the working year, he can get it.

Nonetheless, there is ample time to pursue interests outside of basketball. After all, a normal workday for us in New York consists of only four hours. Dick Barnett uses his free time to go back to school for a Master's degree in Urban Affairs from New York University. Willis Reed likes to run small businesses. Although he always manages to find time for fishing and hunting on his 300-acre farm in Pennsylvania, he must be on top of his affairs. A contract with Uniroyal requires one appearance a month. Various other endorsements take time, and his liquor store, his restaurant, his summer camp, and his apartment building require the rest of his attention.

DeBusschere, more than the others, depends primarily on basketball and his family. He once was a stockbroker but found he disliked the responsibility of handling other people's money. Much of his off-time is spent with his family at home. He loves to cook and play with his kids. Occasionally, he will make a TV commercial for clothes or hairspray or candy or cars. He studies investments and makes his decisions on them with little counsel. He has many friends in the corporate world, and he likes New York restaurants, considering himself a bit of a gourmet.

Activities outside basketball, for all of us, are largely dependent on winning. When things go poorly, commercial offers decrease precipitously. Fewer people want to become acquaintances. Daily encounters with the public become painful. Walking down the street as a winner invites hellos and congratulations. Walking that same street after losing produces criticism and derision. That is the way of our world, and that is why, when we are losing, I do a lot of reading.

## 8

$T$UESDAY EVENING IS THE NIGHT OF A CRUCIAL GAME
against Boston. If we are to have a chance for first
place, we must win tonight. Inside the Employees'
Entrance I mug at Frankie and say hello to Slick, the
elevator man—"Hey, what's happenin', Brother Bill?"

"You got it, Slick."

"Go get 'em tonight."

I get out of the elevator on the fifth floor, the arena
level.

"Hi, Emil, Joe—floor down yet?"

"Naw, the circus was late today."

During two months every year the circus lives at
Madison Square Garden. For me the circus was a
traveling show that came to a small Midwestern town
in the spring. The horse-drawn cages filled with tigers
and the bright colored wagons wound their way
through the cobblestone streets. Enthusiastic crowds
applauded the procession. Outside the town limits,
tents covered what two days before had been a baseball field. Roustabouts raised the big top for its three-
night stand. Two-headed cows. Fire-eaters. Sword
swallowers. Giants. Other assorted country Houdinis.
I would watch enthralled as a barker stood before a
burlesque tent describing the sexual excitement that
awaited a customer just inside the tent flaps. At center ring, the trapeze never seemed as high as the ones
in the movies. The women were never as beautiful
and the lion tamer never as brave. The tents smelled
of oil and mold. Under the flaps of the mess kitchen
you could glimpse dwarfs and fortune tellers, clowns
and roustabouts sitting at a table arguing with the

men in business suits as they ate their evening meal after the main show. Those days of the circus were in outrageous contrast to the daily life of a small Midwestern town.

Many summers there were other tent shows—religious revivals to which my mother would take me. The preachers frightened me. I couldn't carry a tune. The tents were dry and the wooden folding chairs pinched my behind. During the excessively long prayers, I kept thinking of baseballs, basketballs, and tigers in cages. At the collection, when I turned to observe just what the people behind us were contributing to the Lord, I was jabbed in the ribs and told to concentrate on my shortcomings. There was no way for the revival to replace the circus for me. I was twelve years old.

Circus people fill the hallways of Madison Square Garden. Changing areas are established with curtains that look like thick bedsheets. Trunks crowd the corridors. Doors have circus names on them: Gunther Gebel-Williams, RBBB, The Flying Oleos, Petite Phillipe. Other doors belong to the Knicks, the Rangers. Women in tights with heavy muscular legs and rugged faces talk in Rumanian. A man carefully studies his face in a small mirror attached to a stilt pole. A beautiful young girl covered with circus make-up, wearing long eyelashes and a see-through robe, sits crying on the lap of an acrobat. A clown stands next to the Garden electrician's room carefully removing his red and white greasepaint. Gunther Gebel-Williams, the lion tamer, strides from his private dressing room with his long golden locks combed as carefully as the hair of any *Vogue* model. Across the arena floor lions and tigers rest in makeshift cages while hump-backed camels and wrinkled elephants stand impassively, their feet in chains. The smell of urine and hay saturates the recycled Garden air. I feel a kinship with these people. Our skills are different, our lives alike.

The Boston Celtics are our special rivals. We replaced them in 1970 as world champions and since then the press writes of a Knick era as they once talked of the Celtic dynasty; even though we lost the championship two of the next three years. The rivalry between us is intense and the competition is fierce. The games are rough and emotionally draining. The battles over the years, though, develop respect among the players.

I guard John Havlicek—by far the most difficult job I have in a season. Havlicek's every movement has a purpose and his teammates look for him constantly. If I am a split second behind him, or respond to his fakes away from the ball, he receives a pass and gets a basket. He never lets down and his stamina seems endless. I've played him for six years. If he gets twenty-one points and I get fifteen, and we win, I think I have done a good job. Testing my ability against his superior skills gives me great satisfaction. Both of us know instinctively how far we can challenge each other without destroying our mutual respect. If he makes a cut to the basket without the ball, I might try to stop him with a stiff arm to the hip. He might respond by grabbing my arm for leverage and hurtling past me. In tonight's game, a regular season contest, we will play hard against each other—each doing some holding and pushing, but never turning the natural aggressiveness of the game into hostility.

The interaction between the two teams is a competition that extends to the level of management. Red Holzman and Red Auerbach, the Celtic general manager, are bitter rivals. Both subscribe to the notion that no advantage is too small to take. They are polite enough to each other at public and league functions, but individual pride sometimes makes courtesy difficult. One time after a Saturday night game, both teams flew to Boston together for a Sunday afternoon game. As we waited in the passenger lounge, players from each team chatted amicably, but the two Reds remained apart. When the flight was called, they got into an argument about who would get on the plane first.

Whenever the Celtics lose in New York, Auerbach stands in the hallway yelling about how the officials won the game for the Knicks. When we play in Boston, we often dress in locker rooms that are either very hot or very cold. If we win in Boston, we never have the same locker room when we return. Whelan claims that the "musical locker rooms" are the work of Auerbach, and I believe it. When things go bad at the hotel in Boston or on the bus to the airport, Holzman occasionally blames the Celtics. Auerbach in particular prides himself on getting these psychological edges. Opposing players dislike him, but for Auerbach the smallest incident can become a test of his machismo. Once, during play-offs against Boston, Auerbach prevented Whelan, Monroe, and an injured rookie from using the Celtic training room for physical therapy. He claimed that unless the Celtic trainer was present they could not be trusted.

When Auerbach coached he would light a cigar on the bench as soon as he thought his team had won. He liked to embarrass an opponent that way. Once, when Los Angeles won the first game in the final play-off series against Boston in Boston, Auerbach announced after the loss that Russell would coach the following year. The next day, which he was flying to Los Angeles for the second game, the headlines carried news of Russell's appointment and not the Lakers' victory. Red claimed a psychological victory.

But no matter how arrogant Auerbach appears, I cannot dislike him. I have a personal bond underneath the layers of competitive antagonism. When I was in college and he was the coach of world champions he took an interest in my game. We would meet on summer mornings and he would explain the finer points of blocking out for rebounds or running the fast break. After each workout he never forgot to drop the confidence-building compliment and he never asked for anything in return. Auerbach loves the sport and, talking with him, one quickly realizes that he understands how to motivate players. I don't agree with those who say Auerbach just had good player talent during his years as Celtic coach when he won eight of nine championships. He is a great teacher.

———

The film of our last game against the Celtics in Madison Square Garden is on the screen. Two policemen walk into the locker room and say something to Holzman.

"What is it, Red?" I ask.

"Never mind," he says.

I look to the special locker-room assistant, who nods his head and forms his thumb and forefinger into the shape of a revolver.

"Is it a warning?" I ask Red.

"Yeah, but don't worry, nothing can happen," he says.

The special assistant walks over after Red is gone and says, "Somebody called up and said they were gonna get one of the Knicks tonight. The place is crawlin' with plainclothesmen."

Other nights in years past phone calls warned of bombs and violence. Occasionally it made the news. More often, it didn't.

We walk out between the tan curtains, past the sawhorses that hold back the crowd, and onto the court. I see eight or nine plainclothesmen surrounding the court, concentrated behind our bench. The Celtics are going through their lay-ups. The fans are alive as usual with jeers, greetings, insults, threats, invitations, and encouragements. "Boston games are like heavyweight championship fights," Frazier says. "People can't wait until the buzzer rings."

———

The New York press proclaims that every player in professional basketball would like to play in New

York. Basketball salaries here are the highest. Ten million people focus their attention on twelve players. Fifty times a year TV carries our faces into the city's living rooms, revealing our pains along with our triumphs. Fifty times a year 20,000 fans jam the Garden to watch us in person. Outside income from basketball flows more readily to a New York player on a winning team because he is accessible to Madison Avenue, the TV networks, and the hundreds of public appearance requests that come from a metropolitan area of fifteen million.

Basketball, according to some pundits, is really a "city" game, and New York is—more than any other— the city. People who grow up on the streets of New York feel they understand the tempo and skill of the game best. The Garden crowd applauds the subtleties of the game. They recognize the well-executed play and the pass that leads to the pass for a basket. They understand that team defense is essential for victory and that when done well it can be exciting. Yet to imply that basketball is only a city game is a fallacy— more journalistic excess than fact. Good professional players come from all over the country including rural areas in such places as Kentucky, Indiana, and North Carolina. Good coaches work in California and Missouri and many knowledgeable fans have never seen New York.

Our Knick team is not the offspring of the city's playgrounds. None of our first seven players comes from New York. Instead, we were brought to the city by a college draft which allocated each of us to the New York team. We had no choice in the matter. If we wanted to play professional basketball, we had to play in New York. Some of us adjusted and even thrived in the excitement of the city life, but we are the city's stepchildren. I am a New York Knick. I am never a New Yorker in the sense that an athlete from Sparta was a Spartan.

New York has been, for me, a city which operates on as many different levels as there are floors in one of its skyscrapers. In the beginning I approached it with the suspicion of a Midwesterner who has heard too many stories about the city's corrupting influences. I avoided strangers and public places (in New York that's difficult). But slowly I realized that New York provides anonymity as well as the spotlight, humor as well as danger, inspiration as well as sordidness. I have come to appreciate the crowds—people-watching is my number one pastime; I like the layers of humanity with diverse backgrounds all living, functioning, and prospering in such a small area. I like the New York police and the New York cabdrivers—both offering their opinions with their skills. I like the rough impersonality of New York, where human relations are oiled by jokes, complaints, and confessions—all made with the assumption of never seeing the other person again. I like New York because there are enough competing units to make it still seem a very mobile society. I like New York because it engenders high expectations simply by its pace.

"When you're dealing with spiritual concepts," says Phil Jackson, "you like to deal in energies because if you believe in God you believe He is probably an energy force. So, one of the things that amazes me is the amount of energy that's in New York. You get no energy from the earth because the earth is all covered up with cement and bricks. There's no place to walk on the earth unless you go to Central Park. The energy all comes from human beings. It's a very high-pitched, nervous energy. It's also very creative and very human, lustful and earthy. When I come back here every fall from the Northwest, I like the stimulation it brings me. The other thing is that no matter what you like or want, materially, you can find it here."

The New York Knicks are a popular and fashionable part of the New York experience and have been since 1968 when the team began to have a winning record. Basketball stars have become celebrities. Details of players' lives are hot copy. Comparisons are made—so help me—between Walt Frazier and Nureyev.

A broad cross-section of people come to the Garden to see and to be seen—to be identified with the success of the Knicks. An already sizable stable of groupies has diversified as it has grown. Point-spread gamblers sit behind the baskets urging victories by nine points instead of seven, six points instead of five. Aspiring starlets parade around the players' benches at half-time showing off their good looks. For two years a bad dancer appeared at courtside to put his hex on opposing teams. (He later sent a bill to the Knicks.) Twenty thousand people—politicians, corporate executives, carpenters, plumbers, magnificently Afroed women dressed to perfection, and movie actors in disguise—sit with their attention riveted to a small, well-lighted strip of wood on which ten highly trained bodies run and jump.

Performed in the midst of a lengthy war, deepening economic woes, and political upheaval, the game gives people a real-life drama that has a resolution. As a form of show business it is completely honest. As a form of human endeavor it is understandable and pure. The performance demands maximum effort, as one sees clearly at courtside. Unencumbered by masks, pads, or hats, the players reveal their bodies as well as their skills. People come and see and know that what they see is real. Fakes do not win championships, or hold opponents scoreless over a quarter, or charge from behind to hit six shots in the last two minutes.

The athlete's honest performance on the court surprisingly produces the phenomenon of a more general credibility off the court. I can't tell you, for example, how many times people have come to me and said that they used me as a model for their children. I guess that's all right, and often I have been flattered by such comments. But the people don't really know me. Parents see me play and hear about a few aspects of my off-court life. From that they create a model which frequently distorts normal living and often conforms totally with their own views as they relate not just to dictates of diet and physical fitness but also to larger questions of politics, sexuality, and religion. In stripping the athlete of all individuality the parent provides a pure but sterile model for his children— more a playmate than an adult.

I think our believable professionalism on the court also leads to the phenomenon of women (not groupies or surrogate mothers or happy young wives) who regard us as show business figures with a particular brand of masculinity. An athlete can recognize the absence of interest in him as a person. He, more than most males, understands the unnaturalness of being a sex object.

The only thing which differentiates an athlete from other men is his performance on the court. When fans take that performance beyond its own legitimate boundaries, from the court to their fantasy land, they seem to create a monster that says more about their own lives than the athlete's. It is as though people, by transferring their personal dilemmas and problems to the athlete, seek to redirect their explosiveness. If a father fails to instill values in his child, and tells the boy to be like Willis Reed or Dave DeBusschere, trying to stretch the simple example of a normal person's professional excellence into the core of a boy's moral training, he possibly short-cuts his own responsibility to serve as a model. In so doing, he exploits the athlete who performs well on the court, out in the open, ripe for any fan's unarguable interpretation.

And then there is the athlete returning the favor, attempting to exploit the public's belief in his professional integrity, seeking to transfer his general credibility to commercial products. As a spokesman for corporate entities he can generate consumption; his high salary enhancing his basic value as a marketing vehicle. With the rise in athletes' salaries and with the publicity owners and the press gave those salaries, the athlete has taken on a credibility that goes beyond the elemental success of the court and the clean-cut victory. He has become a financial success in a materialistic society which believes money earned accurately measures accomplishment. The athlete not only achieves the obvious success of a warrior on the field of battle but then as if to reinforce his position, receives the appropriate reward from his society. The higher his salary, the more the popular mind legitimizes him. His accomplishment is clear. Envied, perhaps, and certainly well known and widely acclaimed, he becomes a celebrity perfectly cast to tickle the consumer appetites of affluent America.

Fran Tarkenton, the professional football player, always talked about his "relationships" with corporations as if they were well-remembered lovers. He carefully cultivated a stable of executives who had their firms pay him big fees for socializing with fellow executives. Almost every aspect of his life was covered by a "relationship": Delta Airlines gave him free travel, Eastman Kodak gave him clothes, Coke gave him prestige in Atlanta, and *Newsweek* gave him access to media power.

Walt Frazier selects his major endorsements with care. He has become the corporate spokesman for Ripley Clothes, Puma sneakers, Seamless Basketball, and Pioneer Stereo. Each company pays Frazier for the use of his name and image. Willis Reed endorses Pro Ked shoes and Alka Seltzer. Monroe has Volkswagen and Simba Clothes. DeBusschere has M & M Candies, Miss Clairol Hair Coloring, and Lite Beer. Lucas does United Airlines and Jackson has Webfeet Shoes. It takes one day for a player to do a TV commercial for which he can earn as much as $30,000. For a luncheon he can make $2,500—no speech, just chitchat.

"Promptly after December 31 in each year commencing December 31, 1967, Player shall pay to Club 25 percent of net income (after applicable expenses but before income taxes) received by player during the 12 months ended on such December 31 from any sale of his ancillary basketball rights and services made at any time after date hereof and on or before May 31, 1971. For purposes hereof, income from sale of Player's ancillary basketball rights and services shall include, but not by way of limitation, all income from endorsements, pictures, public appearances, books, magazine and newspaper articles, and radio and television programs, provided that such income shall be directly related to Player's activities as a basketball player."

My negotiations with the Knicks in the Spring of 1967 had reached an impasse until that clause solved all the problems. My attorney, Lawrence Fleisher, and I were sitting in a dark booth in the Oak Room of the Plaza Hotel with Irving Mitchell Felt, Ned Irish, and Bill Jennings, the respective presidents of Madison Square Garden Corp., The New York Knickerbockers, and The New York Rangers. They suggested that they would meet my contract request if I agreed to give 25 percent of my ancillary income to Madison Square Garden. I was 22 years old. I looked at Fleisher, a man I'd known only two months. He was looking at the table. The salad was crisp, the seat soft. "Twenty-five percent of my ancillary rights," I said. "Well, let me think about it." We left the hotel, and as we walked toward Sixth Avenue, Fleisher said, "Well what do you think? You ready with the ancillary?"

"Ancillary?" I said, "What are ancillary rights?" I had almost asked at the table but remembered my Abe Lincoln.

"That's the money from commercials and endorsements," he said.

"What? I told them I wasn't going to do any; in fact I insisted on that clause about limiting my publicity appearances."

"Looks like they don't believe you," said Fleisher.

"Looks like I got what I wanted; 25 percent of nothing is nothing," I said.

Two days later, I signed a four-year contract to play professional basketball.

Agents have told me that by choosing not to do endorsements I lose fifty thousand dollars every year I play professionally. I have had some unusual offers, and a few times I was close to agreeing to a deal, but when it came down to the crunch I said no. Perhaps I wanted no part of an advertising industry which created socially useless personal needs and then sold a product to meet those needs. Maybe I felt that endorsement offers came to me because I was a great white hope for some people and not because I was a great player, and that offended my sensibilities. Chalk one up for America's two favorites: original sin and guilt. More probably, I wanted to keep my experience of basketball pure, as innocent and unpolluted by commercialism as possible. For many years basketball was my only passion in life. I was immune to the normal profusion of interests that accompany adolescence. I pressed my physical and emotional life into basketball alone, and it made for a very intense feeling. I felt about the court, the ball, and playing, the way people feel about friends. Playing for money compromised me enough. Taking money for hocking products demeaned my experience of the game. I cared about basketball. I didn't give a damn about perfumes, shaving lotions, clothes, or special foods.

---

"Bill, is DeBusschere there?" said the man from the Knick office.

"No. Why?"

"Got an offer for him."

"Tell me."

"No, you're not interested in this stuff."

"Yeah, I am, maybe, tell me."

"Well, there's this broad who's looking for a Knick to go into business with. She's operating a hair salon on Eighth Avenue. I'll give you the address."

I took the elevator to the top floor and then walked directly into a shag-carpeted waiting room. Dark, heavy Spanish furniture cluttered the small space. (Do they really have this kind of taste in Spain?) A

girl with a pallid complexion stood behind the glass
display case, silhouetted against a large mirror with
thick iron borders. The only light came from a few
spotlights, shining on the magazine rack and on the
ties arranged on the top of the glass case.

"Hi, I'm Lois," said the woman. "You're Bill Bradley.
Come on back to my office."

We walked past some rubbing tables and into the
barbershop area, where two snow white manicurists
with big red lips and tight uniforms were helping
the barber care for a customer. We entered a cubicle
8 by 8 and sat facing each other across her desk.

"Let me tell you. My friend, he's from down on
Wall Street you know, and me, we want to start a
health club. I know him personally. You see, he set
me up in this and said it was mine all alone and he
only wanted 50 percent of my shares. I trust him. He's
smart. He knows finance. I know the clientele—the
Jewish men from the garment district. I know their
mentality. I know what they like and that's why this
place is decorated like it is.

"But how to get 'em here is another question. That's
where you come in. If we called up one or two places
over there and told 'em that Bill Bradley of the Knicks
was getting his hair cut here or just hung around
here for a few hours in the afternoon, they'd be over
here in a minute. That's just the way they are. We'd
give you 20 percent of the business for doing that.

"We expect to make most of our money with the
line of clothes in the boutique. You know, we'd have
Bill Bradley ties and shirts. We expect to franchise
this all over the country after we get going, so there
could be some big money in it for you; $20,000 a year
minimum."

"I'll think about it and let you know," I said as I
rang the elevator bell. The button I pressed was nes-
tled carefully in the crotch of a carved wooden nymph
nailed to the wall.

"Yeah, fucking A," said the ad man, "I know what
you mean. You want somethin' that will make money

and yet not compromise your values as a person. I see. Yeah, we'll think about it."

Two weeks later at a window table in the Four Seasons around 3 P.M. after a long lunch he said, "You want somethin' that's class, and sports, and still you. Here it is." His partner unveiled a 3' by 4' placard on which were written the words: BILL BRADLEY BRAINSTORMS INC. "You can put anything under that. It can be a holding company for operations like a computer school for ghetto kids, an education film company, or anything else. We would provide the advertising and some of the business management.

"We'll want 80 percent. See, we have to have 80 percent for our own conglomerate reasons."

"You will appear three times in a national magazine and all you will say is that you drink milk. How can milk be bad? It's as American as apple pie," said the man from Campbell Ewall in Detroit.

"Who pays me to say that? I asked.

"The Associated Milk Producers of America and The American Dairy Association."

"Hi, Bill. Stan here. Let me explain a little about us. I came over from Random House to manage this operation here for *Playboy*. The magazine is called *Oui* and it has sold 200,000 copies in three months. It is so good it's frightening, but this market has been hurt by the recent surprise court ruling on pornography. During the last month we've cut deliveries to a couple of places in the South. Overall, though, there's enormous demand for our product. We've conducted an in-depth survey on American sexual mores, an update of Kinsey. We want *Oui* to aim at the sophisticated college student, cosmopolitan and young. There's a gap between the *Playboy* audience and the *Oui* audience. Europe will be a real part of *Oui*, both in style and stories. We have correspondents in the big European capitals."

"What do you want from me?"

"We need image help. We want you to speak at

selected luncheons in New York, Chicago and Los Angeles. Our key advertisers will attend. You won't have to push the magazine or have pictures of you in it. We want to keep it subtle; low profile, you know. Just talk about sports or politics and answer questions. It will be good exposure for you. We'll pay $2,500 a speech and guarantee you ten speeches a year, at least. Let me assure you that even if some people in Canton, Ohio, or Springfield, Missouri, don't like *Oui*, the fact remains we sell a lot of copies there."

Every good Celtic team has run a fast break, which means moving the ball downcourt before the defense gets ready. Rebound, outlet pass, pass, lay-up. The Knicks and Chicago use defensive pressures, but Boston generates offensive pressure, creating situations in which one defensive man must cover two offensive players converging on him at full speed from different directions. Every time you shoot against the Celtics your team must worry about retreating to counter the stampede which will ensue if the shot misses. If you get into a running game with them, you're finished: An opponent will work eighteen seconds for two points and the Celtics will match that in five. That's Celtic basketball.

When we force Boston to slow down the tempo of the game, they resort to the same seven plays that Red Auerbach instituted during his tenure as coach. They have maintained a style and approach to the game, even though there has been a generational change of personnel. Their system requires the following kinds of players: an offensive forward who runs well, a defensive (power) forward who rebounds well, a good-shooting forward ready on the bench, an offensive guard who shoots well, a defensive guard who is strong, a swing-man who can play either forward or guard, and an aggressive center who plays defense well and directs the flow of action.

Tonight, Boston is hitting. Havlicek, who gets two

quick baskets, does not usually assert himself this much in the first six or seven minutes. The Celtics run three plays in to Cowens, clearing a side of the floor and allowing him to work at the low post on Lucas. Jo Jo White, the offensive guard with great quickness, hits two jumpers and beats Monroe to the basket on a drive. Havlicek then scores two more jumpers and two foul shots. The Celtics blow us out and win by thirty points. We say to ourselves afterwards that we lost because Lucas was feeling sick and Monroe was injured. But being candid, I wonder if the Celtics are not better than we are this year. The locker room is quiet.

The press files in.

"What happened to the offense?"

"Will you be able to beat the Celtics in the play-offs without Willis?"

"Where would you say they beat you? Rebounding or defense?"

"Have you ever seen Havlicek play better?"

I shower and dress quickly, saying very little to the reporters. Because we are in second place with only 15 games remaining in the season (and because Willis has made little improvement), they expect us to provide a witty observation about our own funeral. The only alternative is to parrot comments on the game as if our sputtering efforts are of no concern to defending champions. On my way out of the Garden, near the big automatic aluminum door on 33rd Street, I sign twelve autographs for young fans. There are fifty asking. I keep walking and signing, until I'm at a cab in front of the Garden. One little kid starts screaming, "Come on, Bradley, I waited. Don't be like Monroe. Come on, Bradley, come on." His voice has the tone of petulance. I've heard it before, too many times. Suddenly, I turn on him and say, "Why don't you learn some manners? If you would have asked politely I might have signed it." (And I would have.) As I get into the cab a teenager says, "Why don't *you* learn somethin'?" and another yells, "What's the matter, we only want your autograph, not your money, you bum." As the cab pulls away and moves through the New York streets to a restaurant where I'm meeting some friends for dinner even my conscience turns on me. I begin to feel sorry for the little kid. He looked surprised when I scolded him. Maybe I was too abrupt.

The game depressed me. I keep saying to myself that we'll be ready when the playoffs come, that these games only qualify us for the post-season competition. Yet, I can't convince myself to take *this* evening's defeat so cavalierly. Injuries affect our play but they are not our main worries. Timing and teamwork can't be turned on and off as if they were spigots, and we didn't have much of either tonight.

The cab pulls up in front of the restaurant, and as I pay the driver, he says, "You're Bradley, right?"

"Yeah."

"You guys better get on the ball. The play-offs start soon. Shit, what am I sayin', forget the play-offs, I lost fifty dollars tonight. How's Reed? Gonna play next week?"

The talk at dinner turns to things other than basketball. Good friends always bring up other things. I begin to forget the worries of the cab ride. We make plans for a summer trip. The conversation rooted in years of close association is about family and friends. The economy is damned, briefly. Money worries. Political anecdotes. Music. A long story about the training of quarter horses. Laughter. A few sarcastic puns. Communal eating.

In the middle of dinner a woman walks up and asks for my autograph. I tell her I'd be glad to do it later, after dinner. She walks away. Two minutes later, a man about 5'11" with husky shoulders and a flat nose walks up to me at the table. "Hey, Bradley, you Bradley," he says. He's had too much to drink. I smile, thinking of the time a drunk reporter walked with his coat to the front of a plane on a transcontinental flight and told everyone he was getting off. We were over Kansas.

"What's the matter, think you're too good?" the

drunk blurts. "The lady just asked for an autograph. I was pro fighter. I ought to knock you out, you son-of-a-bitch. You're all alike. Lady has a kid. . . ." He can't stand still. He sways back and forth as he talks. I take a piece of paper without even nodding at him, scribble my name on it, and thrust it in his pocket.

"Okay, champ, you have it now," I say with a wink.

"Who knows," one of my friends says as our visitor staggers around tables heading for the reassuring darkness of the bar, "if he was a boxer maybe you got off easy."

When we leave the restaurant a man on the street recognizes me. He approaches and says simply as if he were an ordered antidote to the boxer, "Thank you for all the wonderful evenings you have given me. I think the Knicks are class." I say thanks for the words and we walk our separate ways.

———

There is no question about it. Being a member of a successful New York basketball team is a mixed blessing. The notoriety forces one to look at the world differently from other people. It provides money and access. At the same time, it sets one apart from the rest of society and denies one the privilege of being an equal member of a crowd. There is little chance, for example, for a public figure to fail without people knowing it, and no one grows without failing. Many avoid the embarrassment of public failure by never placing themselves in positions where they might fail. Therefore, they never grow. My constant problem is to find places where I am allowed to fail in private. Everyone does not thirst for fame. For me, fame holds as much danger as it does benefit.

If you are famous you get special service at banks, passport offices, and airline ticket counters, and come to expect that service while not respecting yourself for wanting it. Fame is being paid a lot of money for what people think about you as well as for what you do . . . having strange women approach you and say they want to meet you, know you in every way, right now ... misassessing the amount of interest other people have in you ... trying to find yourself while under the scrutiny of thousands of eyes ... reacting instead of acting, being passive instead of active ... having people tell you what they want you to do with your life ... learning to understand what others want from you ... sensing people in a restaurant whispering and pointing toward your party ... forgetting how hot the subways are in August ... having someone write that if you visit this kid who is dying in a hospital he will get better ... having strangers constantly test you and probe for the dimension of your "real" personality ... coming into contact with ten times more people in a year than most people do in a lifetime ... remaining unable to escape those few minutes or several years when what you did made you famous. ...

The American historian Daniel Boorstin in his book *The Image* has observed:

The very agency which first makes the celebrity in the long run inevitably destroys him. ... The newspapers make him and they unmake him— not by murder but by suffocation or starvation. ... There is not even any tragedy in the celebrity's fall, for he is a man returned to his proper anonymous station. The tragic hero, in Aristotle's familiar definition, was man fallen from great estate, a great man with a tragic flaw. He had somehow become the victim of his own greatness. Yesterday's celebrity, however, is a commonplace man who has been fitted back into his proper commonplaceness not by any fault of his own, but by time itself.

The hero was born of time: his gestation required at least a generation. As the saying went, he had "stood the test of time." He grew over generations. ... Receding into the misty past, he became more and not less heroic. ... Men of the last century were more heroic than those of today; men of antiquity were still more heroic. ...

The celebrity, on the contrary, is always contemporary. The hero is made by folk-lore, sacred texts and history books, and the celebrity is the creature of gossip, of public opinion, of newspapers, magazines and the ephemeral images of movie and television screens. The passage of time which creates and establishes the hero, destroys the celebrity. One is made, the other unmade, by repetition. The celebrity is born in the daily papers, and never loses the mark of his fleeting origin.

The other Knicks and I got to our present positions of celebrity through similar routes. There are many encouragements for a boy to be an athlete while in high school. The good athlete is popular among his classmates, but the star athlete develops a reputation outside high school. Townspeople, adults, single him out for attention and interest. Teachers might favor him even if unconsciously. Growing up, when most young people struggle to define their tastes and develop their own sense of right and wrong, the star athlete lies protected in his momentary nest of fame. The community tells him that he is a basketball star. For the townspeople his future is as clearly outlined as his record-book past. They expect him to become an even greater athlete and to do those things which will bring about the fulfillment of what is wholly their fantasy. The adolescent who receives such attention rarely develops personal doubts. There is a smug cockiness about achievements, or a sincere determination to continue along a course that has brought success and praise. The athlete continues to devote his energies to sport. Compared with the natural fears and insecurities of his classmates, he has it easy. His self-assurance is constantly reinforced by public approval.

The athletes who succeed in making college teams have the high school experience duplicated on a grander scale. The few who excel on university teams find that admiration comes then, not from high school friends and adult family friends, but from the national press and from adults they have never met. They begin to see that they can make a good living simply by playing the sport. Self-definition again comes from external sources, not from within. While their physical skill lasts, professional athletes are celebrities— fondled and excused, praised and believed. Only toward the end of their careers do the stars realize that their sense of identity is insufficient.

# Part II

"I need not tell you what it is to be knocking about in an open boat. I remember nights and days of calm, when we pulled, we pulled, and the boat seemed to stand still, as if bewitched within the circle of the sea horizon. I remember the heat, the deluge of rain-squalls that kept us bailing for dear life (but filled our water cask), and I remember sixteen hours on end with a mouth dry as a cinder and a steering oar over the stern to keep my first command head on to the breaking sea. I did not know how good a man I was till then. I remember the drawn faces, the dejected figures of my two men, and I remember my youth and the feeling that will never come back any more—the feeling I could last forever, outlast the sea, the earth and all men; the deceitful feeling that lures us on to joys, to perils, to love, to vain effort—to death; the triumphant conviction of strength, the heat of life in the handful of dust, the glow in the heart that with every year grows dim, grows cold, grows small and expires— and expires, too soon, too soon—before life itself."

(From YOUTH, by *Joseph Conrad*)

THE TRAFFIC TO JFK AIRPORT SLOWS TO A CRAWL for the last five miles of the journey. Two cars have crashed at the intersection of the Van Wyck Expressway and the Southern State Parkway. Normally non-rush hour driving time from Manhattan is thirty-five minutes. Today I will be lucky to make it in fifty. I make most flights with little time to spare, and this delay could prove costly. The Knick's rule is that if a player misses a flight he must pay a hundred dollar fine plus his own fare. Since we fly to Los Angeles today that could mean a four hundred dollar mistake.

Arriving at the American Airlines terminal ten minutes before departure, I throw my bags to the ticket agent and run for the gate, only to find a line at the security checkpoint. After waiting another five minutes I go through the metal detector and make the plane just as the gate attendant is closing down the flight. The whole group is assembled as I walk into the fuselage. My arrival draws applause. "Too bad, I was hoping you'd miss, Bill," Holzman says good-naturedly. "You'd have to dig deep for four hundred bucks. Maybe you'd have to go to that stone house where you keep the money from your first paycheck, right Danny?"

"Riiight," Danny says, stretching the single syllable word to an exclamation which falls somewhere between a battle cry and the sound made during a throat examination.

"Red," Danny continues, "Bill says it's twenty minutes to LaGuardia and thirty-five to JFK. Now Red, Bill knows. You got it perfect don't you, Bill. No mistakes, just right down to the minute. Bill probably got his doughnut and coffee at that greasy spoon on 8th Avenue, read *The New York Times*, then cabbed it to meet the fellows. Almost missed though, didn't you, Senator?"

"Take it easy on him, Danny," Red says. "Remember the job. It's not too long now."

"Oh, yeah, the job. Remember Bill, Red and I get the first two jobs when you make it big in politics. You know, the high-paying no-show at the beach. The one you promised. I'll call you and say, 'Hello Bill, Danny here. Yeah Bill, the water's still in the ocean and it's still wet. How about the Atlantic? Bill, have you checked with Red today? and, Bill, don't forget to mail the check.'"

The plane rolls out to the take-off runway and we are quickly on our way to L.A. for the first stop of a five-game western trip.

Shortly after we are up the stewardess comes around for drink orders. Holzman sets no rules about liquor so each player follows his own inclination.

"Good afternoon," the stewardess says to Monroe and Jackson, "and what would you like to drink today on our red carpet service to Los Angeles?"

Jackson stares at her, smiling until she is finished, and then says with a straight face, "On our red carpet service to Los Angeles I'd like a glass of orange juice and 7-Up mixed."

"And you, sir," she says to Earl who's reading *Rolling Stone* magazine.

"I'll have tea with six sugars and lemon."

"Well, well, six sugars, sir. That's a lot. Are you sure? The three gentlemen in front want the same thing. We might run short on sugars."

"I'm sure," Earl says.

After the meal DeBusschere talks with one of the sportswriters on the trip. Willis reads a book on estate planning. Frazier reads a book on how to improve vocabulary. Earl, Phil, Barnett, and a rookie play cards with Lucas keeping score. Barnett is the moving force behind the game. "Deal 'em," he says to the regular players and the game begins. Using the table in the front of the first class section of a 747 (or the aisle floor of a 727 with a blanket thrown over it) the four gamblers face each other in whatever game the dealer chooses: whist, bid whist, tonk, hi-low middle, or the staple game, poker. Stakes are relatively small but not insignificant. On a New York–Los Angeles flight a player can win as much as four hundred dollars.

Barnett says he gambles for relaxation and to pass the time—not to win big money. He began playing cards at home with his family while listening to radio programs such as Inner Sanctum and Gang Busters. Outside home he didn't play cards much until he got to college. And then during his years in Los Angeles with the Lakers he got into games with doctors and lawyers in which three to four thousand dollars might change hands in one night. Poker is his favorite card game. Ask him why and he says, "It reflects a lot about an individual. It is a personality clash more than luck. It gives you an opportunity to make a choice, which is like a lot of things in life—either you can play or you can get out."

Jackson has the deal. Poker is the game. Phil lost the previous hand on a showdown with Barnett. Phil's big hands fumble the cards and the eight of clubs falls on the floor.

"Better get a crocus sack to shuffle those cards in," Barnett says. "Jealous man can't work and a scared man can't gamble. Deal 'em, chump."

The public address system comes on and the captain says, "We hope you are all enjoying the flight. We are flying at 30,000 feet and place ourselves two hours from Los Angeles. On your right is Durango, Colorado, and in the distance you can see Pikes Peak."

"Rich just 'Humphrey Bogarted' that last pot," says Earl, "just took it for nothing."

"Look at there," says the rookie, "he already spread three kings this time; that's gonna be tough to beat. You should drop now."

"Yeah," says Phil as he throws in his cards.

"Way to dig deep, turkey," Barnett says as he picks up the pot with a toothy smile.

"Better stop countin' the dollars, Rich, or they'll get away from you," says the rookie. "If Phil had one more club in that hand a while back he'd been over."

"I'm hip," says Earl.

"Two in a row makes the rooster crow," Barnett retorts. "You a real Koufax, Earl, pitchin' good cards to me."

The captain makes another announcement: "Shortly we'll cross the Four Corners—directly above the place where Arizona, New Mexico, Utah, and Colorado meet at a single point."

"Your deal, Rich," says Phil. Barnett selects five card stud, deuces wild, and takes his time with the cards, careful to demonstrate in great detail his shuffling ability.

"Way to shuffle the cards," Earl says, pausing, "to death!"

Everyone looks at their hole card and then at each other.

"Cost you ten to go," says Earl, who opens with ten dollars on the strength of a pair of fives showing on three cards. Everybody stays.

The fourth card is dealt. Sixty dollars now sit in the pot.

"Tryin' to stare a hole in 'em, man," Barnett says to Jackson and the rookie. "Either drop the money or drop out. Put some money in the game and you can talk."

"Can't stand your love," the rookie says as he drops.

With the fifth card there is no more excitement. Earl with a deuce as his hole card shows three fives. He wins the hand, taking Barnett with him to the end.

"How's it read, Computer," Dick says to Lucas.

"Barnett up $35 on trip, up $346 on year, Jackson down $26 on trip and up $115 on year, Monroe up $54 on trip, down $85 on year, rookie down $30 on trip, down $43 on year," Lucas concludes.

The captain comes on again, "Ladies and gentlemen, if you look out on the right of the aircraft you'll see the main canyon of the Grand Canyon. If you look up the Colorado River along the edges of the canyon you'll be able to see what looks like a green area. I know it's hard to see due to the snow, but that's the Havasupi Indian Reservation. They live on the bottom of the canyon."

DeBusschere looks up: "What's with the guy? He's a real tour guide." Willis sleeps.

The next hand of poker pits Jackson against Barnett in a head-to-head duel. The game is seven card stud with deuces wild; the first two cards face down. After the sixth card Jackson has two kings showing. Barnett has two aces. The seventh card, dealt faceup, is a deuce for Jacksons and Barnett gets an eight of clubs. They glance at each other and then back at the cards. Jackson raises $40. Barnett calls and raises $30. Jackson calls and raises $25. Barnett calls. By this time the tension is visible in both. Jackson's hole cards are a six of hearts and a deuce. Barnett shows an ace and a deuce. Jackson loses $300.

The captain makes his next announcement. "On your left is Lake Powell. The Glen Canyon dam on the Colorado River created this enormous lake in southern Utah. It has a coastline as long as the western coast of the United States from Tijuana, Mexico, to Vancouver, British Columbia."

The last hand ends just as the plane touches down in L.A.

"Hey, Dollar," shouts Barnett as I walk by. "Let me have ten until my brother straightens out. He's a humpback."

"Who won?" I asked.

"Rich," says Phil.

"Earl," says Rich.

"Phil," says Earl.

"Who?" I ask again.

"The rookie," says Lucas.

The team gets its bags and registers at the Sheraton Airport Hotel. We left New York at noon and ar-

rived in Los Angeles at 2:30. The three-hour time
change assures each of us fewer hours of sleep for
two nights. I'll wake up around 8 A.M. no matter how
late I go to bed tonight. For me going East to West
is always the more difficult direction. After checking-
in, I head directly for the International Hotel Health
Club. I ask DeBusschere if he wants to come with
me to get a massage, and he gives his usual negative
reply.

Occasionally during a season I will realize that I
have done nothing for two weeks but use and care
for my body. Games and practices bring injuries, and
travel brings fatigue. Hot whirlpool baths, diathermy,
ultrasound, ice packs, elastic wraps, aspirin, cold
pills, vitamins, and sleeping pills are all part of the
life. The body is constantly battered and ground
away. During this year alone I have had a jammed
finger, inflamed facia of the arch, a smashed nose
cartilage, five split lips, an elbow in the throat that
eliminated my voice for a week, a bruised right hip, a
sprained ankle, a left hip joint out of socket, and a
contusion of the left wrist. With all these I consider
myself lucky that I have been free of serious injuries,
which would have prevented me from playing. Still,
minor injuries take their psychic toll. From the beginning of the season I feel relaxed, until I'm injured.
Then every workout brings the fear of re-injury and
every night brings the hope for tomorrow's improvement. I wake up in the middle of the night and flex
my knee to see if there is pain, or knead my thigh to
see if the charley horse has begun to heal. I have often
thought, while sitting in a whirlpool with an injury,
that I would stay there twenty-four straight hours if
only it would hasten the healing time.

The element of time separates our injuries from
those of the weekend athlete: We must return to action as soon as physically possible. Some players, De-
Busschere for one, have a very low pain-tolerance
level, while others, such as Monroe, can play with
excruciatingly painful bone chips. The constant question is how soon to return after sustaining an injury.

To come back too soon risks re-injury and a further loss of time; to wait too long in a competitive environment can mean a drop in the team standings or loss of a position to a teammate. Doctors explain that many players can play again after serious operations like spinal fusions, sewn knee ligaments, or repaired achilles tendons because they work harder at recuperation. For example, when Dick Barnett snapped his achilles tendon in 1966 a lot of people thought his career was over; few athletes had ever made a complete recovery from that injury. But Barnett worked to save his playing life. Every day for four months he did a thousand toe raises, ran five miles on the beach and fifty times up ten flights of stairs, and jumped up and down in a swimming pool for an hour—a total of four hours a day working on his foot and leg.

A professional basketball player must be able to run six miles in a game, a hundred games a year—jumping and pivoting under constant physical contact. My body becomes so finely tuned that three days without workouts makes a noticeable difference in timing, wind, and strength. I believe that basketball is the most physically grueling of all professional sports.

Only the athlete himself really knows if he feels well enough for competition. Doctors don't always understand the athlete's healing time schedule. Sometimes I have been told I could play when I knew I couldn't, and sometimes I have been told I couldn't play when I knew I could. I usually consult three doctors when I have a fairly serious injury. After getting their opinions, which often differ, I decide, myself, whether I can play without danger or permanent damage.

Injuries after thirty occur more frequently and they are less responsive to treatment. Top condition is harder to regain and maintain. The real pro is not the twenty-five-year-old who can whip back into shape with two weeks of careless work but the veteran who tests his body each year to see if he still has it, knowing that someday he won't. During the first week of training camp DeBusschere (age 33) went straight home to bed after every workout. The week was equally difficult for me. After running a mile twice a day for three weeks prior to the camp and shooting an hour a day for twenty-one straight days, my body still wasn't ready for the two-a-day workouts under Holzman. The first day my calves felt as if a knife had split them open. My quadriceps the next day went into spasms so that each step felt as if the muscles had been replaced with armored plates. Pain spread to the back of the legs and around the knees. Two days later the back pain began along the sciatic nerve. It was a tiring pain, not sharp, but it felt as if the strands of a string were breaking until only one remained. Then there was the overall fatigue, which only sleep can cure, and there was never enough sleep. Finally, after the first two scrimmages, I realized that four months of normal life had ended, for I was so bruised that when I rolled over in bed I found my body studded with pain.

Most mature athletes have developed their own warm-up and training techniques, their own cures, their own diets. Ice seems to be the only remedy common to all. Applied immediately after injury ice can reduce the recuperative time for a sprained ankle from ten days to two. On late night flights many players sit with ice taped to their ankles or knees or feet throughout the flight. Whenever I get the first throat tickle of a cold I take nine thousand milligrams of vitamin C for four days. The remedy gives me immediate and positive relief. My diet is heavy with meat—steak, pork chops, calf's liver. The only thing I stop eating in the off-season is desserts. With all the running during the season, I never worry about calories. Frazier eats a lot of health foods—vitamins A, B, C, E; protein powder, cod liver oil, and much liver, chicken, fish, carrots and spinach. Jackson tries to eat mostly fish, chicken, and vegetables, with very little meat. Lucas takes 27 pills a day ranging from six vitamin E's to iron. DeBusschere cuts down on beer in the off-season. The club gives each player $19 a day on the road for food. No one starves.

Teammates often joke about the shape of my body

and its limited athletic capabilities. They say I'm the only player in the league with the body of an eighty-year-old man. I am not well-proportioned, and even when I am in peak condition I can't manage relatively simple physical exercises, I can't do twenty push-ups, and I would need a winch to lift most barbells. Standing, legs straight, I can't touch the floor with anything but my feet. With my physical equipment, just playing in the pros is a minor miracle.

Basketball is such a specialized skill that I restrict myself to it exclusively. I don't swim or play tennis, or hike or ride bicycles, or lift weights during the season. Each sport calls upon a different set of muscles and physically I am concerned only about my profession. After each game or practice, ice packs and whirlpools and sometimes anti-inflammatory drugs like endicin or butazolidin save the body for another exertion. A friend likens my body to a jet plane. When it is aloft it can accomplish things with power and speed. When it is on the ground it is helpless, unmaneuverable, and in need of repair. As I sit with my feet in a barrel of ice or my back pressed to the whirlpool in a tub of hot water the comparison becomes reasonable.

One of the Knick team doctors (we have had seven in my eight years with the Knicks) classifies all athletes as tight or loose. A loose athlete is very limber, even when inactive. He can touch his toes and stretch without worry of muscle tears or pulls. For him even yoga represents no challenge. Danger for the loose athlete comes in the joints. While he never has muscle pulls, he frequently does have cartilage or ligament problems because his joints are loosely structured. Joe Namath, for example, is loosely structured. Fran Tarkenton is tightly structured. The tight athlete often has a longer career, free from serious injury but it is filled with nagging little pulls and tears. I am a tightly muscled athlete who has to do stretching exercises the year around to maintain muscles that won't tear when overextended quickly in a jump or lateral pivot. "You might try stretching morning and night," the doc-

tor said as I was recuperating from yet another pull.
"Also running in sand is good, or jumping under water. Massage helps particularly—when the masseur
knows his craft."

―――――――

I have had hundreds of massages in health clubs
and massage salons in every league city. My normal
routine after arriving in a town the day before a game
is to find a facility where I can get a steam bath,
whirlpool, and massage. The masseurs are adequate
at the Washington Athletic Club in Seattle, the Phoenix Country Club, the University Club in Houston,
and Postl's Athletic Club in Chicago. My regular
masseur in New York is Yick Pon Huey, who teaches
at the Swedish Massage Institute. He is the best
quadricep man in the United States. The best all-
around health club in the country is the International
Hotel Health Club in Los Angeles and Lou Jorn, the
chief masseur there, has no peer.

I arrive for my appointment with Lou at 7 P.M. After a ten-minute steam bath, a cold shower, five minutes in the mineral whirlpool, and another cold shower, I walk up the stairs to the massage room, a glass
cubicle in the corner of the weight room. It is 10 P.M.
in New York; the flight was tiring and my body is just
beginning to loosen up. I say hello to Lou and hop
onto a table. A small man (5'8", 160 pounds), he is
one of the dying breed of legitimate masseurs caught
between modern physical therapy which requires the
use of machines under doctors' supervision and the
burgeoning "massage parlor" front for the oldest profession.

Lou says that a good masseur has to know anatomy
—the muscle structure and where the nerves hook
up. He must know how much pressure to apply and
where, and he must remember that since no two bodies are alike no two massages should be alike. Lou
works with his legs, not just his fingers, saving his
energy by using leverage like a weight lifter. He says

that the human hand conforms with any contour of the body and that the secret of massage lies in his fingers, which he conscientiously protects. "When I pull the muscle away from the bone," he says, "my fingers hit the nerves and dilate the blood vessels in the muscles. No one else can do what I do with my fingers. They are like those of a great musician who never had a lesson. I was born with the talent." Thirty years of concentration, intelligence, and trial and error have produced the Jorn Technique.

In his platoon-sergeant manner, Lou issues quick commands for me to roll over, put my head down, lift my legs—orders that are given without hesitation and that never allow a question of his purpose. I lie on my back with a towel covering my groin. Lou starts with the neck in order to loosen tension. His firm strokes hit the muscle knots "about the size of a pea" along the cervical vertebrae and stop at the base of the skull, where veins and nerves bunch on their way to the brain. Other masseurs redden one's ears, put too much pressure on the clavicle, or fail to distribute their strokes over the entire region, especially rubbing the side of the neck where the veins are instead of the bunched muscles along the vertebrae.

Next he takes my arm, and using his thumb and fingers, he splits the triceps, pulls them away from the bone, and squeezes them. The ability to straighten the arm comes from the triceps so everytime I shoot or pass they get used. Danny Whelan used to give Dick Barnett a pre-game massage of his triceps, just as he had done for baseball pitchers who won twenty games.

From the arms Lou goes to the feet where thumb and index finger rub along each side of the heel and into the arch. The strokes are short and hard. He detects some knotting in my arch. I react to the pain when he touches the area. He puts on less pressure but keeps up the jabs, widening them to the outer arch areas. Slowly he returns to the troubled area; gradually the knots break up. But, they don't disappear. He tells me this indicates a problem in the calf.

According to *The Story of Feet*, which is the best book Lou ever read about massage, all reflexes of the body end in the feet and each area of the body has its accompanying pressure point in the feet. Touching each area of the feet gives the masseur a quick preview of the painful weaknesses in the rest of the body. "The better conditioned an athlete is," says Lou, "the more flexible his feet will be."

He turns to the quadriceps and concentrates on the knee area and then asks me to turn over on my stomach. He splits the calf muscle with his thumb and says I need to strengthen my calf if I want to solve my arch problem, for the calf affects the arch as the forearm affects the palm. If the muscle is weak, too great a burden is placed on the arch, he says, and a muscle spasm and an inflammation of the fascia develop.

His size ten hands never leave the body. They move with long smooth strokes toward the heart. The pressure is constant until he encounters a knotted muscle in my lower back. There, he lets up, then returns, lets up, then returns again until it loosens and he can cover all areas with the same pressure. "If you ever bent a water hose you cut off the flow of water," he says. "That's what a muscle spasm does to blood circulation in the lower back. Americans sit wrong and wear bad shoes."

After the massage, which takes an hour, Lou splashes hot alcohol over the body and towels it dry. The hot alcohol evaporates but, unlike cool alcohol, it doesn't startle. He puts the rubber club shoes on my feet and finishes the massage with a slap on the heel. Now it is just a matter of showering, dressing, and returning to the hotel—rejuvenated.

## 2

THE NEXT MORNING RIGHT ON SCHEDULE I WAKE UP at 8:15. When I get downstairs to the coffee shop I notice Earl Monroe sitting alone at the end of the counter. Earl and I began to talk. He has a lump under his left eye. I noticed it on the plane. I ask him how he got it. He says that after the last game in the Garden, day before yesterday, he ran into a little trouble trying to get a cab at 8th Avenue and 31st Street. It was raining, he says; and Tina, "my lady," was standing under the canopy that extends from one of the Garden entrances to the street while he was in the street trying to flag a cab. Four white guys standing on the curb started shouting, "Hey, boy! Hey look at the boy in the rain." Earl said that he ignored them but they kept it up. When a cab came by and splashed water on him it seemed to set him off. He turned, walked to the curb and shouted, "I ain't no boy; don't you ever call me boy again." Pow! One of the whites hit Earl, who staggered back, quickly regained his balance, and came at his assailant. When Earl wrestled him onto the street the man's three buddies started to join the brawl, but Tina held them off with a spray can of mace. Earl was landing the blows when a black man—a stranger, either a Garden employee or a worker in the post office across the street—recognized him. He came over and pulled him off with the words, "Come on, Earl, you don't need this. Here's a cab." Earl and Tina got into the cab and left. As Earl thought about it he became more angry and wanted to resume the fight. He got his car and returned to the scene. No one was there. "It be's that

147

way sometime," Earl said as he ate his eggs, staring at the plate.

How many times, I thought, will racial hatred erupt unexpectedly before I learn that it is a part of the American experience. Two hours after Earl thrills 20,000 people with his skill and reaps significant financial gains for doing so, he is just another "nigger" to part of white America—even a half block from center court. These years in professional basketball, which is 65 percent black, have made an indelible impression on me.

I have been living in a world blacker than any with which I had contact as a boy. Crystal City in the 1950s was still a border town—unsure of its Civil War loyalties. I had relatives who fought for the North and some who sympathized with the Confederacy. The Union Army honorable discharge paper of my great-grandfather hung on my bedroom wall. When I was eleven a Civil War hat craze swept the country. In my class the mix was nearly even between kids who wore Confederate hats and those who preferred the Union blue. No one knew what the respective sides stood for except one wanted slavery and the other did not.

I had no idea about the horrible facts of slavery until I studied them as a history major in college. All I knew at home was that my parents said it was wrong. Likewise, my first-hand knowledge of black people then was superficial. I had noticed the black faces of convicts on road gangs in Georgia and Alabama while driving with my family to Florida for the winter. I had heard the usual racist jokes about blacks' intelligence and physical characteristics. I had known several blacks through sports and school but none well. Once in southern Missouri our teenage baseball team walked out of a restaurant when the owner refused to serve our black catcher.

But of all the blacks I knew Alex best. He was a Negro who assisted our family for fifty years. Due to my father's severe arthritis, it was Alex who gave me boxing lessons at age eight and raised my first basketball hoop at age ten. Although he became a part of our family, he never talked much about his own life. Nothing then, not even a careful reading of American history, had prepared me for the impact my teammates have made on me.

Living together eighteen hours a day for six months a year forces one to see a person, not a race. Sure there is black language, and black attitudes, and black suspicion, but each man is different. Generalities about race become unacceptable against the diversity of human traits. And yet I have changed in some ways because of my black friends. It is hard to say exactly how but after witnessing their joys, fears, perceptions, and spontaneous reactions for seven years I am different. I regard authority a little more skeptically than I once did. I am more interested in experiencing life than in analyzing it. What happens to me today and tomorrow is more important now than it used to be when I worried about the next decade. And, I feel less guilty about the black man's experience in America, realizing that though some of my friends have come from a poorer background, it did not lack in the richness of family love and joy. I not only think less in terms of a black race but also in terms of other group labels. But, above all, I see how much I don't know and can never know about black people.

"How's the record business," I ask Earl.

"It's a challenge, it keeps me moving," he says with a smile. "It's almost like playing ball because you have to fight guys and block out guys just to survive much less to reach your goal."

Earl Monroe is an independent record producer. The name of his company is Scorpio Rose; Scorpio because that's Earl's astrological sign and Rose because that was his mother's name. He controls everything related to his main musical group, Meng-US. Earl gets a professional arranger to refine the group's original composition and once that sound meets his approval, Earl then "runs with the tape" to several record companies. If one of them likes the recording it will try to sign the group to a three- or five-year contract, under which the record company takes 22 percent of all revenues derived from record sales and agrees to pay for all the expenses of the studio. In his contract discussion with one record company, Earl noticed that the company's 22 percent came from 90 percent of the total revenue instead of 100 percent. He says that the discrepancy occurs because the standard recording contract was written at a time when phonograph records had a 10 percent allowance for breakage in transportation and that now with acetate records the hedge is unnecessary. Earl expects to alter the clause in his future negotiations for Meng-US.

Earl arranges for promotion of the group by getting their record played on radio stations. After the record makes the airwaves and people start to request it in retail stores, Earl must assure adequate distribution. "They'll only go to the record store once for it," he says. Finally, he handles all bookings of his group, having successfully placed them in the Howard Theater in Washington, D.C., and at several places in the Virgin Islands. Ideally, Earl would like to have enough groups to take his own show on the road, hitting the big arenas in each city. Right now, however, he is just trying to do a good job with Meng-US. "Talent will come to you," he says. "It's just a matter of getting out there and getting a track record."

Even with his gradual approach Earl sees the music business as a natural way to fortune. Calling himself the "music man" he points out that Elton John and Stevie Wonder are making millions of dollars annually from their records, publishing rights, royalties, and public appearances and that even during the Depression the entertainment business prospered. Earl does not exaggerate the possibility of big money. He hopes that when he is finished playing basketball he will be in the music business full time. He prepares himself by doing the detailed, mundane work of his profession, making valuable contacts and learning from experience, which he hopes won't cost too much. In his first year with the group he lost $50,000, but now he is breaking even and sees bright days ahead.

"I don't believe in saving for a long-range future," Earl says. "Whatever I do I want to do it soon. I want to make it and do things between now and when I'm forty. If I'm not all right after that, then it's my own fault. I want to spend my middle years at leisure. I'll make my own decisions and then I don't have anybody to blame but myself."

---

Shortly after breakfast the team leaves by bus for practice at Loyola College. When I get onto the court Barnett is challenging rookies. He is dressed in a tan rubber sweatsuit and although he has only been shooting fifteen minutes he is soaking wet. "Come on chump," he says to a rookie, as he fakes a shot and drives past him for a basket. "Five, four, three, two—good!" Although the other players leave after practice, Barnett stays, going through his routine, shooting the hook, showing the ball, faking a drive, stopping, pretending to jump into his imaginary man and shooting—swish. Later, he sits in the training room and says, almost as if he were a rookie, "So this is the NBA. Shit. I remember when I got my first uniform in grade school. I took that motherfucker home and put it in the drawer and during the night I got up four times to try it on and make sure it was still there. It's a long way from there to here."

"Barnett's a brother from a different part of Africa," Phil Jackson once told me. "He never follows the pack; he's a lone wolf. He came into the league with gold teeth, no hair, spats, a bowler hat, and a cane. He toned down his dress but he's still not run of the mill. He claims he had the original Afro when he let his hair grow in 1964. I loaned him an electric shaver one night in 1968 to cut his fifty facial hairs and he hasn't shaved since."

Barnett launches into a story about the time he

played former football great Jimmy Brown one-on-one. Brown and Barnett happened on the same night to be at a nightclub in Los Angeles called Maverick's Flat. Brown, who considered himself the greatest all-around athlete ever, walked up to Barnett and challenged him to a one-on-one game outside behind the club on a concrete court. Barnett did not agree to it. Brown insisted. Barnett agreed to play when they set a $100 game stake.

"How was he, Dick?" I ask.

"He was holdin' and shovin', but he was a pretty good player."

"Who won?"

"I won by four or five. He never paid me though. I'm still waitin'."

"Don't hold your breath," someone says.

After practice, I head for a conference with a tax lawyer about my current income tax situation. He has been proposing a tax shelter in real estate.

"In me younger days," said Peter Dunn's Mr. Dooley in "Opinions," "'twas not considered respectable for to be an athlete. An athlete was always a man that was not strong enough for work. Fractions drove him from school and the vagrancy laws drove him to baseball." Today Mr. Dooley's assessment of professional sports seems outdated, undemocratic, and definitely unprofitable. Sports has become a world-wide $100 billion a year industry that has remained comparatively unknown as a business. "The professional sports industry," begins the Brookings Institution report, *Government and the Sports Business*, "provides a fascinating subject for students of the relationship between government and business. Virtually every major public policy toward business—antitrust, labor relations, taxation, even the constitutional prohibition against slavery—has a potentially significant application to sports."

Details about the ownership of professional sports franchises have been, like those of other lucrative businesses, obscure to the public. As long as attention can be focused on the game and its personalities, the men in blue suits only have to count the money and parade through their communities as if they are public benefactors. After all, it has been claimed that pro sports does everything from insuring community pride to contributing to social stability. Predictably, the men who write laws are only too eager to accommodate the proprietors of fantasy land. Tax laws provide owners with loopholes big enough to drive a Sherman tank through. They allow for depreciation of people (players) on the theory that we are property belonging to the owner. They also allow an owner to determine what percentage of his purchase price is for players (depreciable assets) and what for the cost of the franchise (equity). Thus an owner might purchase a team for $4 million and arbitrarily state that the property cost $3.5 million and the right to operate the franchise half a million. The selling owner, however, in the same transaction might state that the property's value is half a million dollars and the franchise is $3.5 million. He chooses to allocate as little as possible to players (property) because that portion of his sale is taxed as ordinary income while the franchise sale is given capital gains treatment. The truly outrageous aspect of the transaction is that buyer and seller are permitted legally to declare different values for their own tax purposes. Owners also benefit directly from the public coffer. Arenas are often constructed with taxpayer's dollars through bond issues. They are justified frequently by claiming that such public generosity will make a city "big league"; a nebulous term to say the least. In addition, owners often derive revenue from control of concessions at their games and, in the few private arenas, from building rental.

The financial considerations are considerable but until 1967 the control of player movement was an even greater bonanza for owners. Unlike other businesses, a player could not move freely from job to job. He was arbitrarily sent to a team by an impersonal draft and, once there, was perpetually bound to that team by a reserve clause, de jure or de facto; the only way he could leave was if the owner wanted to trade him. These restrictions gave assurance that there would always be a cheap, predictable flow of talent to stock the teams. The league assigned a franchise to a city and gave the owner an exclusive right to operate in that city. Likewise the owner control of player movement gave the businessman a monopoly over talent. If a player wanted to play he had no choice but to acquiesce in the system. Big TV contracts gave owners sums never foreseen by the early operators of professional basketball, and with the brighter prospects of pay TV the future seemed even more profitable. But as with many monopolies, it was too good to last. The mass exposure alerted other businessmen to the profit opportunity and in 1967 they started a second professional league which bid vigorously for players' services. Also, at about the same time the players finally grew up and started a union.

The early days of the Players Association were rough, just as in any other union. Owners applied pressure, threatened, and advised players against joining together. They were unsuccessful. Finally, they recognized the union and in 1967 signed a collective bargaining agreement providing for a pension. During the next several years players made significant gains at the negotiating table. Black players, who are the leaders and form the majority of the union, found it easy to doubt the lofty promises offered by owners as substitutes for meeting player demands. Many white players, accustomed to father/son relationships with white coaches, general managers, and owners, hesitated at first but then slowly realized that major gains were possible only if everyone stayed together. The highlights of our achievements are easily understood. We obtained per diem money, severance pay, disability insurance, medical insurance, increased pension benefits, better playing conditions, first-class air travel and moving expenses. Simultaneously we began a licensing program which generates large annual sums from various product endorsements made by the union and its members; the proceeds of which go into a fund to be distributed to players ten years after their retirement. But, our most serious effort during these years was to preserve the rudimentary stirrings of competition which the second league had brought to players. Around 1969 there were whispers that the two leagues would merge, as the football leagues had in 1966. To prevent that, all the players in the NBA entered into an unprecedented class action lawsuit against the owners. The suit sought an injunction barring a merger and a judgment eradicating all existent restrictions on a player's right to move freely from job to job in the practice of his profession. When the judge granted an injunction, the owners petitioned the U.S. Congress for an exemption to the antitrust laws. After lengthy testimony from all interested parties, the Senate Anti-Trust Subcommittee of the Judiciary Committee issued a report which recommended that no exemption be granted until the reserve system of player control was totally abolished. I will never forget the day Senator John Tunney told us he opposed the merger. He said that had his father, Gene, not been able to end restrictive agreements with promoters and managers, he would have lost the bulk of his million dollar earnings from his two fights with Jack Dempsey. "An athlete, like any other American, should be free," he said, "as free as my father was." Needless to say, the owners who had, I heard, spent almost a million dollars in their lobbying efforts, ceased to push for an exemption in Congress. It was clear that the exemption could be obtained only after meeting the players' objections on the issue of player movement. The player-owner confrontation is now back in the courts. There have been several efforts to settle the case, but in all of them when it was decision time the owners would not accept free player movement. The result is a collision course for eighteen basketball businessmen and two hundred players.

Throughout the existence of the Players Association, the general counsel has been Lawrence Fleischer, who works for one-third the salary of his counterparts in baseball and football. He was a schoolyard basketball player in the Bronx during the era of the championship teams at CCNY and LIU. He was a leftist in politics during his youth, a graduate of Harvard Law School at 22, and a financial vice-president of a major U.S. corporation at 34. Working for the association allows the concurrence of his idealistic drive, his childhood passion, and his knowledge of big business. Without his honesty and guidance. I can imagine that players' rights would still be ignored and benefits non-existent.

I suppose it was inevitable that the big business of basketball should be countered by the big labor of players, and if the conflict between the two becomes intractable, no doubt big government will intercede. Sports are followed by more Americans than practically any other issue (except perhaps war and the economy) and it arouses fierce passions. When the player–owner dispute really angers the fan he will demand action from his elected representatives, who will take to the airwaves. (Any politician knows sports is a high visibility issue.) The result will probably be a government commission set up to control or regulate professional sports. Ultimately it would not surprise me to see municipalities or states owning teams, thus going back to sports ownership patterns last seen in the 1890s.

All in all, though, the player has benefited handsomely from the competition of two leagues. He is being paid more than ever before. The average salary in the NBA is $91,000, with many players making more than $150,000. The question is the same for every newly enriched player. Who should he trust with his money? There is no shortage of eager advisers now that basketball has reached the financial big time. They lurk around schoolyards and on college campuses. Many specialize in one thing only—persuasion. A successful lawyer doesn't have time to play the courting game with 20-year-old kids. Thus, novices and crooks swarm to potentially wealthy young players as bees to honey. Many players have lost money unnecessarily. In some cases agents took fees as high as 20 percent, up front, before the player got anything. If a contract called for $200,000 over four years the agent got $40,000 before the player got anything. Other operators used their player-clients' money to buy inflated assets in which they themselves had an interest. Frequently tax-shelter investments proved to be economically unsound. After the Internal Revenue Service investigated, they also proved to be unsatisfactory as shelters. So the player ended up with a worthless asset that sometimes had accumulated bills and with a lien on future earnings to pay past due taxes. With these abuses it is understandable how some athletes have discovered that the million-dollar contract of yesterday is virtually worthless today.

During the next few years there are bound to be scandals involving mismanagement of funds by agents. Illegality in investments often takes time to surface. The real tragedy lies in those athletes who will discover only at the end of their careers that their advisers were corrupt. Gradually, through a process of painful trial and error, most players will settle with good counsel.

"Total service management" provides for the receipt of an athlete's check by the agent who pays all the player's bills and sends him a monthly allowance. Everything is prepared for the athlete by the agent's office, from insurance to taxes, from corporate plans to investments, from budgets to marriage contracts. Occasionally the athlete will be consulted about the general direction of his portfolio and the degree of risk desired, but rarely does the agent's office consult him on every investment. Walt Frazier is a believer in total service management. In fact that's one specialty offered by his firm, Walt Frazier Enterprises. But W.F. E. makes it a point to consult clients on every investment; that way, if they lose, they shoulder some of the responsibility. Frazier has 50 clients. "We provide a complete package," he says. "What the company is good for is holding guys back. If you want to buy a house or a car you have to contact the company first because you might not be able to afford it. For exam-

ple, I wanted a Rolls Royce two or three years before
I got it. Guys got to learn that some things you just
have to wait for."

Earl Monroe believes in the opposite kind of management. He hires specific people to do specific things.
He pays his own bills. About the plight of the younger player and the alternative of total service management he says, "I think a guy has to do something for
himself. It's not good for guys coming out of school to
put everything in their agents' hands. They should find
out things for themselves. That way if something happens you're not left out in the cold. I know some
guys that couldn't read their account books and what
not, even if they were to go to the agent and ask to
look at them. If somebody audited the books for them
they'd say, 'Wow, I've been getting ripped off here.'
You have to handle your money to be able to handle
your money."

━━━━━

After my meeting with the tax lawyer, I drive back
to the hotel during rush hour. The pace of the traffic on
the freeway in Los Angeles reminds me of giant
turtles moving in mud. Cars—bumper to bumper—
with only one person in many of them. A man in the
car next to me reads a book as he commutes. Few
drivers leave their windows down. Rush hour rock
stars move their lips, singing along with the latest hit
that blasts from their car radios. In the distance I see
snow peaked mountains. A strong March wind has
blown away most of the smog, leaving the valley with
an atmosphere that conveys what Los Angeles must
have been like before it became the nation's dream fix
and/or exhaust pipe.

DeBusschere and I have an Italian dinner with a
screenwriter and later go to a party at a female movie
star's rambling house, set high in the hills overlooking
Los Angeles. My natural suspicion for movie people
lessens. I enjoy myself, marvel at the poses assumed
by the guests, and assume a few of my own. I never

really overcome my uneasiness but leave with a pleasant memory and a touch of fancy for the hostess.

I never sense much professional kinship with movie actors. They have no feel for a live audience or knowledge of the instant gratification it delivers. Even politicians know more about the "crowd."

Shortly after Joe DiMaggio and Marilyn Monroe married, she went on a tour of military bases in Korea while he remained in Japan. She returned ecstatic and said, "Joe, there were 50,000 soldiers applauding and screaming. It was wonderful. You just don't know how it felt." Joe looked at her, smiled and replied, "Yes, I do."

Stage actors are more my compatriots, for their work, like mine, disappears in the air as soon as it lives. The final curtain makes it just a memory. As years pass people either forget the performance or distort it beyond recognition. The late show provides us with no reminders of our accomplishments.

The experience of basketball players and stage actors differs, though, during the few minutes after a performance when the performer stands before his audience and receives its applause. Sitting in a theater, clapping enthusiastically, I have a tinge of envy for the actor or musician or dancer taking his bows. Chills course up my spine. I sense I know what he feels, but I'm not sure. "Mass love vibes," a friend of mine calls that applause. At first the performer takes his bows as a part of the show. Then as the noise reaches a crescendo his professionalism breaks and he receives the audience as a lover. He smiles; he waves; he bows; he throws kisses; he cries; he laughs —he accepts as long as the audience gives. The basketball player, on the other hand, allows himself limited, fleeting contact with his audience, even after a magnificent evening. Occasionally he is applauded when he comes out of a game but he rarely responds. There are no curtain calls. The athlete is taught early never to acknowledge the audience. He runs from the court and crowds into the locker room with his team. Just once I would like to stand at center court after a great game and take my bows and feel the "love vibes" other performers experience. I would like to accept that audience as a lover for just that night without fear that it will turn on me tomorrow.

## 3

I MANAGE TO SLEEP UNTIL 9:15 THE NEXT MORNING. IN the hallway outside my room stands a man about 25 who shows up every time we're in Los Angeles. He is holding publicity photos and magazine articles about me which he asks to have autographed.

"What do you do with all these autographs?" I say, signing four pictures.

"Aw, I don't know," he says, "I just collect them."

"Trade them ever?" I ask.

"Yeah," he says, "I trade them with the other kids."

As the elevator takes me downstairs, Danny Whelan gets on at the sixth floor. He is wearing Florsheim shoes, gray double-knit pants, a brown sports jacket, a wash-and-wear white shirt and his omnipresent plain dark tie. He walks with a pronounced bounce, newspaper under his arm, a cigar in his mouth. In his job Danny is a rock of dependability and away from it he likes the good life, insisting always on first class. Flights, hotels, restaurants, and vacations must be the best. He never mentions money personally but he freely talks about the public's money that crooked politicians pilfer. His penchant for offering his own succinct interpretation of the latest public scandal, and his appreciation of luxury led players to nickname him "Big Time."

Danny is a man of routines. He rises every morning at 8 A.M. He loves the New York skyline and takes a Circle Line boat tour around Manhattan four times a year. He also frequently visits the major tourist spots: St. Patrick's Cathedral, Wall Street, the Stock Exchange, Statue of Liberty, Fifth Avenue, and

Tiffany's. He has been to the top of the Empire State Building twenty-three times in seven years. Every day we're in New York, rain or shine, Danny walks the thirty-five blocks from his apartment to the Garden and the thirty-five blocks back. On game days he only walks to the Garden, preferring to take a cab back at night, to his favorite eatery, P. J. Clarke's saloon.

His road habits, evolved over thirty years as a trainer in professional sport, have a continuity despite the changing environment. He begins each day perusing the morning newspaper and watching the "Today Show" with a breakfast of coffee and orange juice. If he notices that there are any big criminal trials in process, locally, and one looks particularly colorful, he will go sit in the courtroom for two or three hours listening to the story of the case unfold. Always, though —early if there's a trial, later if not—Danny takes a walk. Rarely selecting a destination he paces the streets of a town for three hours. He takes no other exercise. I kid him, calling him the Irish Harry Truman.

═══════

Holzman has scheduled a film for 11 A.M. The Knicks tape each team in their first visit to New York. Unless a team plays in our division or becomes a probable play-off opponent, the early season film replaces scouting for the rest of the year. Films serve an invaluable function only in the play-offs. Then, when two teams might meet seven times in three weeks, they reveal weaknesses that are missed in the heat of a game and they suggest possible adjustments in style. Today, during the regular season, particularly with a West Coast team, the film's purpose becomes more psychological than tactical. Injuries, trades, and rookie development have forced changes in the Lakers' lineup since their visit to New York in November. The film will give us little hard information. Still, the hour with the team, together, watching basketball will help us to begin thinking about tonight's game and the other weekend games in San Francisco and Seattle.

Helping one to focus on the game in Los Angeles is important, for it is an easy place to lose concentration. The change in weather encourages one to get away from the hotel and onto the beaches or tennis courts. Every player has his own set of personal distractions —family, friends, business, and unusual kicks—that are more plentiful in the nation's second largest city. More than one game has been lost in L.A. because the team was not ready to play by gametime.

"Hey, Clyde, don't sit under that chandelier," Holzman says to Frazier in the hotel ballroom where the movie is set up, "it might fall."

"It wouldn't hit Clyde," I say. "He's too fast."

"No," Jackson interrupts, "Red would catch it before it got to Clyde."

———————————

Jack Kent Cooke, who owns the Los Angeles Lakers, emigrated to the United States in the 1960s from Canada. He made his first million before he was twenty-nine. He prides himself on his million-dollar art collection, his eighteen-thousand-acre ranch, and his impeccable vocabulary. He bought the Lakers from Robert Short for $4 million in 1966. Cooke, a smart but ruthless businessman, rarely sacrifices profit to personal considerations. Dick Barnett, talking of his brief terms as a Cooke Laker gets right to the point, "Man was down on the bench wipin' sweat off me with a towel and two days later I was traded to New York."

Shortly after he purchased the team, Cooke embroiled himself in a major dispute with the City of Los Angeles over his rental of the municipally owned L. A. Sports Arena. When the city officials would not budge from their position, Cooke decided to build his own arena. He bought a tract of land next to Hollywood Park Race Track in nearby Inglewood and constructed The Fabulous Forum. (It had to be a forum; Los Angeles already had a Coliseum.) Never mind

that no athletic events were ever held in the forum of
Rome, after which Cooke named his monument. But,
when it comes to things like the usherettes, they wear
*mini* togas to keep up with current fashion *and* the
historical motif. Such compromises create the usual
southern California jumble—seen elsewhere in monumental restaurants with terrible food—where one can
never be sure of the interconnection of money, style,
and function.

For all its pretentiousness the Forum is my favorite
building away from Madison Square Garden. It makes
me appreciate Cooke's drive, success, and imagination.
There is real evidence of planning for the players'
needs, beginning with the simple convenience that
players can park their cars very near the employees
entrance. The locker rooms are spacious with mirrors,
showers, wash basins, toilets, and benches built for
people over 6'5". A man under 5'6" can't see his face in
the bathroom mirror. The hallways and playing area
are kept spotless. There are private press rooms for
interviews and a luxurious club for post-game drinks
and dinner. The air in the arena is cool. The baskets
are suitably loose. The portable court (laid over hockey ice) gives slightly with a player's weight since it is
separated from the ice by a four-inch layer of air. It
is easy on the legs. The lighting promotes a feeling of
distance from the crowd. The press are not permitted
at courtside.

I carry my suitcase to the game along with my basketball bag. We will leave from the Forum for a
12:30 A.M. flight to San Francisco. I am the last one to
arrive in the locker room. The evening's conversation
has already begun.

"Aw, come on Danny, how big?" says DeBusschere.

"I swear to God, as big as this," Danny says, grabbing each elbow with the opposite hand and making
his arms into a circle. "Their balls swelled up as big
as this."

"How did they walk, then?" asks Frazier.

"They used to have to carry their balls in a wheelbarrow. That's how tough it was for some guys in the South Pacific during the war."

Barnett walks up to DeBusschere, who is on the taping table, and asks, "How's the stock market?"

"Shitty," says DeBusschere.

"You know, some guy wanted to sell me stock at the beginning of last summer," continues Barnett, "and two weeks ago I pulled into a gas station and there he was readin' the meter and pumping gas."

"We're all lucky to have a job," adds Whelan.

There is a moment of silence, then Willis and Barnett get into a discussion of the movie *Superfly*, which is about a black who sells drugs in the ghetto. Barnett maintains that the guy should be shot; force is the only way to clean up the drug problem in the ghetto. Willis says that the guy is just "a brother gettin' over," that the real enemy is "the man," and that any way a black man can get ahead is okay with him. Barnett grimaces, shakes his head and says, "No, man, not no sellin' horse to brothers, that's not gettin' over, that's murder."

On the other side of the room two rookies talk about a newspaper account of a fight between two players on Philadelphia and Portland. Both teams apparently joined in and several players were seriously injured. That discussion leads to accounts of other fights and boils down to comments on the greatest fight ever seen. Barnett tells the story of one player who held a grudge against another for winning an MVP award in college. During a game in his second year in the league, the recipient of the MVP award drove for a lay-up against his old rivel—but never made it. He landed in the third row of the audience, with what turned out to be a career-ending back injury. When the first player was asked why he had deliberately injured his opponent, he said only, "I deserved to be MVP."

DeBusschere tells the story of Reggie Harding, the 7-foot center with a high school education whom he coached in Detroit and who later died of gunshot wounds sustained in pursuit of a heroin fix. During one of his several suspensions from the team, Harding came to a game in which Detroit played Wilt Chamberlain's team. Harding, who usually gave Wilt a good game (though not as good as he himself believed) stood on the sidelines half drunk, baiting Wilt: "Hey, big fella, I'm gonna stick your dick in the sand. You're lucky I ain't playing tonight." Wilt ignored the taunts, and no fight developed—which may have been a good thing for him because Harding often carried a gun.

A whole series of one-sentence stories follows featuring well-known players in one-punch fights: "Out, he knocked him out," or "He killed him, oh my God it was pitiful," or "He just can't fight. He will, but he loses," or "He sucker-punched him, before he knew it," or "Pow! it was over," or "He's a bad motherfucker, make no mistake." The younger players do most of the talking about fighting. After you've heard the stories ten times they sound like a search for manhood, a litany of youth. When the discussion turns to the most memorable moments of basketball violence, it inevitably touches on Al Attles's fighting knowledge, Wilt Chamberlain's unchallenged strength, and the night Willis Reed knocked out the whole Los Angeles Lakers team.

"Part way into the first quarter it looked like someone jumped on Willis' back," Phil Jackson says about the film of Willis' Los Angeles massacre. "Suddenly Willis totally lost control of himself. Anything that moved he hit. After five minutes he had knocked out two Lakers, broken the nose of a third, and downed a fourth. Finally a Knick teammate about his size snuck up behind him and said, 'Take it easy, Willis, it's me!'" The story of that night made the rounds of the locker rooms. No one ever challenged Willis again.

Thirty minutes before game time Red asks the reporters to leave. There is a surprising amount of ten-

sion in the air. We have been on a losing streak, and a
win tonight will keep us in the running for first place
in the East. Waiting for Holzman to begin his pregame
talk each player has his own nervous habits. I bite my
nails. Willis tapes his fingers and adjusts the hydroculator pad on his knee. Lucas keeps counting with his
thumb touching each one of his fingers in rapid order
as if he were filing their tips. DeBusschere and Earl
stare straight ahead. Some of the rookies concentrate
on chewing gum. Jackson scratches and scratches
his leg.

The Lakers field a less interesting team than in the
recent past. From Cooke's triumvirate of Jerry West,
Elgin Baylor, and Wilt Chamberlain, only West remains. The regal threesome never won a championship
together. Only when Elgin Baylor was forced into retirement and Chamberlain had one of his most peaceful, satisfying, and successful years did Los Angeles
finally win it all. That year the Lakers beat the Knicks
four games to one in an anticlimactic title series. I
was very happy for West, a man of quiet dignity and
prodigious talents. I felt the championship was more
his than Wilt's, whose talents and personality even in
victory stood apart from the team.

The highlight of those play-offs was the Los Angeles–Milwaukee semifinal pitting Wilt against Jabbar.
Wilt, in that series, at last became a popular big-man.
He defeated the proud, independent Muslim, who for
a brief moment due to his size, outspokenness, and
misunderstood religion became the designated villain
that Chamberlain's arrogance and size had always
made him in the public mind. Wilt had finally become
an American hero.

For fifteen years Wilt Chamberlain was the dominant single *individual* in professional basketball, a
*team* sport. His massive height and weight (7'2", 260
pounds) sometimes made him seem a colossus. It
brought almost incomprehensible achievements. During one year he averaged 50 points per game and in
one game he scored 100. He averaged 30.1 rebounds
per game for his career. Against Boston once he got 55.

He led the league in rebounding eight times and once in assists. In practically every department of the game for which individual statistics are kept, Wilt's name is etched in the record book.

Wilt played the game as if he had to prove his worth to someone who had never seen basketball. He pointed to his statistical achievements as specific measurements of his ability, and they were; but to someone who knows basketball they are, if not irrelevant, certainly nonessential. The point of the game is not how well the individual does but whether the team wins. That is the beautiful heart of the game, the blending of personalities, the mutual sacrifices for group success. No one man can dominate every aspect of a game—serving as a daddy and assuring victory through his effort alone. The essence of the game is selectivity, knowing one's limitations and abiding by them. Some players are capable of exercising several skills but often their team situation requires that they concentrate on only one. If an individual claims superiority in everything, then it is impossible to avoid the ultimate responsibility for victory or defeat. A team wins or loses; an individual who audaciously claims pre-eminence *must* win. Wilt could not eat his cake and have it too. If he had been a part of the team he alone never would have been blamed for defeat. But, since he sought statistics to justify his superiority in *every* aspect of the game, he could not avoid responsibility for the game's outcome. So the more often Wilt lost (perhaps because he did have mediocre teammates) and tried to absolve himself by referring to his individual achievements the more he became, in the eyes of fans, a giant who should never lose. What seemed like a paradox was really a misunderstanding of the game. It was as if Wilt were a big tank fighting in a jungle, possessed of all the latest equipment but unable to win a guerrilla war. The more Wilt accomplished individually, the more he came to symbolize failure.

Accompanying Wilt's statistical self-justification was a veneer of sportsmanship. It seemed as if Wilt almost choked on the familiar aphorism about sports taught to all American children: "It's not whether you win or lose but how you play the game." Wilt apparently applied this prescription selectively to professional basketball, where its reverse is true and where aggressiveness is essential for success. Some people even say that the reason he didn't win every year was because he played too passively. He never developed the killer instinct necessary for team victory. In his rookie year he was constantly battered, kneed, elbowed, tripped, and gouged. He did not hit back. Instead, he threatened retirement. In his duels with Bill Russell he patted him on the behind when Russell made a good play, showing what Wilt thought was magnanimity. It was as if he were paralyzed within his enormous body, unwilling to strike out for fear of injuring an opponent or demeaning himself. Above all, Wilt, sensitive to being called a bully, made sure he never took unfair advantage. If someone said Wilt could only score by dunking, he retaliated by taking fall-away jumpers. If critics questioned his passing ability, he stopped shooting and rolled up the assists. He seemed driven to be the best, and on everyone else's terms.

Another familiar aphorism heard in America is that a man is free to fly as high as his ability will take him. But, a person born to vast inherited wealth has a better chance to succeed than a poor man. Likewise, a man with unparalleled physical equipment is more likely to succeed at sports than a man with an average body, no matter how hard the latter works. Although we continue to teach the democratic ideal of equality, inequality surely exists in abilities and power. Those few people who are more fortunate—Rockefellers or Chamberlains—receive the average man's resentment together with his admiration. If their work exposes them to public curiosity, they must be prepared to handle that resentment in all its intensity.

Wilt has dealt with the public for over twenty years. When people started showering favors and money on him as a 6'11" fourteen-year-old, he learned to manipulate them to his own advantage. Though he rarely failed to get things his way, he must have felt the fans' resentment. They asked for his autograph and then told him that anyone seven feet tall should be able to score thousands of points.

To those who weren't fans and didn't recognize that his size meant superior physical ability, he was regarded as a freak, a giant, labeled different and weird. His height alone subjected Wilt to stares, pointing fingers, and inane questions. A man whose head rises eighteen inches above the crowd can never have a normal existence. Add the fact that Wilt is black in a racist society and it is easy to see how he had to retreat inside himself, if only for protection.

Wilt's personality survival kit apparently included a decision to confront his public. It seemed as if his only chance to escape the resentments attached to his career was to win the fans over with his ability and conquer the non-sport public with his fame. Clearly a team championship was not sufficient for Wilt's personal needs. He seemed determined to become one of the best-known bodies in the world. Homes, women, cars, money, only provided accompaniment to his primary quest—celebrity. Only widely publicized supremacy in all statistically measured areas of the sport or life could suffice. Then and only then might he soften the resentment that his style and size had engendered.

I have the impression that Wilt might have been more secure in losing. In defeat, after carefully covering himself with allusions to *his* accomplishments, he could be magnanimous. Sometimes waxing philosophic he would wonder publicly why the American character insisted on victory. He would relate objectively the limitations of his own team. He would imply that basketball was just a small part of his life, a life which encompassed presidents and queens, millionaires and movie stars. He would be polite with writers, talking with them as if their interest in him was somehow unconnected with the game's outcome, or even with basketball.

Acceptance of defeat had been Wilt's final error. If there is anything the American public hates more than its villains, it is a favorite who flaunts it and then blows the victory. Wilt's emphasis on individual accomplishments failed to gain him public affection but made him the favorite to win the game. And, simultaneously, it assured him of losing. A team hero who loses receives sympathy, compassion, and understanding, like Jerry West or Willis Reed. An individual star who loses only gets a derisive laugh of good riddance, until he loses often enough to become a symbol for losing, the ultimate insult.

Each game has a pace of its own. One can never be sure of how a game will end by checking the score at half-time. I have been on teams that lost 30-point leads. I have come from 25 back to win. The score means little. What is important is being able to sense the mood of the opponent. What I feel is his will. A team sometimes gets behind 20 points and caves in; it just gives up. The team tries but its execution becomes sloppy; the players don't get back on defense as fast, or play as tenaciously against their men. They take bad shots, start to bicker among themselves, and in their ultimate discouragement talk to their opponent about their own teammates' shortcomings.

I sense tonight's game against the Lakers is over by half-time. We have a 21-point lead. During the third quarter the Lakers make their move, cutting it to 12. We hold and then increase our lead to 18. With six minutes gone in the third quarter, I know we have it.

For the rest of the third quarter, I just watch Frazier. Occasionally he infuriates me when he doesn't pass the ball as much as I would like, and DeBusschere sometimes, after running six times up the floor without getting a shot, will throw up his arms in anger and shout "pass the god damn ball." But there is no denying Clyde's ability. I am on the same court but I'm a spectator. He plays with smooth and effortless grace, as if he were a dancer revealing the beauty of a body in movement. It's somehow right that he doesn't sweat much. His build is perfect for basketball: tall, erect, and thin. He can move with deceptive speed. The jumper, its fake, and the drive are his repertoire—he does not have a lot of moves like Monroe. He is classic in his economy of motion, though an occasional behind-the-back dribble shows there is still a flirtation with flamboyance. Holzman says that people should get to see him practice, for that's where he plays complete basketball. Tonight he's doing a pretty good job of it in Los Angeles. He shoulder fakes and hits two jumpers; a third time he draws the foul, and follows with a baseline drive and a fadeaway, at which several players on the Los Angeles bench shake their heads in awe. The next time downcourt he uses a change of pace dribble that makes the defensive man look ridiculous: Tonight he could make anyone look bad.

The crowd excitement at games brings out Clyde's supreme efforts. "It's like dancing," he says. "When you hear a certain record you dance and you can feel it. That's the same way I feel about the roar of crowds. They help me get psyched up. If the game is tied in the last five minutes and I make a basket, I'm telling myself, 'You're ready now, Clyde. Now you're going to come up with the steal, or get the rebound, or make three more baskets.'"

Confidence and determination are big parts of Frazier's personality. The confidence is displayed with unmistakable bravado. The determination, which the public rarely sees, rests at the core of a kid from Georgia who went to a predominantly white college and made it against the odds. "I wanted to go home that first year," he says. "I was shy and talked different from the other kids there. In class it seemed like everybody was staring at me; it seemed like me against the world." The results of his poor preparation and difficult adjustment showed after his freshman year when he became academically ineligible and had to sit out his sophomore year of basketball. He soon noticed how people's attitude toward him changed. The coach gave him no academic help, forced him to work out everyday playing *only* defense, and refused to help him get transportation to Atlanta at Christmas. Frazier says that, with the help of a kind black teacher, he discovered himself, as a person, that year. He married. He learned to study and to accept responsibility and by the end of the year pulled his grades up to the B— range. "I made everything I got," he remembers. "It's like in sports: You don't quit, you keep fighting back. Before the year of ineligibility I was like my father, riding with the punches and believing anything goes. Then, I became more like my grandfather. I married and took on responsibilities."

One can see Clyde's determination even in aspects of his financial affairs. Treading a fine line between extravagance and caution, he doesn't *feel* he is flamboyant. The Rolls Royce, the New York co-op, the Atlanta house are investments to him; the mink and sealskin coats were free. Becoming an overnight millionaire is not his style, he says. "I would rather save my money. Like I have a lot of tax-free bonds. You don't get a hell of a return but you don't lose. That is my primary concern, not losing. Some people say, 'Get in the stock market. You will double or triple.' I don't care about that."

Toward the end of the game Frazier makes three steals and two difficult drives. He finishes with 44 points and wins the knitted shirts as star of the game.

"Why were you so hot?" asked one reporter.

"Is this your best effort of the year?"

"What are you wearing tonight, Clyde?"

"Are the Knicks going to catch the Celtics?"

"Let's go," says Whelan. "The bus leaves in ten minutes."

We arrive at the airport fifty minutes before departure. Players wander into the coffee shop and newsstand. I sit opposite the departure gate reading a book about Nova Scotia. A section I had read on the flight to Los Angeles discussed the Oak Island mystery, raising the possibility that the pirate Captain Kidd buried some of his treasures on this small island in Mahone Bay off the Nova Scotia coast. I see Lucas standing alone at the empty air insurance counter and, since I had mentioned the treasure to him, I walk over and say jokingly, "Want to be partners with me in a search for the Oak Island riches?"

"I've got my own goldmine after these past two days."

"In what?" I ask, "puzzles?"

"No."

"Magic?"

"No."

"Well, what is it then?"

"Hyperberic medicine."

"What's that?"

"Ralph," says Lucas, "my plastic surgeon friend out here in Hollywood—the one with the gorgeous wife —told me about it last fall because he'd been using it. I told him to get all the figures together. This trip he did and I haven't slept in three days it's so fuckin' great!"

"What is it?"

"The Navy doctors have researched it for two years. Their findings are going to be made known in September at a medical conference in Canada. Once it gets out, the shit's gonna hit the fan. Vickers, a company in England, makes a hyperberic chamber, which means a pressurized oxygen chamber. You sit in it for fifteen or twenty minutes a day, for a week and you're a new man. One treatment lasts six months. I've seen pictures of burns healed overnight at the naval hospital in San Diego. It grows hair—makes you feel younger. Guys come out of there and they want to screw everything that moves—that's what it does for your sex life. It also helps concentration. It does it all."

"So, how do you make money?"

"I'll get a loan for 90 percent. It takes six months to deliver right now, we only need sixty chambers to get started. Ralph and I could finance that."

"How?"

"Shit, Ralph makes $600,000 a year as a Hollywood plastic surgeon. He operates every morning from 9:30 to 1 P.M. and charges $1,500 for fixing tits and $1,200 for noses. He made $400,000 last year from tits alone. If everything works out after September everybody will want to climb into these chambers, and if I work it right we'll have a corner on the market for the machines. We'll get locations near hospitals and country clubs and we'll hire a pulmonary physiologist to run each one for a salary plus percentage. There is *no* way we can miss."

"Who miss?" asks Jackson.

"Luke," I reply.

"Oh, I thought you meant Clyde."

"Yeah," I say, "that was some game. The Lakers really miss Wilt."

Chamberlain had slowed down a lot but he was still intimidating during his last year, before he signed a $600,000 contract to coach in the ABA. Players would test his quickness by challenging him and when Wilt bent to gather himself for the jump, the challenger would shoot the ball before Wilt could uncoil. That act was called "freezing him." Other teams tried to have their center set a screen for a good shooter; Wilt never switched out and the shooter had easy seventeen-foot jump shots. At the end players were willing to test his finesse and quickness, but no one tested his strength.

"Wilt is probably laughing in the living room of his million-dollar house, the one with 20-foot ceilings that remind him of the Baptist Church of his childhood," I say to no one in particular.

"Laughing all the way to the bank," a rookie says.

And then Barnett adds: "People out there in the streets starvin' and this sucker goes and builds himself a million-dollar house."

━━━━━━━

By the time we pick up our bags in San Francisco it is 2 A.M. We board a bus which will take us to a motel near the arena in Oakland. San Francisco is Danny Whelan's hometown. He grew up during the 1920s in the Mission district where his father ran a grocery store. "If you had a couple of dollars then, you were a millionaire," he says. Every time we get into town he sees his kids from a first marriage, often bringing them to the game, and he visits some of his old friends: carpenters, bartenders, brewery workers, who still live in the district. San Francisco has changed since he left. The Mission district is no longer the Irish Catholic neighborhood where, as Danny remembers, "200 people stood in front of the radio store listening to the Dempsey–Tunney fight and pulling for Tunney all the way." The district still has the best weather in San Francisco according to Danny, and although it has become a Hispanic ghetto, it's home for him and he relishes the thought of his return, even at 2 A.M.

As the bus speeds along the freeway, Danny seizes the microphone and gives us a guided tour, pointing out the Cow Palace, Candlestick Park, Alcatraz, and the Golden Gate Bridge. A card game begins. Barnett, wearing a blue denim jumpsuit, plays with Earl and Phil.

"Dick, did you jump into that suit while it was standing up against the wall?" Phil asks. "You gonna change it this trip?"

"Deal 'em," Barnett barks, "don't let that chump distract you. But in answer to your question, I brought five jumpsuits."

"Yeah," needles Earl, "all the same exact kind."

There is laughter, then silence.

"Gonna see that Nazi broad here, Phil?" asks Barnett.

"Who?"

"You know, the one who moved here from Milwaukee. The one with the boots and helmet."

The bus crosses the bridge leaving San Francisco, heading toward Oakland. Phil shouts, "Big Time Danny Whelan, this is your town."

THE NEXT MORNING I WAKE UP IN THE OAKLAND Hyatt House at 11:30. There is no bathtub in the room —only a shower—so I can't soak my aching muscles. Even though I've slept seven and a half hours, I don't feel rested. Sometimes I need sleep more than food, and I learn to take it where I can—on buses, planes, in airport lobbies—and when I can—early afternoon naps, pregame naps, at midnight, or much later. With the constant travel, I usually get to bed at the hour I did last night—around 3 A.M. After four of these nights in five days in four different cities, I sometimes wake up to an early morning phone call not knowing what town I'm in or what day it is. My confusion is increased by the similarity in hotel decorations. All the hotels we stay in except one provide double beds for us. I sleep in so many different beds in a year that the one in my apartment seems no more familiar than any other.

DeBusschere is not in the room. He has different sleeping habits and usually gets up by 9:30 no matter what time he gets to bed. When I finish my coffee and doughnut in the restaurant and return to our room, DeBusschere is reading the morning paper. We talk briefly about the day's news events—a murder in Marin County, an earthquake in South America, an environmental campaign in the Bay area, and a statement on the economy by the President. The phone rings. An old classmate of mine who lives in San Francisco says hello and asks if I have any complimentary tickets for the game. As soon as I hang up the phone rings again. Gerri DeBusschere, Dave's wife, is calling from New York. I pitch the phone to Dave, who begins talking. I immediately tune out of his conversation. After eight years as roommates, the telephone calls reflect an unspoken yet comfortable distance between us. We hear but don't pay attention to each other's conversations. Neither of us is rude enough to ask questions about the other's calls, and both of us tend to carry on our end of a conversation with monosyllables just in case the other's interest perks up.

I have only twenty-five minutes before lunch, not enough time to get back into the book I've started, but plenty to finish the magazine in my bag. I ponder the decision for a minute or two, looking out the window at the cars passing on the freeway. I luxuriate in small decisions such as these. Making a choice has always fascinated me, and the delight in weighing each side and then acting remains the same for me however insignificant the decision.

After lunch I take my book to the Hyatt House courtyard where I sit alone, enclosed on all sides by the four-story motel structure. Astroturf edges the shimmering rectangular swimming pool. Scrubby pines and ten-foot palms dot a more distant area covered by worn soil. Bright red wastebaskets and green vinyl sun chairs add touches of emotion to the courtyard the way games highlight the away schedule. The newly watered sod smells fresh and clean. An occasional airplane roars overhead, but mostly the sounds are of birds and of trees blowing in the wind. The breeze drops the temperature to the fifties, while occasional bursts of sun provide a soothing warmth. It's not exactly a walled monastery garden but it's a quiet niche and on the road that's pleasant.

In the locker room that night at the Oakland Coliseum everything goes as usual except that Danny's son, Pat, stands enraptured, watching his father work. Barnett sits next to Frazier as Danny tapes DeBusschere's ankles. Danny says something to his son, who replies, "Okay, Dad."

"That gets you every time, doesn't it, Dan," says Frazier, "when a little boy calls you Dad."

"Yeah, it sure does," says Danny. Both smile and shake their heads as if in agreement over a fundamental truth.

"Stop it, Clyde," interrupts Barnett. "You're making me cry."

"What's the matter, Rich, you never felt that way?" asks Frazier.

"No, not the way you two go at it."

The conversation changes quickly to a movie star who follows the Knicks. Each player ventures his opinions of the star: his life, his approximate income, his hang-ups, his best roles, his dress, his appearance, and his knowledge of basketball. Finally Frazier asks, "Is he doin' it with the girl that has the frizzy hair?"

"Yeah," says Barnett as he leaves the room for his workout, "he be the instructor and they experiment with wild herbs."

While Barnett is on the court everyone talks about his age and his battle to stay in shape, as if each of us was a wife looking at her husband's changing body.

"He's never gonna lose weight eatin' all those nuts," Frazier says. "He says he only eats fruit, then I see him buyin' a candy bar."

"I asked him last week and he claims he's at 198," says Jackson. "That's just three pounds heavier than his playing weight."

"Shit," says DeBusschere, "he must have redistributed it awful fast to get those rolls of fat around his hips."

———

Going through warm-ups I don't have my concentration. Only the game itself, played properly, will kindle my excitement. That's one of the advantages of being hooked on the team game; it can be a source of inspiration. Winning is a necessary constant in a happy team life. But there are nights when style, meaning a *team* victory, is more important than competitiveness, which accepts any kind of victory. I can never tell which nights just winning will be enough. Tonight I know that my enjoyment will increase in direct proportion to the extent we achieve a team-style victory.

Unpredictable as it is, such an approach makes games more interesting, for there are gradations of victory. But it makes the practices harder. My determination to practice three hours a day from age fourteen to twenty-one came primarily from my competitive drive to be the best possible player, not from a sense of enjoyment for the game. When I practiced in high school and college I would break down my shots into their components. I would execute my moves and then repeat; think and repeat, until I had them. While practicing, my basketball fantasies would emerge—putting a move on Oscar Robertson, hitting a running hook shot to win a game, using the reverse pivot in the championship. When I returned after two years away from the game in 1967, I couldn't sustain basketball fantasies for a long practice, much less the sheer concentration necessary to master new moves or shots. I found myself, instead, thinking about things other than basketball as I moved around an imaginary semi-circle twenty feet from the basket, hitting fifteen shots from each of five spots on the floor. My mind wandered to politics, movies, money, women, food, the future. The longest I can practice alone now is about forty-five minutes.

With my dedication to lone practice gone, the team is everything. How the team does affects my feelings about the game and myself; sometimes, I think, too much. I am obsessed with my work of team basketball. In a way my personality, formed as it was on a steady diet of Calvinist religion, is amenable to the idea of team play. Self-denial is nothing new for me. The conflict comes because I have to interact with others to accomplish my goal of team play. My problem is that my aspirations demand that I create something I cannot control completely. I do not depend on the outside for recognition. The press and public approval mean little to me. What is important is my own judgment as to whether the team plays according to my estimation of how an ideal team should. My actions are often determined by what I feel will bring about the ideal and victory. It is a more complicated process than simply playing or being the star. Some friends say I am functioning in a world that bears little resemblance to reality. At times I feel as if I am an artist in the wrong medium.

But there are a few games every year when I am neither personally competitive nor in pursuit of my team ideal. I simply play for the joy of the game, shooting and passing without calculation. I forget the score and sometimes go through a quarter without looking at the scoreboard. I don't *think* about my movements. I feel good running and bumping, and I get an overall sense of whether we are playing well, executing intelligently and precisely, by the crispness of the passes, the timing of the plays, and the enthusiasm with which we communicate. On those enjoyable nights fatigue is a stranger.

There is a dimension of the game that only the players and maybe the fans in the first couple of rows can appreciate—the sounds. I hear the court noises of sneakers squeaking, 230-pound bodies hitting the floor and slapping into each other, the ball bouncing up from the floor, the quick staccato shouts of play numbers, the long whine of complaint to a referee, the hoarse voice of a coach baiting officials and bellowing instructions, the fan noise of shouts, and in the background the loud roar of applause and cheering. Tonight I hear:

"Hey, baby. What's happenin'?"

"You guys ready? Okay, Reed, get in the circle."

Tweet, tweet—clapping—

"2-1-F. 2-1-F." Thud. Thud.

"Screen, screen, watch the pick."

Squeak—roar of waterfalls.

"Defense! Defense! Defense!"

"Force him to middle, get over screen."

"Blue, Blue, Blue!"—Pop!

"Number 24—intentional foul—two shots."

"What . . . I just tried to steal."

"That's enough—nobody runs my game. Two shots. First one is dead."

"How's your leg, Jeff? How're the kids? What are you doing after the game?"

"Reed, you're finished—DeBusschere, you're getting old—San Francisco will win it this year—a Knick funeral."

"Nate the hat trick man, one more and you took the collar, big fella."

Swish—"In your eye."

"Willis, Willis, out here, here go Will."

Thud, Thud, Thud, Thud—"Break to the middle."

Whoosh! Twap—swish.

Buzzzzz—"Final score: New York 102, San Francisco 96."

The star of the game is Willis Reed, for the first time this year. He wins two knitted shirts and a swarm of reporters.

"Do you think you got it back tonight, Will?"

"How did your knee feel?"

"When was the last time you had twenty points?"

---

We arrive at the San Francisco airport at 11:30 for a 12:30 flight to Seattle. At midnight the place is quiet, so quiet it is eerie without the monotone departure announcements, the sounds of powerful jet takeoffs, and the bustle of crowds. Now, there is only the murmur of scattered groups. A family of American Indians sits across from me in the waiting hall, casting disapproving glances at a long-haired youth passing their bench. The woman constantly pulls at her dress in a vain attempt to get it below her knees. A serviceman sleeps on an empty bench. His buddy says they are waiting to be first in line for military fare the next morning. Muzak filters into the background. Three teen-agers in jeans and safari jackets prowl the airport alert and curious. Phil talks to a girl in the coffee shop. Willis treats three girls to drinks in the bar. Red and Danny drink scotch at a corner table. DeBusschere, a writer, and I stand at the bar. I drink two beers. DeBusschere is drinking scotch. A gambler seated next to us prepares for a 2:30 A.M. flight to Las Vegas where he hopes to repeat his $15,000 win of the previous month. He refuses a beer and drinks Southern Comfort.

After twenty-five minutes we make our way to the security checkpoint. The players are allowed to skirt the body search segment. A sportswriter walks in our group. I get the guard's attention.

"Hey!" I say, "this guy's not with us." The security man stops the reporter for a body search. We laugh. I say that I was just kidding but the guard says he better search him anyway.

When the reporter catches up with DeBusschere and me at the plane, he says, "I'll be around when Bill Bradley is just another answer to a trivia question."

Inside the plane the card game has started, with Earl, Rich, Phil, and the rookie "talking trash" and laughing. The reporters, Danny, and Red play the "old-movie" game.

"Who played Rafael in 'Desert Song'?"

"Which movie had the butler who always said 'Mr. Worthington'?"

"Who was Errol Flynn's first wife?"

"What was the real name of the sheriff in 'Gunfight at the OK Corral'?"

I ease into a seat next to DeBusschere. We sit quietly until after drinks are served. The game was hard. We are tired and a little tipsy. Dave turns to me and asks, "Do you think we'll still be friends after basketball?"

"Yeah," I say smiling. "I'm sure we will."

Friendship on a team is often misunderstood. People talk about teams as families, as groups that eat, sleep, work, and play together. But on many teams the friendship aspect is overblown and even hypocritical. I could never understand owners who treat players as sons in public and cheat them on salary in private, or owners who are surprised when players whom they have cheated later resent them for it, or coaches who talk about their "family" and then the next year trade players away, or teams that one year publicize a unique meshing of personalities and then the next year have players who won't pass the ball to each other, or coaches that switch roommates to prevent cliques and produce angry, isolated players.

I have heard people say that dissension developed on a particular team because the players never saw each other off the court and didn't care about each other as human beings. Outsiders envision players as having intense personal relations with each other, sharing innermost thoughts, fears, and hopes, sort of an extension of summer camp into adulthood. That's not the way with the Knicks.

Each player on the Knicks has his own territory. Frazier, Willis, and DeBusschere are the voices of the Knicks to the press. Lucas and Barnett are the promoters. In addition, DeBusschere and Frazier never put themselves in a position where they may appear to be competing with a teammate. For example, they often relax in shooting games and never play one-on-one with teammates; everyone understands. Each player brings his own personal strength to an area and it is different from every other player's. All realize that the greater freedom to "do your own thing" comes only from the interest generated by winning, so no one seeks to take all the credit or seize all the opportunities; anger and dissatisfaction never last.

Greil Marcus in *Mystery Train*, a book on rock and roll music, says of The Band, "Friendship can be a means of community. But if one does not live in the world, then one will feed off the small world of friendship until there is nothing left." Partly because we rarely see teammates in New York off the court, the road becomes a pleasure enhanced by the absence of personality conflicts. Our contact with each other is rationed to the phones, buses, hotels, and arenas where we live as a group, drawn together and bound, but not like pressed steel. It is as if we come together for mutual reinforcement and then disperse into the world, each following his own separate interest. Roommates, though, are a different story.

I am somewhat stunned by DeBusschere's question. Will we be friends? I hope so. There is so much in our relationship that is left unspoken, but it is hard to imagine it ending. Living together makes for a strong bond. All the telephone calls, nights out, shared toiletries, mutual kidding; all the knowledge of mundane things like sleeping, drinking, and eating habits, clothes preferences, sexual preferences, pet peeves. Each of us has much to tolerate in the other. Sometimes we keep our luggage in the same room in a town and never see each other. But that is precisely what is good about our friendship. There is no need to feel guilty for not socializing together every night on the road. We have different interests and friends. I don't ask a lot of personal questions, and he respects my privacy. Within the boundaries of that friendship there is much room for good times, affection, and deep respect.

We share basketball and our complementary views of the game. When that is gone I believe that, unlike a lot of professional athletes who are friends for the moment, we will remain close through the post-playing years. Since meeting Dave, I feel easier with small groups of strangers. I can relax over a beer, even with people I've just met. His honesty, friendliness, and total lack of pretension are constant sources of the strength of my feeling for him. I can't believe those qualities will change. Yet the fear is there; the fear that what is now so good and true and strong will prove to be just one more elusive human contact, that we will pass through each other's lives and out, that somehow the self-contained protective world of basketball has been too generous to us, and that the real world may prove too strident, too troublesome, too fragmented for even our friendship to bear.

I WAKE UP THE NEXT MORNING AROUND 11:00 IN THE Washington Plaza, a 40-story circular building in downtown Seattle, my favorite hotel in America. From our thirty-second-floor room I look past the Moore Theater and the Calhoun Hotel, both over 40 years old, past the Public Service Insurance Co. and a new 20-story condominium, out to Puget Sound where under brilliant sunshine a ferry crosses to Bremerton, and hundreds of sailboats move briskly over the whitecaps. In the distance Mount Rainier and other peaks in the Cascade range stand like guardians at the gates of this fresh, green city on the water. It is the kind of day that exhilarates by the sheer force of its beauty. I go downstairs to breakfast and then sit in the lobby reading the Seattle newspaper.

Local news fills our travel like patches in a quilt— the writing of a new state constitution in Texas, a public-housing scandal in Cleveland, a freeway siting in Atlanta, a skyrocketing crime rate in Detroit, an earthquake in Los Angeles. Today I read that the city of Seattle proposes to close the Pike Street Market and build new office buildings in its place. The historical society and environmentalists are opposing the move, but the state's lawyers say they are fighting a lost cause. The story saddens me, because I really like the market. Every time I'm in Seattle I take an afternoon walk through it. Now, I put my paper down and wonder if today's visit will be my last.

The market is an old wooden structure at First Avenue and Pike Street. First Avenue looks like a scene from an Edward Hopper painting except the frame facades are filled with unlikely tenants: Sansoni's Wig Boutique, DiLaurenti's International Food Mart, and the Green Parrot Theater. The market proper is an open area covered by a roof and divided into shops, stores, and stalls on several levels, all overlooking Puget Sound. Young craftsmen off the main market aisle sell their own products: candles, leather work, turquoise beadware, necklaces made from the feathers of pheasants and peacocks. One of them used to make chokers of beads and yarn in the woods of southern Oregon. He moved to Seattle when the paper mills closed and economic conditions soured. Further into the market sits a young female artist named Susan, who paints portraits while you wait. She arrived at Pike Place via Minnesota, Europe, school in the East, marriage in San Francisco, and a separation in Seattle.

I have discovered that I like people much more than I used to when I self-consciously fled from the public. Being the subject of public curiosity has paradoxically made me more curious. I go toward people with less inhibitions. Traveling around the country as we do, I enjoy approaching a stranger with questions. I learn from the life stories of ordinary people who want to talk about themselves if asked. I ask.

The March air is cold but the Japanese-American vendors still offer their products. "I got crab $1.39 a pound—Romaine lettuce usually 39 cents, but for you 20 cents to make your buy an even buck." A crowd buzzes around the stalls. Collard greens, cabbage sprouts, spinach, watercress, new potatoes, sugar peas, hubbard squash, red chard, mustard greens, and chives are for sale. On platforms covered with ice the Pike Place Fish Co. displays Columbia River smelts, ink squid, Dungeness crab, white perch, and jumbo shrimp—arranged as if with the assistance of an art director. "Send the salmon back East, an ideal gift, a souvenir from Puget Sound, 8 to 10 pounds, guaranteed to arrive in good condition." The scene reminds me of open markets in England. The temperature makes my nose red and numbs my sense of smell, but I feel more invigorated than if I were walking through a suburban supermarket.

Two men—one Indian and one white—approach me and the white says, "Hey, partner, how about a dime or two." Three Indian buddies lean precariously against a nearby wall passing around a bottle of Bokay apple wine.

*"I grew up full of discrepancies about the Indian,"* Phil Jackson has told me. *"They were supposed to be dirty and weren't to be trusted and they had no concept of civilization. My grandfather had that boarding house near the reservation at Wolfpoint, Montana, and he used to always say Indians were drunks just standing outside bars or in the middle of streets, ready to steal anything if you left your car unlocked. Two Indians were in my sixth grade class at Williston, North Dakota. They lived on the flats down along the Missouri River."*

I ask the white man about his life. He says that he is a hook tender on a logging crew, waiting two more weeks before Archie McDougall of the Alaskan Logging Employment Agency sends him up to Prince of Wales Island near Ketchikan at Thorn Bay to work the summer for Georgia Pacific. The Indians leaning against the wall are Aleuts and they are waiting for work, too. He says that a lot of Indians work in Alaska, logging, and mostly they are Klamath, Aleuts, and other Alaskan and Canadian Indians.

*"As I learned more about the Indians,"* said Phil, *"their self-sufficiency appealed to me, particularly since they lived without the inventions of the white man. Many Indians were nomads living on the prairies. Everything they got was wild—fruit, vegetables, meat, herbs—and yet they lived quite at ease in very harsh country. Boys were taught the ways of*

*animals. Storytellers passed on the tradition and history. Body movement was as important as words. The whole concept of life was how to stay in tune with your environment."*

The logger says that he spends winters in Drain, Oregon, collecting unemployment, but every summer since 1956 when he was discharged from the army he heads north to pull the big logs out of virgin forest. He tells me they get up there by plane; sometimes as many as 5,000 men a summer are living in barracks, two in a room. "Archie furnishes you a ticket and you pay him ten percent," the logger claims. "Say he puts out $100, you pay him back $110 out of your first check. It's worth it. Hell, loggin' is what this country is built on."

I walk on past a tall, thin boy dressed in jeans, plaid shirt and derby hat, holding a guitar. He stands next to a pole and plays Bob Dylan's song "Just Like A Woman" too rapidly. As I pass the Philippine Cafe, a white girl, her face painted red, white, and blue like a clown, stops a black woman shopper and asks her to contribute to a fund that will fight drug addiction among young people. Inside the Athenian Cafe I take a booth at a window overlooking Puget Sound and order beef stew; this is the only place in the league where I don't have my usual pre-game meal. Big menus over the counter list beers from fourteen countries, and on the side of my wooden booth is carved the word "Peace," above which is penciled "54–40 or Fight." The meal is as good as the day. The cafe is full even though it's 2 P.M. I divide my attention between the brightness of Puget Sound and the bustle of the cafe, watching the people, and with the help of my imagination constructing their life stories. As I drink my coffee I know that today is one of the delicious by-products of playing professional basketball. Moving through America sampling its diversity and vitality and yet seeing it as a whole is as much a part of the life as loneliness.

I often ask myself why I continue to play. I was convinced that in 1967, when I first signed, I would play no more than four years, the length of my initial contract. After eight years I'm still playing. One reason is the money. There is no question that it gives me a sense of security, and a greater feeling of freedom, mobility, and accomplishment. Yet it also forces me to consider how much money is enough and what is the true value of my basketball services.

As a small boy I used to watch baseball in St. Louis. The Cardinals were my team and Stan Musial was my favorite player. One day at old Sportsman's Park he struck out in the bottom of the ninth with two runners on base and the Cardinals one run back. A fan behind me shouted, "You get $80,000 a year—for that? What a waste." During my first year in the NBA when I heard similar comments directed at me, I often thought of the Musial incident and then considered the question of what a player should be paid and for what.

There are some things in our society that are crazy. Among them are show business salaries, our dependency on lawyers, and the pomp of the evening TV news. Imagine a boy like me from the Midwest who plays basketball constantly for every conceivable reason except money. Suddenly he is told he can make over $100,000 a year playing. It's lying on the ground like a seashell at the edge of the ocean. Am I going to pick it up? Sure. It wasn't my idea for basketball to become tax-shelter show biz.

It is unlikely that a basketball player contributes as much to the social good as a teacher, a doctor or a member of the clergy. He works just as hard and has a brief career that frequently leaves him crippled, but if you believe that people should be paid according to the amount of social good they contribute (if that could ever be objectively measured), then probably a basketball player is overpaid. But the only way to rectify such an injustice is to admit that the marketplace erred, which is to say that the way economic activity has been organized in this country is wrong. But who, under another system, would determine the salary level of basketball players or doctors or teachers? Would it be the doctors or teachers? Would it be chaos or caprice? Would it be a government salary commission instead of the judgment of individual businessmen? Would any of those alternatives be better?

I heard a player say, "Money alone makes you more of what you were before you had money." Ultimately it is your work and the struggle that surrounds its daily practice that is important, much more so than money, because it is work, as Joseph Conrad has said, that provides the "sustaining illusion of an independent existence." Although I play basketball for money, and the amount of money is important, it is not the sole reason I play. The answer is not so easy to uncover. It lies much deeper in the workings of the game and in me.

A couple of minutes after I get back from Pike Street Market, I take a nap, sleeping through the departure of the bus. DeBusschere and I take a cab to the arena and when we arrive in the locker room Danny is taping ankles and talking: "We used to go to Alcatraz as kids to play ball," he says. "Every time some guy from the neighborhood would be there and he'd always have the same story. 'Gee, I don't know what happened. I was just standing on the corner and some cop comes up and says I was robbing a bank and plants a gun on me. You know I wouldn't do that.'"

Barnett is next on the table for a quick tape job. He is reading a book, *Building Black Business*, while Danny works. Phil walks in, distracted, two minutes before the deadline. Red tells him how lucky he is; how close he came to being fined. Phil closes his book on Zen love, hangs up his plaid lumberjack shirt and Wrangler jeans, scratches his beard, and replaces his wire rim glasses with contact lenses. He puts on his jock, walks over to the taping table, and notices what Barnett is reading.

"You believe in capitalism, Rich?" he asks.

"Why, Phil?" interjects Lucas defensively. "Don't you?"

Phil smiles.

"Do I what?" Barnett asks, irritated because he has been interrupted.

"Do you believe in capitalism?" repeats Phil.

"No, Phil," Barnett says in exasperation, "I believe in love."

Barnett then tells a story about his Tennessee State team playing Philander Smith College in Arkansas. Tennessee State was nationally ranked and had beaten Smith by 70 points in Nashville. The gym in Arkansas was small and the rims had no nets. When Tennessee State scored, the officials occasionally ignored it. If a long shot went through without touching the rim, the officials frequently called the shot short; Tennessee State lost seven baskets that way during the game. At the buzzer Tennessee State was up by one and the team dressed hurriedly and left. "On our way back to Tennessee State the next day," Barnett says, "we read in the paper that Philander Smith had won by one point on two free throws, given because of a double technical the official had called on our coach at the buzzer. We kept it as a victory in our yearbook and they kept it a victory in theirs."

━━━━━━

Bill Russell coaches the Seattle Supersonics with an authoritarian hand. His young players do not play well, and the frequent defeats put him, after years as a champion, in the unfamiliar position of being associated with a losing team. Even so, he seems unaffected, still walking with a pronounced stoop and laughing often in his unique cackle. He remains the competitor of the century. There is no way his team can continue to lose for long.

As a player, Russell was a remarkable innovator using his perfect timing to block shots and his exceptional quickness to dominate an opponent defensively. Until Russell's entry into professional basketball, team defense counted for little. There were individual defensive stars, but rarely were there five men who worked as a unit defensively as well as they did offensively. Russell changed that. He played the middle on defense and encouraged his teammates to overplay their men. He always stood behind them, poised to stop an opponent who broke free. The Celtic defense became more aggressive as it revolved around the "eagle with a beard," as an opponent once called Russell. And defense in general became a more important part of the game.

Red Auerbach, Russell's coach during those years, states unequivocally that Russell was the greatest player ever to play the game. He recalls that some nights Russell could "play a whole team" defensively. He could hold any one player scoreless, but he was more interested in stopping five. He could get anything within fifteen feet of the basket, blocking as many as four separate shots on one play. The rest of the game he might just imply an intention with a fake, a step, or a raised arm—the grace notes of basketball—causing an offensive man to throw up a wild shot in fear that this time Russell was going for the block. No other big man ever had his lateral quickness, and few players, big or small, had a personality like his.

He saw early that the key to basketball was not individual statistics, but winning the game. Armed with that knowledge, he applied his enormous competitive energies to orchestrating victory. The advertisement he once did for Equitable Life Assurance, pointing out that becoming number one is easier than remaining number one, touches on a theme that seemed to fascinate him. During eleven of Russell's thirteen years, the Celtics won the world championship. He developed a great pride from his dominant role in the Celtic dynasty—a fact which constantly brought him into conflict with the more publicized Bob Cousy. When reporters asked Russell why Red Auerbach was a great coach, Russell would reply that he, Bill Russell, was the main reason.

Russell uncovered another dimension to the game beyond the pure physical skills of shot blocking and defense. He plumbed the depths of an opponent's personality, looking for the weak spot. He delighted in the mental aspect of basketball. Once he encountered a young opponent in a restaurant the night before they were supposed to play. The young player smiled and nodded; Russell ignored him. The next night the opponent played poorly, out of his rhythm, trying to make an indelible impression on Russell.

I remember a time in my sophomore year in the NBA when Russell was playing his last season, and the young Knicks, one year away from a championship, were playing the Celtics in the play-offs. I had hit three jump shots in a row and the Knicks were threatening the Celtic lead. Just prior to a free throw I was lined up next to Tom Sanders, who was guarding me, and across the lane was Russell. Russell caught my eye, looked directly at me, then at Sanders and shouted in an exasperated tone, "Come on, Satch, stop him," and then nodded at me. Suddenly I did not feel as confident, or maybe I felt more determined to meet the challenge he threw at me, but at any rate I scored very little the rest of the game.

Tom Heinsohn, Russell's teammate for nine years and now coach of the Boston Celtics, recalls that Russell's greatest psyche jobs were on Chamberlain. When Wilt's team came to Boston, Russell frequently invited him to dinner, softening him up for the game and making it difficult for Wilt to muster the personal antagonism he needed to play aggressive basketball. Russell, as audacious as it may seem, made sure Wilt always had plausible excuses for losing. He always told reporters that Wilt was the best center. Perhaps he said it because he sensed that as long as the Celtics continued to win no one (including Wilt) would believe the praise. Or maybe he realized that even he might not be able to stop an enraged Wilt for forty-eight minutes.

Wilt was stronger and offensively more potent, and though Russell could play even with him for most of a game, he never allowed Chamberlain a clear comparison. Heinsohn refers to the times when by the third quarter the Celtics would be up 20 and Russell would have outscored and outrebounded Wilt. Russell would go the bench; Wilt would score 20 in the last quarter to outscore Russell for the game and then, according to Heinsohn, Wilt would "go to the locker room and bitch about his *team* not being as strong as the Celtics."

Oscar Robertson recalls another facet of Russell's mental game. When Wilt had the step advantage for a dunk shot Russell rarely tried to block it. Instead, he released toward the other basket so that when Wilt slammed the ball through, a Celtic would grab it and throw a long pass to Russell for an easy lay-in. There was no way Chamberlain could recover fast enough to prevent the lay-in. He could only chastise his teammates for not covering.

Russell's commitment to the game was different from other players who treated basketball as a job and had difficulty developing the killer instinct. For Russell there seemed to be no separation between basketball success/failure and the rest of his life, which in part explains his nervous vomiting before games, his conflict with Cousy, and his insistence, year after year, that he, not some jockey, or football player, or golfer, was the greatest athlete of the sixties.

Russell never got as much recognition as he deserved. Race was one reason. During the early sixties no black artist got adequate publicity. Then, too, perhaps pro basketball did not have the national following sufficient to merit enormous press attention. Most probably, I think he was overlooked because his greatest accomplishments were in the game's subtleties and in seeking to guarantee team victory in a society which tends to focus attention on the individual achiever.

===

Seattle's inexperience shows in the first half as we spurt to a twelve-point lead. Frazier misses his first two shots in the third quarter. DeBusschere hits a driving hook but his man scores three quick baskets. Seattle is relaxed. They have nothing to lose. If they don't make a comeback, no one will be surprised; but if they can overcome our lead they'll be heroes for the night. Willis can't move well tonight. He misses two shots and has trouble getting up and down the floor. A Seattle guard makes two long jump shots and an incredible drive. The fans begin to sense a move. Our defense plays listlessly. The difference dwindles to two points, then Seattle takes the lead. Frustration shows on our faces. Seattle has shot fourteen free throws to our six during the quarter. With one minute left in the third quarter Earl Monroe gets his fourth foul. He argues with the official, who promptly assesses him with a technical foul.

"Why'd you do that?" I say to the official. "He didn't embarrass you out here."

"Yeah," the ref barks back, "but he said the magic word."

"What!"

"Anytime someone says motherfucker on my court, I'll give a technical."

"Why, you never heard it before out here?"

"Every time I do it's a T."

"Oh," I say, "but you wouldn't if he said shit-face or son-of-a-bitch, you mean if he called . . . you . . . a *motherfucker*, that's the only time you'd give a technical. Not if he called you just an asshole."

The referee's face reddens.

"O.K., O.K.," I say, "I just wanted to know so I could tell the team. Thanks."

Basketball is impossible to officiate well. Most of

the calls are dependent on judgment, which in turn is dependent on the official's vision, his angle, his emotional state, and his partner. The result is colossal inconsistency. Sometimes I can make contact with hands all night without being caught and the next game the official calls three quick fouls for the same kind of play. Sometimes I can jump into my defensive man on the shot and get a foul, while the next night the same move is called charging. Players universally complain about officials. Too many fouls slow the game; too few calls make it physically dangerous. Each player has his own favorite official and his worst enemy. The players' union has considered black-balling the poorest officials, but it is impossible to reach a consensus on who they are. The problem is experience. Pro basketball is very different from college, and only by officiating in the pro league can an official get experience. Teams of three or four officials would cover the game more thoroughly, but they would cost more money than the owners are willing to spend on the game. About the only thing that can be done is to eliminate personal idiosyncrasies and vendettas from officiating. There is no place for player baiting or quixotic technical fouls. A good example of how referees abuse their power is in their treatment of rookies, telling them to be quiet or to expect no breaks their first year. When I was a rookie I saw little action, averaging sixteen minutes a game. The first game I played in during the last quarter was at Boston. With a minute to go, I was fouled. I had one and one, two shots, and the Knicks were up by one. Needless to say, I was nervous. The referee, Earl Strom, handed me the ball at the foul line and said with a smirk, "Now we'll see what you're made of."

———

Seattle opens their lead in the fourth quarter to eight points. Everything we do goes wrong. It is as if no one wants to touch the ball, much less shoot it. No one will take the offensive responsibility. When one of us finally asserts himself, it is outside the flow of the team and leads to forced shots. Holzman calls time out and berates each player.

"You gonna let that guy go around you again, Clyde?" he says. "All defensive team, my ass, their rookies can't wait to get you."

"Goddammit, box out!" he says to me. "We can't let 'em keep getting three and four shots! They'll push you right off the court if you don't hit back! They get the ball anywhere they want it.

"Yeah, I know, those dumb cocksuckers," he says pointing to the refs, "they aren't gonna give us anything. Don't waste your time again! I'll do that. Let's go out now and play some defense. Stop poundin' the fuckin' ball into the floor, guards; it's gotta start with you. And you forwards, don't stand around with your thumbs up your ass! Move to the open spot. O.K., let's go."

With three minutes left in the game Seattle leads by twelve. Suddenly we catch fire. Frazier steals two passes. Earl hits two jumpers. I hit one and DeBusschere gets a tap-in. It's a four-point ball game now. The intensity of the game has doubled. They are beginning to panic. Russell calls time out with one minute to go. Upon returning to play, they hold the ball trying to play for a good shot, low, just before the twenty-four second clock expires. The ball rims the basket. Lucas, now playing center, gets the rebound, passes it to me. I feed Earl, going to the basket for a fast break lay-up. Seattle didn't have anyone protecting. Now we're just two points back with forty seconds left. They hold the ball again; the crowd is on its feet. Their young guard dribbles cautiously looking at the clock. Suddenly, as quick as a frog's tongue, Frazier slaps the ball away from him, gains control, takes six dribbles, shoots and scores. The game is tied. The same guard immediately dribbles the full length of the court and fires a clumsy shot from the deep corner. It is a flagrant "get-backing" and as he launches it I figure we'll have a chance to win when it misses. But, it goes in, eliciting tumultuous approval from the crowd. We call time out and set up a last-second play to try to tie the score. Twelve seconds remain. The play calls for me to shoot from the corner. Frazier in-bounds to Earl. When I come around Willis's screen, the center switches on to me. I'm cornered. Earl begins to penetrate to the basket, sees DeBusschere, passes it. DeBusschere takes a 16-foot jump shot. It misses. We lose by two points and pandemonium breaks out in the Seattle Coliseum.

"Why you guys waited," Holzman says in the locker room, "until three minutes left in the game to start playing defense, I'll never know. We should have won by twenty. It's a shame to let a bunch of rookies be heroes. Get a shower; bus leaves in thirty-five minutes."

Two things strike me about the game as I shower. If Dave had hit the last shot we would have won. I know it. Yet to think he lost it is wrong. We all lost it in the third quarter when we stank. The important thing about a last-second shot is not just to make it but to have five guys willing to take it; ready to shoulder the responsibility. No one criticizes Dave; he accepted his role tonight. But our play in the last three minutes is more of a mystery. Why did we wait? The road, the time of the season and place in the schedule provides only a partial explanation. Some games need a spark to come alive—a fight, an embarrassment, a referee's call, or an inspiring individual effort. Tonight we waited too long before we decided that indeed we might lose. Good teams have a tendency to be complacent. It is as if we tempted fate, sure of our ability to rescue any situation before disaster. The realization that a loss was imminent jarred us to action, but too late.

## 6

THE NEXT MORNING THE BUS LEAVES THE HOTEL AT 7:00 for the airport. Most of the players are half asleep as we move through the wet, deserted streets of early morning Seattle and pull onto Route 5 toward Tacoma. Below and to the right of the freeway is the site of the new Seattle Superdome. A little later we pass the Boeing development center. Big 747 and 727 jet planes stand unattended on runways bordered by enormous repair hangars. On the other side of the highway is an abrupt incline crowned with apartments and houses. A sign on the side of one house says, "Jesus is coming." As we approach the vicinity of the airport, Danny grabs the touring microphone in the bus for a little early morning entertainment. "On your left," he begins, "is the Lewis & Clark bargain clothing store where Clyde—Clyde, wake up—for $15.95 you can get a whole suit, shirt, cuff links, an extra pair of pants, shoes, socks, underwear, and everything. On your right you will see a little white frame house with a picket fence; that was my birthplace."

"Tell it, Big Time," shouts a rookie.

"W. C. Whelan, do it," says another.

The bus doors open and we stroll through the airport, wasting the forty-five minutes at the newsstand or coffee shop before departure to Phoenix. I buy a magazine and head for the gate. After take-off I open it to a story about Mickey Mantle at his home in Dallas, Texas.

"'At night,'" the author, Roger Kahn, quotes Mantle as saying, " 'my knee can hurt so bad it wakes me up. But first I dream. I'm playing in the stadium and I can't make it. My leg is gone. I'm in to hit and I can't take my good swing. I strike out and that's when it wakes me. Then I know it's really over.'

" 'I loved it,' he says, 'his voice throbbing with intensity. Nobody could have loved playing ball as much as me, when I wasn't hurt. I must have fifty scrapbooks. People sent 'em to me. Sometimes after breakfast when the boys get off to school, I sit by myself and take a scrapbook and just turn the pages. The hair comes up on the back of my neck. I get goose bumps. And I remember how it was and how I used to think that it would always be that way.' "

The words seem to jump off the page at me. I remember the last time we were in Portland, Oregon, when Mickey Mantle was staying at the same hotel. He was in town as part of his job with a Dallas-based insurance company. Five years out of baseball, he was the principal guest at a luncheon honoring the great Indian quarterback for the University of Washington Huskies, Sonny Sixkiller, who had just joined the insurance company. Mantle stood in the lobby for over an hour on that stormy afternoon. He chatted with Danny and said hello to some of us players, but mostly he just stared at the rain. As I watched from across the lobby and listened, the rain beating against the window began to sound like thousands of hands clapping in wild applause.

There is terror behind the dream of being a professional ballplayer. It comes as a slow realization of finality and of the frightening unknowns which the end brings. When the playing is over, one can sense that one's youth has been spent playing a game and now both the game and youth are gone, along with the innocence that characterizes all games which at root are pure and promote a prolonged adolescence in those who play. Now the athlete must face a world where awkward naiveté can no longer be overlooked because of athletic performance. By age thirty-five any potential for developing skills outside of basketball is slim. The "good guy" syndrome ceases. What is left is the other side of the Faustian bargain: To live all one's days never able to recapture the feeling of those few years of intensified youth. In a way it is the fate of a warrior class to receive rewards, plaudits, and exhilaration simultaneously with the means of self-destruction. When a middle-aged lawyer moves more slowly on the tennis court, he makes adjustments and may even laugh at his geriatic restrictions because for him there remains the law. For the athlete who reaches thirty-five, something in him dies; not a peripheral activity but a fundamental passion. It necessarily dies. The athlete rarely recuperates. He approaches the end of his playing days the way old people approach death. He puts his finances in order. He reminisces easily. He offers advice to the young. But, the athlete differs from an old person in that he must continue living. Behind all the years of practice and all the hours of glory waits that inexorable terror of living without the game.

I have often wondered how I will handle the end of my playing days. No one really knows until that day comes. DeBusschere says that as long as one doesn't puff up with the unnatural attention given a pro athlete, and keeps a few good friends, the adjustment should be easy. I don't know if he really believes it. Tom Heinsohn says you don't realize how much you love the game until you miss it. Forced into a premature retirement by injury, he yearned for the life again so much that he took a 75 percent cut in salary to coach the Celtics. One retired player told me he noticed the end at home in his relationship with his wife. The fears and resentment that were formerly projected into the team now fall on wife and children, making life miserable for all. Holzman says that he never regretted the end, for when it came he had had enough basketball and wanted out. In my case, I've been preparing for the end since my first year, but even so I can only hope that I will manage easily the withdrawal from what Phil Jackson calls "my addiction."

When DeBusschere announced his retirement after getting a ten-year contract to become General Manager of the New York Nets, many newspapers said that he was retiring at his best. Once, after a speech I gave, a man came up to me and said, "Retire while you're still at the top. Whizzer White did it. Jim Brown did it. Bill Russell did it." DeBusschere talks about how sad he felt for Willie Mays struggling at the end of his brilliant career. He calls Mays' play embarrassing. He also says of several players that they played one year too long.

In the same way that it is difficult to watch your father grow old, it's difficult to watch your favorite player become increasingly unable to do the small things that made you admire him. But unless a man has a better opportunity, why should he stop doing something he loves? Fans want stars to retire on top in part to protect their fantasies. That makes no sense; consider Jerry West or Oscar Robertson, whose last two years of struggle didn't diminish the twelve previous years of achievement. In a way it made them more likable than if they had sought to retain an heroic level through early retirement. The decline is sad but human, for it is the one thing that strikes ineluctably in professional sports. To miss it makes a pro's experience incomplete.

The end of a player's career is the end of the big money and big publicity, and at that point the future depends on past prudence and levelheadedness. The specter of Joe Louis or Sugar Ray Robinson haunts many players. DeBusschere believes that of all the Knicks Frazier will have the most difficulty adjusting to the post-playing days. I'm not so sure. "My biggest motivation not to go broke," says Frazier, "doesn't come from the example of Sugar Ray or Joe Louis, but from my father. When he lost all of his money, he lost everything. The new 'Caddies' and other presents that used to arrive at the house stopped coming. I hold back spending too much money more than I would if I hadn't been around when something happened to my father." Frazier clearly has thought about the change of living standard but DeBusschere wonders also whether Clyde can adjust to a life of less publicity after nearly ten years in the New York spotlight. Though his life seemingly focuses on externals, and remains naively vulnerable to the quixotic taste of strangers, I believe Clyde does seem to understand the precarious path he treads and he confidently prepares for the end with little concern for the potential terror. Maybe no fall can be as hard and damaging as that which he witnessed his father take many years before.

Perhaps the last word on the end of a player's career comes from Danny Whelan. "When the fan is kissing your ass and telling you that you're the greatest," says Danny, "he hates you. They want to get you down on their level and they can't when you're on the top. After you retire just go to that guy who was buying you drinks when you were a player and ask him for a job. He'll show you the door. The fan likes to step on a player after he's finished playing if he gets a chance. A good example is Sweetwater Clifton. Just the other night some guy says he remembers Sweets with the Knicks and asks me if I know what he's doing. I shut up. If I had told him that he's driving a cab in Chicago the guy would have got his nuts off. Players would be better off to change their names and start anew."

---

The plane flies from the lush greenery of the Pacific Northwest to the desert of Arizona. A city comes into view; it appears as a greenish-gray geometric design placed in the middle of brown blotting paper. "If you look out the plane to your right," the captain announces during the descent, "you will see the London Bridge at Lake Havasu, near Phoenix, Arizona."

A warm, dry wind blows steadily as we leave the plane. Inside the antiseptic terminal, we pick up our luggage and move to the bus outside, opposite a row of taxis. DeBusschere reads the Phoenix afternoon paper while the bus moves along the palm-lined drive to the airport exit. I ask him to let me see it when he's finished. Passing through a poorer section of town, manicured lawns disappear. Small yellow-gray frame houses with front porches that sag on each end, stand in the middle of dusty plots of land. "We've just passed the projects," says a rookie.

Another player hums Otis Redding's hit, "I've Been Loving You Too Long," and a third, hearing the song, reminisces, "Hey, remember J. R. on Saturday night radio out of Nashville, brought to you by Randy's Record Shop?"

"Yeah, I remember," a rookie says. "Jimmy Reed be singin' 'Just 'A Runnin' . . . Just 'A Hidin'" [he begins to sing]. . . . That's blues."

"Yeah, man," another player says. "I've seen motherfuckers down South sittin' next to that radio on a Saturday night cryin'. Especially if they got a little white lightnin' in them. They'd be listenin' to the blues and shaking their heads, 'Oh, my, yes.'"

DeBusschere throws me the paper opened to a story about a house owned by the Phoenix Suns' Dick Van Arsdale, who was my roommate during my rookie year. He is a handsome man, 6'5" and blond, with a personality as sturdy as his durable legs. I had returned to Oxford after the 1967–68 season to take examinations for my degree, when one morning at breakfast I read in the *International Herald Tribune* that the Knicks had sent Van Arsdale to Phoenix in the expansion draft. It was my first contact with owner-controlled player movement. My reaction was sadness at losing a good friend, but, in retrospect, the most important effect was that I came to understand the power of owners. "They can send me anywhere overnight," I thought. "How can you form close friendships if the next day you might be gone?" I had always seen trading from the fan's viewpoint, but then I saw the human cost involved. I don't like the fear their power over me evokes. I don't like the idea of a man owning, selling, and buying another man as if he was an old car.

The Van Arsdale deal occurred during the off-season and Dick had time to relocate his family. If the trade had taken place during the season, Van, like any other player, would have had 48 hours to report to his new team, whatever the hardship. By signing a contract, players automatically agree to the possibility of a forced move without advance notice. Sportswriters jokingly refer to the movement of "horseflesh." General managers point out how trades benefit all parties, as if they were the "invisible hand" of basketball. Owners call their control of players essential to the structure and integrity of professional basketball. After Van's departure I realized that no matter how kind, friendly, and genuinely interested the owners may be, in the end most players are little more than depreciable assets to them.

The lobby of the Del Webb Townehouse is filled with suntanned ladies and men wearing brightly colored alpaca sweaters—the professional golfers are in town for the Phoenix Open. The size and blackness of our group creates a minor sensation until we escape to the elevators. After telephoning a local friend I go to the lobby and rent a car for our two-day stay.

Having a car encourages a kind of exploration, particularly in the West. I know the physical layout of nearly every city in the league. I form many impressions from behind a steering wheel. Sometimes I spend a whole afternoon just cruising the streets and countryside.

I notice Danny talking with the bellman, a retired army sergeant. I ask him where he is heading and he says Scottsdale. He's meeting some baseball buddies.

Five professional teams have spring training in Arizona. I offer him a ride and he accepts, talking of lawyers and trials the whole way.

"When I was a boy in San Francisco," he says, "I used to cut school to go to the courthouse and listen to trials. The best criminal lawyer I ever saw was Jake Erlich. He used to put me in the front row. I knew he had a winner when he wore a white shirt and big diamond cuff links. The jury couldn't take their eyes off the diamonds during his summation. He'd win every time."

"Did you ever think about becoming a lawyer?" I ask a little self-consciously, thinking about all the times the same question has been posed to me.

"No," Danny answers, "I just went to listen to the stories."

"What was the most dramatic trial scene you've witnessed?" I ask in a different version of the "What was your greatest game?" question.

"That would be in the Errol Flynn rape trial. The prosecutor got up and established this and that and made it pretty convincing. Then Jerry Geisler, Flynn's lawyer, got the woman involved on the stand and said, 'You were lying in bed, right?'

" 'Yes,' the woman answered, as Geisler, himself, fell to the courtroom floor.

" 'And you had your legs spread like this, right?'

" 'Yeah,' she said, and Geisler starts movin' like he was screwin' right there.

" 'And you were moving like this, right.'

" 'Yes.'

"Shit," Danny says, "he won the case right there."

We finally arrive at Lulu Belle's, an old-fashioned saloon-steak house, with red velvet interior. Danny gets out, ready for a night of baseball reminiscing and serious drinking. I head back to Phoenix, somewhat wishing that the game were tonight. A weekend of three games in three nights is physically tough but there is little dead time. The road can be a bore without games. I remember five days in Kansas City when the walls of my Holiday Inn room seemed to laugh at me in the way prison walls must mock the expectant parolee, telling him that his departure will necessarily be decided by someone else, and that in the meantime, only dreams can reduce the monotony.

## 7

I HAVE COFFEE WITH DEBUSSCHERE AND A SPORTS-
writer, during which the discussion deals with the difference between basketball today and in the 1950s.

"In the fifties," Dave says, "basketball was a power
game with big muscle men around the basket. Defense was mainly for the guards, maybe because the
jump shot wasn't widely used by big men. There
wasn't much finesse. Then along came Wilt and Russell who controlled the inside. Opponents had to do
other things. You had to break down the floor before
Wilt or Russell could get set, and you had to be good
from the outside. Quick men and coaching also became a bigger part of basketball. The concept of
team defense resulted from big men cutting off the
traditional way of scoring. You had to learn how to
defense the guys other than Wilt or Russell. You had
to press and double team so that guys wouldn't be as
effective even though they kept getting better and
better at shooting."

I always thought that the use of a small forward
was the biggest innovation of my career years. In the
past other teams had used players such as Frank
Ramsey, George Yardley, Cliff Hagan, and John Havlicek, but when I came into the league most of the
forwards were 6'6" or over. I had to play guard.
Because I wasn't quick enough I got burned often;
when I had a chance to return to forward I was re-
lieved. When writers asked Holzman how he could
play me, a small 6'5" forward against men 6'9" he
told them that a disadvantage was often an advantage. What he meant was that when an opposing

team saw the difference in height they often forced the action toward my man, thus disrupting the normal flow of their offense, and forcing my man to take a bigger scoring responsibility. Often their hopes of taking advantage backfired when my man missed shots, or passes went awry when they tried to get the ball to him. Meanwhile on offense I was quicker than the bigger man and could maneuver for shots more easily. After Holzman used the small forward successfully, every team accepted his redefinition of the game and put men 6'4" to 6'5" at one forward position.

The balanced team defense is also a Holzman innovation. Boston had a team defense, but its practitioners were allowed a larger margin of error with Bill Russell under the basket. Willis Reed and Jerry Lucas are not as dominant, so the margin of error for the Knicks is smaller. Each defensive man has to accept the responsibility for his own man and also to aid a teammate in trouble. Once he understands that and acts on it, the various types of presses are simply technical adjustments and our double teaming becomes a well-executed, known defensive maneuver. With team defense understood, pressure defense is assured, and with pressure defense the game's emphasis shifts from muscle to quickness, from pure individual physical skill to coordinated, intelligent group responses.

━━━━━━

I pick up a Phoenix friend for lunch and we drive along Central Avenue to Indian School Road, named for the Phoenix Indian School which is in the center of town. He tells me there are forty Indian tribes living in Arizona. In the early days of statehood most of the Indians lived on reservations where there were no schools. Indians termed "promising," as my friend put it, came to Phoenix where they lived in dormitories and attended classes. Today they still come from grade school age through high school, looking for the magic skills that will allow them to assimilate gracefully into modern America. The trees and green fields surrounding the school provide a pleasant environment. Up Central Avenue a few blocks stands a Jesuit high school, a reminder of the first white men to penetrate the Indian civilization.

"When guns are outlawed," a sign says on a passing car, "only outlaws will have guns."

We turn onto Arcadia Drive where 60-foot eucalyptus trees tower over our car. All the streets off the drive are lined with low-slung homes set in comfortable green and surrounded by Phoenix palms and orange trees with trunk bottoms whitewashed as if they were the legs of horses taped for a race. The only influence of the desert here is the dry air and the parched mountains in the distance. We stop for lunch at the Old Hatch Restaurant in Scottsdale. Sitting outside at a table on the balcony in the warm March sunshine, with Camelback Mountain backdropping the two-story buildings of Scottsdale's Fifth Avenue section, I sense why so many people have left their homes and migrated here.

Fifty percent of the people in the Phoenix area have been here less than 10 years. In 1950 Phoenix was a town of 50,000 people; now 800,000 live here. Scottsdale has increased from 10,000 to 100,000. The Valley of the Sun—Scottsdale, Phoenix, Sun City area—has grown from 100,000 in 1950 to 1.3 million. Such rapid growth produces unevenly scattered development. Private enterprise, unfettered, built Phoenix and many of the rugged individualists still remain. Barry Goldwater's house and the Wrigley mansion are two prominent landmarks. For them, and their kind, economic freedom is America's most cherished ideal. Government is anathema. They have yet to feel the compelling need for belonging to a group, brought on by the limits of individualism in a crowded, complex, technological world. They have not confronted the twin yearnings, unity and freedom, felt by so many Americans equally and simultaneously. For Western conservatives, belonging is less important than freedom. In this sense, Phoenix is a simpler and perhaps a healthier place than Chicago; yet it is young. As more and more people flee the weather and regimentation of the urban East for Phoenix, this single-minded dedication to economic freedom will end. One can already see what lies ahead as surely as the smog hangs over the city three days out of five. Phoenix is in the terminal phase of the American frontier spirit.

We turn onto Van Buren at 40th and come face to face with "The Strip." Thirty-eight motels dot the next 16 blocks of Phoenix. The first motel built in the United States was near San Luis Obispo, California, in 1924. Today there are over 43,500 motels in the United States accounting for over two-thirds of all commercial lodges. Some of the places on "The Strip" existed before half of the present Phoenix population arrived. All seem to be flourishing as more transients seek refuge in the cool anonymity of a motel room—a home for those Americans whose only mobility is horizontal. A sign outside Chuck Meyer's House of Television says, "Work for the Lord, pay is small, retirement benefits are out of this world."

A short distance from the State Capitol we turn left and head into the mountains, passing through pungent orange groves and clumps of giant cactus and beginning to climb the steep road leading to the lookout of South Mountain Park. We see no other cars in the park. From the metal map at the summit you can see downtown Phoenix, with its houses and offices arranged in small, neat squares, and sitting under a cloud of smog. As the squares of farms surrounding the city get larger and greener, the smog decreases. Beyond, vast expanses of desert, pierced only by the highway to the mountains, show how much room is left for settlement by the twentieth-century pioneers now poised in the motels. We stay a few minutes in the afternoon breeze and then I head back to the hotel for an hour's sleep before the game.

"Did you ever see a rabbit do it?" I hear Willis Reed ask as I enter the locker room later that night. "Shit, it's over before it begins; the female, she lies down like she was shot. Horses are different. Once we had a mare and we bought a visit from a stud; that motherfucker was this big [stretching his hands apart at least three feet]. You got to guide him into the mare. We missed and he shot his load all over us, he was so excited."

I put my bag down, undress, and begin taping my ankles as Barnett picks up the conversation. "Hey, Luke," he says, "ever hear from 'the breath' any-more?" Lucas ignores Barnett's ribbing. "We're in Milwaukee," continues Barnett, "and this bitch calls on the phone, starts goin' into this and that and how she's all hot for Lucas, who's playin Mr. Nice Guy, just listening. She talks on the phone for an hour with this breathing rough-ass voice. Her phone game was together—*too . . . geh tha!* [spoken like three tuba blasts]. She probably weighed 278 or 78."

"Barnett was shouting, 'Give it up, bitch,' as I was talking," says Lucas. "Who knows, maybe she was just lonely."

"Or had the phone between her legs," says Barnett.

"Hey, wait a minute," says Jackson, "did she say she had an older sister?"

"Yeah," says Lucas.

"She called me, too," says Jackson.

"DeBusschere and me, too," I say. "Whoever's in the room she talks to. Last time she said she was out at a motel by the airport where the heat was off and she had to stay in bed to stay warm. I never saw her though."

"Right," says Barnett, "and if you did you wouldn't let us know. She's got to be a chiwollephant."

The soft side of every hardened pro is his experience with women on the road. Locker-room "styling" and "telling the fellas" about the night before are sometimes part of the routine. Occasionally a groupie is passed around and compared until she becomes NBA Jane, or Connie, or Carol. Most players, how-

ever, keep their experiences private; for them discretion is the key. Along with the professional ten-
sions of the road flows a parallel, intensely personal
set of emotions. The women complement the games,
providing a respite from the competition for some and
a chance to regain the confidence lost in a bad game
for others. After the season, the attachments fade and,
though their memory is special, become a part of just
another season. But during those brief encounters life
seems fuller on the road; whatever their duration
such moments are genuine, alive, exciting, troublesome, dangerous, sad, and so unlike much of the
travel through our jet-age America.

Team athletes on the road take their place in a long
line of males in flight from domesticity and its responsibilities of one woman and family. The road
symbolizes the same thing for a basketball player as
the forest, frontier, or sea did for some of America's
greatest writers: Like Rip Van Winkle who escaped
through sleep, or the Pathfinder who blazed trails
through a wild environment, or Nick Adams who escaped through fishing, the pro player escapes through
a life of games on the road. Being away with the
fellas makes up an essential part of the job. No player
glorifies the virtues of male companionship, but when
women reporters first began entering locker rooms,
the furor that erupted was in part due to the en-
croachment of women on a last refuge from their
threatening presence.

But there is no need for the team to serve as a substitute for mother or wife. Each town has its own
supply of women and ostensibly gives to each player
the chance to escape the trap of an all-male world.
Only at the end of his career when the constant motion of away games stops and the player must depend
much more on one woman and family, does he realize
that all the women along the road have not helped
him to mature but rather have allowed him a continued flight from responsibility.

A strong and inseparable bond exists between the

innocent, beautiful girl and the pampered athlete. Both are objects in the eyes of most people. Both are given credit only for their physical attributes, and receive inordinate prizes for them. They are told they are something special, Miss America and the All-American, without understanding what qualities beyond the superficialities of face and body hold importance in life. Both become subject to a dangerous vanity. Both live in terror of the day their glory will end and frequently live life hard and fast in anticipation of the day their age will show. An athlete knows the world of a beautiful girl. Maybe that is why DiMaggio and Monroe stuck in the American imagination as an example of a mythic match.

As the seventies have progressed, athletes have acted more freely and taken on a peacock look, as careful with their platform shoes and hair dyes as any manicured woman. The age of athlete chic has arrived. Jocks are no longer sweaty monsters but purveyors of "manly scents" and transforming hair sprays. Likewise, beautiful women have begun to admit that they, like the athlete, work at their beauty. The female sports movement followed the glamour girls' exit from the workout closet. The bonus babies of the beauty business are the natural progeny of the bonus babies of the sports world.

———

The Knicks take the court in the empty Phoenix Coliseum, one week to the day before chaps-wearing, bow-legged cowboys will be riding and roping calves under the same roof. The crowd gradually fills the arena. We go through warm-ups to musical accompaniment—"Aquarius." The fans begin their own warm-ups:

"Hey, Bradley, you yo-yo."

"Frazier, you better check your money bags, you're too pretty for mugging in New York."

"Red. Hey, Holzman, you *were* the best coach.

Now you run an old-age home. Go back to New York, you bum, and take your overpaid greasers with you."

"DeBusschere—you wearin' your hair coloring tonight?"

"Hey, Bradley, Bradley, go back to Rhodes."

Crowds differ. The Garden crowd during the warm-up before a big game crackles with anticipation; the blasé Forum crowd in Los Angeles often leaves before the game's end—beating the freeway traffic is more important than seeing the final minutes. The public address announcer in Philadelphia captures his audience and visiting players with the staccato timing of his pronunciation; the Boston crowd fills the air of the old Boston Garden with a loving adoration of the Celtics and covers the balconies with simplistic banners such as "Celtics Pride Cannot Be Denied," "Heinsohn's Heroes," and "Celtics —a team for all seasons."

Phoenix is one of the least hospitable places to play. The fans, many of whom don't understand professional basketball, attack referees and visiting players in the way the father of a high school star berates the league's next best player. Their animosities stem from deep-seated prejudices and not from judgment; they frequently boo when the referee is simply enforcing the rules, such as giving a player an extra free throw. The hostility is full of misconceptions and occasionally takes the form of racist remarks.

Under the basket near the visiting bench the same two long-legged women sit every game. They cross their legs suggestively, toss back their jet black hair, stare occasionally at their favorite visitor of the night, and provide distraction if the game turns dull.

I have played basketball before audiences in eighteen countries and hundreds of U.S. cities. On only two occasions have I felt the crowd as a collective body provide dramatic comment on the society outside the arena.

Once Walt Frazier was having a bad game in the play-offs. When he came out for a rest the Madison

Square Garden crowd booed him for what seemed like five minutes. During my rookie year, when I failed to fulfill the public's expectations, I was frequently jeered, ridiculed, and once even spat upon, but never did I receive as vicious a booing from twenty thousand people. Frazier's face twitched as he sat on the bench, the towel placed to his mouth.

"Take the ordinary ethnic, white, working stiff," said a reporter covering that game. (The reporter had once worked for a politician, not uncommon for a sports reporter.) "He works on a dangerous job, leaving home at seven and getting home late in time to face his old lady and a screaming kid. He's too tired to think of sex more than two or three times a month. He saves his money, scrounges for a ticket to the Knicks, gets into his double knits that still don't hide his pot, and goes to the Garden. There he sees Frazier, this black who can get women, white or black, whenever he wants, who is making $300,000 a year for playing—not working—and seemingly doing it easily. Then there he is, playing poorly; so the guy boos, thinking that the overpaid son-of-a-bitch deserves it. I have watched lots of crowds and those boos for Frazier were vicious. They were like the ones Robert Kennedy met in the spring of 1968 when he finally decided to run for President. They were the boos of a powerful resentment saved for the man who exudes sexuality. Kennedy faced it and so does Walt Frazier." Whatever the explanation, the boos seemed to hurt Clyde deeply.

The other unusual crowd reaction occurred in 1965 in Budapest. I was a member of the American team which had just won the basketball competition in the World University Games by defeating the Russians in the final. We stood on a platform at center court where each of us received a medal and a bouquet of flowers. After our first-place presentation we were asked to walk around the infield of the twenty-thousand-seat, outdoor arena. The crowd was yelling, clapping, waving, and throwing flowers at us throughout our triumphant parade. After we finished our walk and stood at one end of the stadium, the second place medals were presented to the Russians, who then followed our path around the interior of the stadium. For them there was no noise. Total silence. So startling was the contrast that I felt sorry for the Russians who had played just as hard. Looking up into the stands I saw why there was silence. The Hungarians were clapping, except their hands missed in midair. Ten thousand people moved their hands in the way a baseball umpire signals safe. The Russians were still the conquerors.

———

After the warm-ups DeBusschere feels sick and tells Red he can't play. He retires to the locker room, his head pounding as if it were the bit on an oil drill. Every player has two or three games a year when the pace and intensity of the schedule prevents him from working. Playing a hundred games a year most players are conscientious about their nights off, waiting if possible until they are out of town with a minimum of TV or press coverage and against a weaker team. Athletes can play on "rest" nights, but probably poorly, and they risk serious injury due to illness and slowed reflexes. If it were a war and the player was a soldier, he would fight and probably make it. But that is the point: Basketball, even at the professional level, is not war and the only thing that the iron-man has to show for his ability to play every game is (maybe) a shortened career. We are human beings, perhaps depreciable, but we don't come with five-year guarantees. I once had hopes of being an iron-man until I realized that the masochism needed to become one prevents me from performing consistently well or enjoying a game. When an arch inflammation or a muscle pull keeps me out, the fans can think whatever they like. After years of limited absence and unlimited effort on the court, I think they must know I'm not dodging it. DeBusschere had earned his right to take himself out, too, through all his years of maximum competitive effort.

Holzman never protests a player's injury assessment. He checks with a doctor, when possible, but ultimately leaves the decision up to the player. That is another aspect of his genius. He knows that after the game the heroes are humans who hurt as much from migraines as anybody else. He protects us.

With Dave out of the lineup Phil Jackson starts at forward and Willis at center. At the end of the first quarter Lucas replaces Willis. The Phoenix team, setting no screens and passing infrequently, plays as if it were an all-star team from Ellis Island. Van Arsdale drives around two men to the basket and, much to his chagrin, no foul is called. He tries it again, and still no foul is called. Van becomes incensed.

Many players feel that referees favor us. ("You can't beat New York, the refs won't let you.") The Knick syndrome is not so different from the Boston syndrome of an earlier time except that there is the feeling that since we are winners from New York we are paid more, publicized more, and pampered more. Occasionally, we blow open a game which should be close because the opponent starts fighting his image of us. There are ways to capitalize on his consequent weakness, by nourishing his self-delusion.

Jerry Lucas understands the mental aspects of the game as well as anyone since Bill Russell. Lucas is a shooter in the ninety-ninth percentile and he passes better than most guards, but it is the things he and I do to opponents with our voices, eyes, and timing that makes it such a joy to play alongside him. For example, we will call a play when our opponents shoot a free throw. The play calls for me to fake a move to the other side of the court, receive a pass, and take an easy jumper behind a Lucas screen. As I begin my move to the other side, Lucas will shout angrily, "Get out of here, Bill. Get the hell to the other side. Go." My man, hearing Lucas, will retreat two more steps in anticipation of the move across court and as I quickly step behind the screen, I am left with an uncontested shot. At other times Lucas and I will talk gibberish to each other on the court, pretending that we understand each other. "E ah se mach e kah," I will say. "Puto res di ah," Lucas will reply. The rookie will retreat a step, break his concentration, or try to anticipate more alternatives than are possible. What are they saying? It must mean something.

Tonight Lucas and I are working our game to perfection; five verbal decoys in a row and I start laughing. I can't control myself. Jackson then runs a screen and roll. It works. The fans yell at the refs and deride us. They don't understand what is really happening. Lucas slips two bounce passes to our rookie guard, streaking back door down the middle. Monroe hits a spin and Frazier swishes two jumpers. We win by 12.

After the game I drive with a friend to Pinnacle Peak about 30 miles outside Phoenix. We eat baked beans, T-bone steaks, and drink beer, as a Country and Western band plays the tunes that ring familiar for so many Phoenix immigrants. The walls of the restaurant are covered with business cards, thousands in just one of the restaurant's rooms. Men wearing blue jeans and women with puffed-sleeve blouses sit at the next table, drinking. They begin to dance, awkwardly at first, then with less inhibition. A girl volunteers to perform with the band and sings "Blue Ridge Mountains"—not so bad. Three beers, three steaks, and two apple pies later we leave, walking through the huge, empty, main room with its giant pot-bellied stove. Outside the night is cold. We walk across the dirt parking lot, across the two-lane blacktop, and out into the desert, passing 15-foot cacti and piled sagebrush. Everything is still and quiet except for the wind whispering around rocks. The sky is speckled with thousands of stars, as if they were reflections of Phoenix at night, glimmering before us in the distance.

## 8

THE BUS LEAVES THE HOTEL AT 5:30 A.M. FOR THE worst flight of the trip—a three-stop jaunt from Phoenix to Albuquerque to Oklahoma City to Houston, where we will play the following night. Everyone staggers aboard the airplane, the exhaustion from last night's game still on them—mouths burning, eyes itching, legs aching, bruises being discovered for the first time. Frazier pulls his tan beret over his head and immediately falls asleep. Willis and Jackson soon follow and Monroe, who sits next to me wearing a blue and white rain cap, begins to nod. The stewardess comes around with hot bouillon. Barnett removes his boat captain's hat and says, "Six-thirty in the mornin'. Time when you want eggs and stuff to stick to your bones and some bitch gives you *boolyan*." The man sitting next to Barnett is startled, but recovering quickly engages Barnett in the worst of all possible conversations: early morning fan-racial talk. After we're aloft for forty-five minutes the man goes to the rest room.

"How'd I get stuck with this motherfucker," Barnett says, leaning up to Monroe and me who are just eating breakfast.

"Learning a lot?" I kid.

"Yeah," says Barnett, who has his hat back on. "All about business . . . and why do you colored fellas wear all those funny hats?"

The man returns from the rest room, stopping to talk to DeBusschere, who feels much better this morning.

"Do you think you'll win the championship again this year?" he asks Dave.

Dave brushes the question off but it has hit a sensitive spot in me. I recall again, for about the fiftieth time this season, how it was. We had won the championship only ten months earlier. On days when I ask myself why I play, I remember those few moments after victory, in the locker room with the team, when there was a total oneness with the world and smiles grew broad enough to ache. The chance it could happen again is a sufficient lure to continue. The money is important but the chance to relive that moment outweighs dollars.

After our first championship in 1970, I got a letter which read, "I have had the great pleasure of watching sports on all levels for many of my 45 years. Rarely have I been privileged to see 12 people work so smoothly and selflessly as a team, and in the final Lakers series, under adversity [Willis had been injured].

"In these trying times, compounded by Cambodia, Vietnam, Kent State, riots, concurrent inflation and deflation, you and your teammates have made millions of fans happy and have given us a small spark of inspiration in the currently rather confused world."

The championship was what one wanted to make of it. Vicariously experiencing the victory can't compare to being Number One. Owners and politicians celebrate in the locker room of a champion but only the players, the coach, and perhaps the trainer can feel the special satisfaction of the achievement. They start nine months earlier in training camp. They play the games, endure the travel, and sweat through the practices. They receive the public criticism and overcome their own personal ambitions. But the high of the championship is unequaled in my experience.

Standing at midcourt in Madison Square Garden, two fists raised, and chills coursing up and down my spine, I realized in May 1970 that we had won the championship. I existed apart from the twenty thou-

sand people who roared their approval. Since I was
nine years old I had played basketball to become the
best. Individual honors were nice but insufficient. The
Olympic gold medal gave satisfaction, but it was not
top-flight basketball. Only the NBA in the early 1970s
was clearly the highest caliber in the world, and there
I was a part of the best team. All those statements
of team solidarity expressed since high school; all the
hours of loneliness, dribbling and shooting a basketball in a gym somewhere in the world; all the near
misses in the smaller championships—high school and
college—of America's sports hierarchy; all the missed
opportunities in other fields; all the denied moments
of personal enjoyment; all the derision by self-
appointed experts and opposing fans; and all the in-
sistent advice to shoot more instead of passing, given
by friends and family who didn't understand my commitment to the group; all the struggling against other
competitors who sought the same prize; all the personal conflicts suppressed and angers swallowed—
everything seemed worth it for the feeling at center
court on May 7, 1970. The championship vindicated
my concept of and approach to the game. I had finally
proved something to myself.

When we got to the locker room after the final
buzzer of that first championship, the owners, the
TV cameras, and the press awaited us. And the champagne. The son of a Garden executive asked me for
my jersey. Everybody did their turn on national TV,
telling America in thirty seconds what the championship meant to them. The players hugged, grabbed,
slapped, laughed, kissed—each other. A player would
rush from one cluster of people to another, explaining
how the victory was accomplished but never getting
close to telling the whole story. Each of us sampled
the champagne; no one drank much; its presence was
symbolic more than functional. Cameramen asked
players to pose for photos and slowly, very slowly, the
bedlam of victory died to the normal hum of the
locker room, except that it was now the place of

champions. We showered, dressed, put our wet clothes in our bags, and left. It was over.

We won a second championship two years later, but it was a more mature victory, savored instead of excitedly consumed. The euphoria lasted during a quiet post-game meal with friends in Los Angeles, through a marvelous night until morning, and through the plane ride back to New York. By the following day it too was over.

I wonder if fans know that all the pressure, work, and excitement makes for only 24 hours of joy. How fast it is gone! Only a memory remains of how our group performed and how it felt to make it to the top together. If there is any broader social meaning to the championship, it is not, as my friend suggested in his letter, that it diverts you from unpleasantness or inspires you to great achievements, but rather that it gives a glimpse of a better world—a world unattainable. A team championship exposes the limits of self-reliance, selfishness, and irresponsibility. One man alone can't make it happen; in fact, the contrary is true: a single man can prevent it from happening. The success of the group assures the success of the individual, but not the other way around. Yet the team is an inept model, for even as people marvel at the unselfishness and skill involved, they disagree on how it is achieved and who is the most instrumental. The human closeness of a basketball team cannot be reconstructed on a large scale. Groups in the real world cannot be like a championship team and ultimately the model of sport is dissatisfying for everyone but the participants.

In the locker room after our second championship, as I looked around at my teammates I thought of how I liked something about each of them. They were good people, and from our sharing these unique moments they would be forever different from other people. I saw our reflections in the lives of nomadic Indian tribes on the Plains, making the group adjustments necessary to exist in a constantly changing en-

vironment, and also in the lives of Western gun-
slingers moving on from challenge to challenge with
the knowledge that one day somebody would be faster and surer. Our friendship was based on deeds
accomplished together. It even seemed at times like
that night to seal the split between the black and
white races. "There warn't no home like a raft, after
all," says Huck Finn. "You feel mighty free and easy
and comfortable on a raft." Being on a championship
team is like being on that raft, floating down the
Mississippi. Neither one can last forever.

Red Holzman stood in the locker room throwing
right hands of jubilation at imaginary opponents. We
had just defeated Boston in the seventh game of the
East Division title on our way to our second championship. "It's days like this that do it," Red said to
me with his teeth clenched. "You get hooked—this
job, this profession, you live for days like this. It's so
great to get them. Everyone was great. We really re-
sponded. But, you know," he said, taking a drink of
beer while in the background players shouted and reporters pushed, "it's not real, all this, the ecstasy, this
isn't what life's about. But you get hooked. I always
have. Seems like I've played 30,000 years but today
was the greatest thrill. We beat Boston in *their* year.
Hell of a satisfaction. Tomorrow I'll call you dumb
cocksuckers again but today, well, today even the
scotch will taste better." He put his head back and
smiled.

The tires squeak as we touch down in Albuquerque.
The landing wakes everyone except Willis. While we
are waiting for the new passengers to board, Barnett
quickly arranges a card game. Earl takes my seat and
I move up to the front row, which has two seats
empty. The deck of cards whir and the game is on.
Lucas agrees to keep score today.

The new passengers file through first class. A few
look twice at the team with a don't-I-know-them-

from-somewhere-look. After about twenty people pass by a man wearing a blue denim suit and white cowboy boots sits down next to me. I take him to be a rancher by his wind-burned, roadmap face and immediately I begin to imagine his life and adventures, but I'm puzzled by his hands. There are no calluses. Don't all cowboys have calluses?

A few minutes later three other men similarly dressed enter the plane. They greet my seat partner and go past to the tourist section. A young black man with skin the color of caramel and a close-cropped Afro smiles as he passes. "Aren't you Dick Barnett?" he asks Barnett, sitting two rows back. Barnett nods. "Hey, I'm Charley Pride. I saw you play in college. Mind if I sit in on a hand?"

"You got money?" Barnett asks.

"Sure, I'm ready as soon as we're in the air."

The plane takes off and I ask the man next to me who Charley Pride is. He looks surprised and tells me he is the hottest Country and Western entertainer in America, that he is his manager, and they are on their way to Oklahoma City for a concert. Pride, he says, has just begun to move up on the charts but he still travels most of the year. By 1979, the manager reckons, Charley should be the biggest money maker in the Country and Western field, and that means millions. He says that even Pride's family had difficulty adjusting to his playing the white man's music, but Charley, who is part Indian, African, and Caucasian, had enough courage just to be himself, Charley Pride, genetic man, American.

I look back at Pride. A handsome man, dressed in tan slacks and a tan sportshirt, he is alternately standing above the game and sitting on the arm of Barnett's chair. Pride wins the hand, but shows a remarkable lack of pretension. He is "talking stuff" right along with Barnett. A rookie gives him a long glance, and smiles as if to say, "Yeah, you a brother for real."

From what his manager says it seems to me that Charley Pride is to country music in the 1970s what Elvis Presley was to rhythm and blues in the 1950s.

Both have tread the musical territory of the other's race and in so doing have affected the whole field, demonstrating that nothing is so narrow as racial clichés. Both Elvis, with his assorted mansions and Cadillacs, and Charley, with his $170,000 home in Dallas, show conspicuously the payoff for following their personal inclinations. Both, simply by their appearance, bring the unexpected. Elvis said that all the sexual energy beating beneath the surface should break out of white America. Let go those Puritan shackles and "get all shook up!" Charley says that quietude, symbolic patriotism, tragic love, and work also have charted the legitimacy of our society. Accept that order of things which preserves the old values and "work for the day is coming." Elvis was more famous, a greater synthesizer, and a bigger influence in the world, but Charley Pride sings of an American future as much as the past. He owes his creative debt to a rough, rambling, American soul as much white as black—a token black he will be only as long as it takes for the next black man with talent to admit that the influences of America are too diverse to preclude *any* creative vision.

The card game continues until the plane lands in Oklahoma City. One of the four men in blue denim and white boots leaving the plane says to Pride: "You lost, boy!" Charley smiles at the comment from a member of his band. He wins the last hand, as he did most during the flight, and, with his manager, he leaves moving gracefully down the steps. The three band members wait below with a new man also dressed in a western suit and cowboy hat. Charley shakes the dignitary's hand, and jumps into a white Cadillac limousine parked a few feet away. His manager and the band join him. Through the back window I see Charley laugh as the car pulls away.

---

After arriving in Houston I have a shower, a massage at the University Club, and a nap. DeBusschere,

Lucas, and I have dinner at the Marriott. Lucas tells us of another idea to strike it rich, though this one is on reserve until he can devote more time to it. "I've worked on it for five years," he says. "If it hits, it's all over. I use a simple mechanical principle to generate energy. It could be a source that would make nuclear energy unnecessary. You want to be on my Board of Directors?"

"How does it work?" Dave asks.

"Simple," Luke says. "I get an incline which I graduate at a certain degree and shape it in the form of a circular track. Then I put a steel ball on that track and attach it to the center by way of a steel rod. The angle causes gravity to move the ball, creating friction, which is the source of energy. You get a big field somewhere in Illinois and build an enormous model and it'll generate all the energy for a town—all the energy you'll ever need."

After dinner Lucas has some calls to make and De-Busschere is tired, so Jackson and I go for a ride. It is dusk as we drive through the River Oaks section of Houston, one of the wealthiest areas in the world—many homes selling for $600,000. At the end of a grand boulevard flanked on either side by palatial mansions stands the River Oaks Country Club. We pull up to the entrance and ask the guard, who wears a holster and a gun, if he knows which house on the street belongs to Governor John Connally.

"Who?" the guard asks.

"John Connally, the former Texas Governor, Democrat for Nixon, and Secretary of the Treasury." We smile at our put-on, for we know Connally lives nearby.

"No," the guard answers protectively. "I never heard of him."

## 9

THE NEXT MORNING I SEE DANNY IN THE LOBBY OF THE Marriott. He is on his way to the trial of Wayne Hendley, the young man accused of 26 murders in the Houston area. Danny says that he has to get there early for a seat; it's a popular trial. Frazier sits at the counter and I join him.

"What'd you do last night?" I ask.

"Went out with a friend."

"Do you think you could live here?" I ask.

"No," Clyde says, "it doesn't seem to have much to offer black people. I still feel the tension of segregation."

"How?"

"Just by walkin' in the stores and how people wait on you; like here at the Marriott, the way the lady gives you change. They're just little things I can relate to because I grew up in the South, and it reminds me of that again. The same thing in Phoenix; the other day I went into a store and four saleswomen just stood there looking at me asking each other, 'Who's going to wait on him?' Anywhere in the South we go on Delta or Eastern Airlines, I can feel the tension between white and black, starting with the stewardesses; it's different when we fly United or Northwest."

"Will the South ever be different for you?"

"It will always be the same."

"Why?"

"Because of the parents," says Frazier. "Kids know no prejudice. They just go out and have a good time playing. Then the parents start saying black is wrong, don't play with black kids, don't be a nigger lover. So they change early in life and that's the problem."

"What were all those leaflets in the Garden last week about your liquor store?" I ask. Frazier and Reed both have liquor stores in Harlem.

"Guy walks into the store one day while I'm there and says he's going to picket my store because we offer Mateus wine for sale in the window, which only supports the Portuguese economy, which allows them to fight in Africa. I told him to go downtown if he wanted to stop Mateus. I don't make much on it anyway. Man, the public is somethin' else. There's no way you can win. Like on our TV games they always ask why I don't smile and then once when the camera caught me smiling, they say I'm not taking the game serious."

"Are you glad the public knows you're a great dresser?" I ask. Clyde has been voted the best-dressed athlete, and he judges beauty contests.

"Sure."

"Would you ever want to be a clothes designer?"

"I have thought of that, but I don't do as much designing as I used to. Now I'm concerned with fabric. I pick them all myself. I like a quiet elegance that you see in the shape of the garment. So it's not jumping at you. It takes me two days just to pick fabrics and buttons for shirts. Suits I never stop buying. This year I've had 14 made. The tailor, like the shirtmaker, has my favorite pattern. With certain fabrics I want a certain style. Like with twill I want a safari look and with gabardine a more dressy look. The fabric is what determines the style of the suit."

Clyde then describes three separate looks in clothes down to the minutest detail. He talks in rapid fire order: Shawl collar suits, turtle necks, burgundy pants, tams, polyester pants, high black boots, single button suits, plaid jackets of beige and rust colors, blue hats, green hats, notch lapels, peak lapels, vents vs. no vents, white straw hats—all fill his conversation as

easily as picks and rolls, or jump shots. I begin to think
that maybe one of America's greatest athletes could
be a designer of clothes at heart.

After breakfast I take a taxi to the home of a
Houston friend. The black driver cannot find the
street. He stops at a gasoline station and waits. No one
comes out to service him. He gets out finally and
goes inside where two white men stand talking.
"Do you know where Pine Wald Lane is?" the driver
asks.

"No," they say, "not exactly. It's somewhere around
here but I'm not sure. Why don't you go down four
blocks and ask at the Esso station."

At the Esso station a black attendant and a black
manager come out.

"Hey brother," the driver says, "you know where
Pine Wald Lane is?"

The attendant says no but the manager says, "Sure,
Pine Wald. Go back up four blocks to the gas station,
take a left and its one block down."

The driver gets back in and as we're passing the
first station he mutters, "The street is one block from
the station. Why'd he say he don't know where it is?
Why?"

Later in the day I sit in the lobby of the Marriott
talking with a Houston friend and his 13-year-old son.
He is an alumnus of Princeton. He tells me how he is
trying to recruit blacks to go to Princeton. "It was
my first time in a black high school. I went in and they
told me that they're different. Yeah, they are different."

"Hey, Charlie," shouts his son, running over to a
black kid on his school football team who is accompanied by his mother.

"Is that your Daddy?" the black woman asks the 13-
year-old.

"Yes," the boy answers, but his father, less than 15
feet away makes no move.

The bus for the game arrived twenty-five minutes late (the driver said he got lost). I munch on a chocolate bar while Barnett tells about a past game. His team, the Los Angeles Lakers, was in St. Louis for a game against the Hawks, scheduled for 8 P.M. The Lakers were still warming up alone at 8:30; people started throwing things on the floor. At 9 P.M. it was announced that the Hawks were on their way from the airport. About half an hour later the Hawks walked in wearing overcoats and hats over their uniforms. They went straight to the bench and the game began. The Hawks won by 35 points. Maybe our bus driver is a lucky charm.

The Houston Rockets is another young team that has not jelled. They shout at each other and at the coach. We play our game as if we are the X's and they are the O's on our blackboard. DeBusschere hits two jump shots and a drive and then calls a backdoor play for me. Frazier throws the ball to DeBusschere and jogs with Monroe to the left side of the court with Willis. DeBusschere dribbles the ball toward me in the far right corner. He approaches at a 45° angle, giving my defensive man the impression that he will set a screen for me to take a jump shot. I take a step and a half toward him and my man anticipates the screen by moving a step in front of me. Pushing off suddenly with my left foot, I cut to the basket. DeBusschere drops a bounce pass to me and I make a wide open lay-up.

Later in the game Lucas runs the same play with our rookie guard who, when his man expects a screen from the forward, overplays to the side only to watch helplessly while the rookie streaks down the middle of the lane for a bounce pass from Lucas and a lay-up.

We move the ball well, no player holding it longer than a few seconds and we have the patience to find the man with the least contested shot. He gets the ball and usually two points. We are a team of shooters. Critics say we don't solo enough. They

might be right but when we play with finesse like tonight we only need to move the ball. Our shooting
touches take care of the rest. In one game in the
play-offs two years ago we shot 70 percent as a team.

During the last quarter we run our plays to perfection, giving the man at the end the split seconds he
needs to shoot. A dribble or a slow pass forces the
shooter to rush. Timing is crucial to a patient offense.
Everything we do seems to work. It's too bad there
are only 2,300 people in the arena and no TV back to
New York. We win easily.

The money and the championships are reasons I
play, but what I'm addicted to are the nights like
tonight when something special happens on the court.
The experience is one of beautiful isolation. It cannot
be deduced from the self-evident, like a philosophi-
cal proposition. It cannot be generally agreed upon,
like an empirically verifiable fact, and it is far more
than a passing emotion. It is as if a lightning bolt
strikes, bringing insight into an uncharted area of human experience. It makes perfect sense at the same
time it seems new and undiscovered. The moment in
basketball depends on the blending of human forces
at the right time and in the right degree. It goes beyond the competition that brings goose pimples or the
ecstasy of victory. With my team, before the crowd,
against our opponents, no one else but me can feel
what it all means. It's my private world. No one else
can sense the inexorable rightness of the moment. A
back-door play that comes with perfect execution at
a critical time charges the crowd, but I sense an immediate transporting enthusiasm and a feeling that
everything is in perfect balance.

Those moments require a childlike imagination. "We
can only know as adults what we can only feel as
children," says Leslie Fiedler. In those moments on a
basketball court I feel as a child and know as an adult.
Experience rushes through my pores as if sucked by a
strong vacuum. I feel the power of imagination that
creates a sense of mystery and wonder I last accepted
in childhood, before the mind hardened. When a

friend tells me that his son cries when I miss a last-second shot, I know how he feels. I cry a little, too. That's why ultimately when I play for anyone outside the team, I play for children. With them the communication of joy or sorrow rings true and through the playing that allows me to continue feeling as a child I sense a child's innocent yearning and love.

## 10

THE FLIGHT FROM HOUSTON IS UNEVENTFUL. DEBUSS-
chere sleeps most of the time. Tomorrow will be his
"night" at the Garden. Throughout the year he has
been honored in each city as he made his last appearance. Most teams gave him plaques, and one,
Cleveland, presented him with a color television. After each ceremony Dave would say a few words of appreciation, never varying his basic response. Now
New York will say good-bye.

"It represents a deep satisfying feeling to be
honored in such a manner," I read him quoted in the
afternoon *New York Post*, as I ride into the city with
Phil and Clyde.

DeBusschere is a little nervous when I arrive at the
Garden for the game against the Philadelphia '76ers
on Dave DeBusschere Night. He chuckles when he
reads one of his letters and pitches it to me.

> For some reason I have always suspected you of
> being a "dumper" along with some others through
> the league. . . . During the radio broadcast of the
> game from Phoenix, I thought I heard the announcer
> say that you begged off because you had a migraine
> headache. You poor kid, did your big head ache a
> little. I certainly hope you are feeling better. Ap-
> parently you have the perfect out when you are doing
> your thing. After all, who could accuse a man of
> dumping a game when he isn't playing. I shall not
> wish you good luck for this obviously is no problem
> from a financial point of view. (You must have plenty
> socked away—tax free, too.)

I wonder if the writer is here tonight to honor Dave.

We take to the court half an hour early. The crowd is already waiting. "Hey, Dave," a kid shouts, "just one picture. My cousin knows your lawyer." The warm-ups are brief. The buzzer sounds and we go to the bench for the ceremony.

The Knick radio announcer serves as the master of ceremonies. He introduces two dignitaries who present Dave with a key to the city and the Big Apple Award. Frazier, not playing tonight due to injury and dressed in a fawn-colored leather suit, presents bouquets of roses to Dave's mother and to Gerri, his wife. Red Holzman gives Dave a portrait done by LeRoy Neiman. Willis presents him a gift from the 1970 championship team.

Next is Madison Square Garden Corporation. Dave requested that anyone wanting to give him something should contribute to the Dave DeBusschere Scholarship Fund, which will provide money for college to needy kids. Dave feels that the Garden executives have tried in subtle ways to minimize the evening because they are displeased with his decision to forgo two more years of playing in order to join the arch-rival Nets as General Manager. Their feelings culminate in a paltry donation to the scholarship fund (the players gave more) and no retirement of his jersey, number 22. Even in the end, basketball is a business and the businessmen have made the decisions based on a narrow loyalty to the company.

After the final presentation Dave steps to the microphone. "Defense, De-fense," the crowd spontaneously begins to shout. For what seems like four minutes Dave takes in their "love vibes," experiencing that rare moment when an athlete can stand before his fans and absorb their adulation. Tonight he receives more than any performer, for their roars of appreciation come not just for a game but for a career; for all the strength, courage, desire, and effort he has exerted before them over the years.

"De-fense, De-fense, De-fense," they chant. Memories of a hundred games come to mind; memories of last-quarter surges to victory and perfect team communion; memories of the road and years together; memories of defeats and rebirths; memories of aspiration fulfilled and challenges met.

"De-fense, De-fense, De-fense." The code word of our years, Defense. It's work, hard work, and unrewarding individually. Only the group wins and only the group plays defense. Tonight symbolizes its passing. My eyes water. "Why am I crying?" I wonder. It's his night. But it's not, really. It's our night; it's the fans' night. It's all of our nights, under the spoked-wheel roof of Madison Square Garden. An era is ending.

"Being with the Knicks . . . ," Dave says after the crowd quiets, "the teamwork we've always conveyed to each other has been genuine; has given me an insight into some tremendous human beings."

I remember the first championship in 1970. Dave's first reaction was to go directly to Willis, who had played the last game with his leg shot full of novocaine, and to hug him uninhibitedly.

"When the final buzzer goes off, win or lose," Dave continues—the crowd starts yelling, Win! Win! Win! the reflex amens of the basketball temple—"it's going to tear me up."

I look up at the balconies where banners hang. "DeBush, DeBest," one says. "Dave, you're nuts for going to the Nets," says another. A third proclaims, "Dave DeBusschere—you're 1 in a million; we love you; we'll miss you."

"Last but not least I want to thank the fans," Dave says. "You are the backbone of our ball club. I know many times your cheers have given me goose bumps . . . memories of playing here in New York have been the greatest memories of my life."

And in mine, too, and in all of our lives; there will be no more Garden filled with the roaring approval of 20,000. No more confusion about who they are and what they mean. No more nights of happy exhaustion. No more tomorrows with another chance. It's over.

## 11

THE SEASON ENDED IN BOSTON AGAINST THE CELTICS with DeBusschere on the sidelines suffering from torn stomach muscles. Now, it is a day in June at 6:15 A.M. As I pull up to Newark Airport, the sun appears as a red ball, rising from behind the two distant towers of Manhattan's World Trade Center. The rest of the sky is dark. I am early for the flight.

Phil Jackson has asked Willis Reed and me to join him in staging a basketball clinic at the Oglala Sioux Indian reservation in Pine Ridge, South Dakota. One year ago on the reservation twelve Sioux warriors, members of the American Indian Movement, forcibly occupied the Sacred Heart Catholic Church at Wounded Knee for two and a half weeks, much to the chagrin of 300 federal law enforcement officers summoned to the scene. The tension still runs high according to Mike-Her-Many-Horses, a friend of Phil's from college. Some of Mike's relatives died at the first Wounded Knee Massacre in 1890.

Ten minutes before the scheduled flight departure a green Oldsmobile stops in front of the United Airlines terminal. Willis Reed steps out. He takes his fishing tackle boxes and his camping clothes from the car (he is going hunting in Montana after the clinic), checks in ("OK, Mr. Reed, glad to have you flying with us to Denver"), and walks to the gate. ("Isn't that Willis Reed? Hey, Willis, how's the leg?") He limps noticeably. We settle into the row with extra leg room at the front of the DC-10's first class section.

After we are in the air for forty-five minutes, Willis and I begin to talk about his leg and his future, both of which at the moment are uncertain. "I went to see Dr. O'Donohue four days ago," he says. "He said that what I was feelin' in the play-offs against Boston was a, what'ya call it, a Baker's cyst or maybe a spur deep inside the back of my knee. If I wanted to play he said that I'd have to have another operation."

"When were you last healthy?" I ask.

"I felt pretty good in the final L.A. series in '73, like, you know, the best since 1971, when I started havin' the tendon trouble in my left knee. With legs like this . . ." he looks at his knees. "No athlete can play unless he's healthy. You want to do it but you can't; it's not severe pain but just enough to prevent you from getting into good shape."

"You going to have the operation?" I ask.

Willis's big left hand moves across the side of his face, covering and then exposing first his nose and mouth and then his cheek. His fingers meet under his chin, where they pause momentarily. His face looks wrinkled as he looks up and says, "I don't know. I don't know. You got to be up for an operation—emotionally up just like for a game. I'm not now. I've had a severely strained shoulder, bone chips removed in my ankle, an operation in my left knee for tendonitis, and an operation in my right knee for a torn cartilage. The pain the first four or five days after an operation is horrible. You just lay there and can't move. You call for the nurse to give you a shot to numb the pain; you sleep an hour and then it's the same thing. On my left knee they put the cast on too soon and the leg didn't have anyplace to go. It swelled up like a balloon. The pain was a monster. With the right knee I had a 103° temperature for three days. I don't know. I don't know if I want to go through all that again, particularly when, if I played after it, I might get a permanent injury. Medicine can't help me now. I guess I need somethin' more. But I got two years on my contract."

"Will the Garden honor your contract if you quit?"

"It depends on whether they say I have to get the operation. They said they thought I was OK. I say,

'hey, I did too, but you see what O'Donohue says.'"
He starts fidgeting with the medal that hangs around
his neck. "I had planned to retire in two years. I'd have
enough money, then, to get by on; no big numbers,
but enough to be my own man. I don't want to quit
now, but with the knee, the operation, and the money
being doubtful, I don't know. I got to decide in a
week."

We switch to Frontier Airlines in Denver. When
we arrive in Rapid City the sun is shining brightly;
the horizon wide open. There are few trees; just grass
and space. It is startling at first. Mike-Her-Many-
Horses greets us at the airport. He wears his straight
black hair in a ponytail. His shoulders are broad and
his hips narrow. He smiles easily. After a brief TV interview at the studio in "Rapid" we drive 50 miles
to the reservation in Mike's pickup truck. Mike says
that he is so used to the rolling open hills that he can't
leave them. One summer he worked in Glacier National Park in Montana but left after three weeks because "the mountains and trees gave me the feeling I
was closed in." We drive slowly through a town called
Scenic on the edge of the reservation; then past the
Long Horn Saloon, the Badlands Jail, and a gas station.
"Since the reservation is dry," Mike says, "here's
where people go to let off steam. There is no law and
in that saloon there are lots of shootings and stab-
bings."

"You carry a gun on you?" Willis asks.

"No, I keep one in the back of the pickup."

The reservation land is 4,353 square miles of dirt
buttes and "cheet" grass; mostly badlands, which
means *bad land.* Originally the Sioux treaties with
the U.S. government had guaranteed the Sioux the
fertile Black Hills, then a holy ground, but when
gold was discovered in them, the treaties were abro-
gated and thousands of fortune hunters occupied and
settled the area with the help of the U.S. Army. Later
when there was a large immigration from Northern
Europe to the West—Phil Jackson's ancestors were in
this group—the reservation shrank further until it has

become land of great acreage but of little productive value for a people who have never escaped their nomadic past.

We pass a fenced-off field of about 200 acres. The man who leased the Indian land from the Bureau of Indian Affairs for $1 an acre has put up a sign which warns Indians—no trespassing, no hunting, no firewood. Mike says there are some deer and antelope in the hills and catfish in the White River, which runs through the land. We pass a house that belongs to an Indian jockey, who lives well on the reservation with his racing winnings. Windmills stand behind houses, whining in the wind and providing energy to pump water. At intervals along the desolate two-lane highway, cars lie abandoned and rusting in the fields as if they were the successors of the dinosaurs that died in the area; as if the Indians drove them to death taking out their fury on the white man's machines.

Driving to Pine Ridge, the reservation's main town (pop. 1,000), we stop at Wounded Knee. The Sacred Heart Church, or what's left of it, sits on a small hill overlooking a little valley through which runs the Wounded Knee Creek. One year earlier hundreds of U.S. marshals with automatic weapons lined the hills and banks of the creek. On the charred foundation of the church are scribbled "AIM Wounded Knee 1890–1973" and "Fuck you Dick _____," the last name is rubbed out. Behind the church is the graveyard, where some of Mike's relatives lie buried. The old souvenir shop and museum have collapsed, and along the road is a monument and sign commemorating the events of 1890, when on the morning of December 28, the U.S. Seventh Cavalry surrounded an encampment of Oglala Sioux and with the help of Hotchkiss guns killed 194 men, women, and children. It was the last recorded skirmish between the U.S. Army and the American Indian. We get out of the car and walk to the sign. Willis limps like a wounded buffalo, each step painful. I wonder how he will get through his demonstration this evening. The wind whips through the "cheet" grass and jack pines, providing an eerie background hum. Willis, Mike, and Phil stand silhouetted against the sky reading the inscription on the sign: "Unrest on the reservation was due to a reduction in beef rations by the U.S. Congress and to the ghost-dancing of Chief Kicking Bear and Sitting Bull, who said that by wearing the ghost shirt and doing the ghost dances of Wovoka, the Piaute mystic the warriors would become immune to the white man's bullets; could openly defy the soldiers and white settlers; *and could bring back the days of the old buffalo herds.*"

"Those days ain't never comin' back," says Willis.

We slowly move back to the car and then on to Pine Ridge. About thirty Indian kids await us in the gym. During my demonstration they are silent and still; quite different from the nervous fidgeting of inner-city kids. They ask me only two questions:

"If a ball player don't get hurt or nothin', how long can he play?"

"What happens if you punched a referee in the mouth?"

Finally, Willis Reed comes on the court, positions himself at the low post, and begins to explain pivot play. "You take the ball with both hands, turn, and shoot. Always keep the ball high. Now if he plays you to the right, you fake and go left. If he plays you to the left, go right. Or, you can turn all the way around like this, and show him the ball and drive. After you drive once you've got him set up for the drop dribble. Face him, fake a drive, take one bounce away from the basket, turn, and shoot. You'll have him flat-footed."

Willis doesn't move much, and when one of the kids asks him if he will play next year, he says yes and he expects the Knicks to be in contention for the title. In closing, Willis gives the group a little lecture about hard work, responsibility, and the need to set goals. He says practice and study go hand in hand with a clean life. He speaks with the assurance of a man whose life has been built upon moral certainties.

He says never to get down when you lose because there is always another game. He is glistening with sweat; though he is still standing in one spot, his tee shirt is wet. The kids are enraptured. "There isn't much these days that hasn't been done," he says. "There's been a man on the moon and somebody has already run a mile in 3:55. But you have a chance for a real first: One of you can be the first Indian to play in the NBA."

## ABOUT THE AUTHOR

BILL BRADLEY was born in Crystal City, Missouri. He is a graduate of Princeton University, where he achieved All-American status. After studying for two years at Oxford as a Rhodes Scholar, he signed with the New York Knickerbockers. During his nine years with them, he has been a starter on two championship teams. He is currently the senior senator from the state of New Jersey. He lives in northern New Jersey with his wife Ernestine.

Shaken by public acclaim for his earlier books, Ron Luciano tempts fate with a new form of baseball reporting: the dugout autobiography.

In his new bestselling hardcover, THE FALL OF THE ROMAN UMPIRE, Ron Luciano is on a new crusade. Why should the superstars of baseball, the Micks and Reggies, be the only players to have autobiographies? This book, dedicated to the unheralded heroes of baseball, will present from his fan's-eye view some of the true and truly uprorarious stories of real, hope-I-don't-drop-the-next-fly-ball players.

If you enjoyed Luciano's books, why not take a swing at THE UMPIRE STRIKES BACK, narrated by Mr. Luciano himself. In it the legendary loudmouth and funniest umpire ever to call balls and strikes, will keep you laughing with anecdotes from his pre-umpire days, his life as the general manager of a minor league team, his career as an umpire and more. Fifty minutes of Ron on tape!